Transnational Coupling in the Age of Nation Making during the 19th and 20th Centuries

Nicole Leopoldie

ANTHEM PRESS

Anthem Press
An imprint of Wimbledon Publishing Company
www.anthempress.com

This edition first published in UK and USA 2025
by ANTHEM PRESS
75–76 Blackfriars Road, London SE1 8HA, UK
or PO Box 9779, London SW19 7ZG, UK
and
244 Madison Ave #116, New York, NY 10016, USA

First published in the UK and USA by Anthem Press in 2023

© 2025 Nicole Leopoldie

The author asserts the moral right to be identified as the author of this work.

All rights reserved. Without limiting the rights under copyright reserved above,
no part of this publication may be reproduced, stored or introduced
into a retrieval system, or transmitted, in any form or by any means
(electronic, mechanical, photocopying, recording or otherwise),
without the prior written permission of both the copyright
owner and the above publisher of this book.

British Library Cataloguing-in-Publication Data
A catalogue record for this book is available from the British Library.

Library of Congress Control Number: 2025936943

ISBN-13: 978-1-83999-639-9 (Pbk)
ISBN-10: 1-83999-639-0 (Pbk)

This title is also available as an e-book.

CONTENTS

List of Figures   iv

Acknowledgements   v

Introduction   Marriage: National Borders and Personal Spaces   1

Part I   "Trading Titles for Treasure?": Elite Marriages during the Nineteenth Century   17

1. The Making of a Transnational High Society   27
2. Emotional Dimensions of Elite Transnational Spaces   53

Part II   "Paris is Free—and So Are Its Kisses": Wartime Marriages during the Twentieth Century   77

3. Longing for the Other through the War   83
4. Transnational Courtship in Spaces of War   117

Conclusion   141

Bibliography   147

Index   157

LIST OF FIGURES

1.1	La Sortie du bal en 1902, Escalier de l'Hôtel du Marquis de Vogué, Raymond, Fournier-Sarlovèze Joseph. CCØ Bibliothèque de l'Institut d'Histoire de l'Art	35
2.1	Portrait de Boni de Castellane et Anna Gould, Davis & Sanford. CCØ Paris Musées / Musée Carnavalet—Histoire de Paris	66
3.1	Advertisement in *Stars and Stripes*, April 4, 1919	89
3.2	"Here's What We're Fighting For," *Stars and Stripes*, September 9, 1944. Courtesy of Stars and Stripes, All Rights Reserved	90
3.3	"This is th' town my pappy told me about," *Stars and Stripes*, September 6, 1944. Copyright by Bill Mauldin (1944). Courtesy of Bill Mauldin Estate LLC	95

ACKNOWLEDGEMENTS

The completion of this work has left me indebted to many. First and foremost, I am tremendously fortunate to have been guided by my mentors who saw me through the doctoral process when I began this project, Thomas Adam and Pilar Gonzáles Bernaldo. The depth of their knowledge is matched by few, and I cannot thank them enough for challenging me, encouraging me, and for keeping me intellectually grounded. I also owe immeasurable appreciation to the other scholars who served as readers and reviewers during that time, especially Steven Reinhardt, Mark Meigs, Kenyon Zimmer, and Pierre-Yves Saunier. Their meticulous feedback and encouragement were invaluable, and the examples they set with their own work were inspiring. For their precise and friendly guidance during my fellowship there, I thank the kind and helpful staff at the New York Public Library. And for their thoughtful comments on earlier conference and workshop papers, I thank Dirk Hoerder, Susan Ball, Mirna Safi, Hélène le Dantec-Lowry, Evelyne Payen, Beate Collet, Thomas Wolfe, and Timm Beichelt.

On a more personal level, I thank my dearest colleagues and closest friends, Isabelle Rispler, Bryan Garrett, and Rufki Salihi for countless hours of discussion, debate, and much needed encouragement. For me, Rufki's memory will forever live on in the pages that follow. Lastly, I thank my husband for his incessant emotional support, but mostly for the hours he spent reading, proofreading, and checking translations throughout my research process.

What follows is largely the result of generous financial support from an Enhanced Graduate Teaching Fellowship from the University of Texas at Arlington; a Trans-Atlantic Summer Institute Fellowship from the University of Minnesota and the German Academic Exchange Service; a Short-Term Research Fellowship from the New York Public Library; a Global Research Fellowship from the Festival of Ideas/Global Research Program; a Dean's Excellence Research Travel Award from the College of Liberal Arts at the University of Texas at Arlington; and a Global and European Studies Summer School Fellowship from the French-German University and the German Historical Institute in Paris.

An earlier version of a portion of this research was previously published as "A Comparative Spatial Analysis of Transnational Coupling during the Nineteenth and Twentieth Centuries" in *The Yearbook of Transnational History, Volume Two*, copyright © 2019 by The Rowman & Littlefield Publishing Group. It has been expanded, edited, and reproduced here with permission of The Licensor through PLSclear.

Introduction

MARRIAGE: NATIONAL BORDERS AND PERSONAL SPACES

Why do people marry? Or better: Why do they couple?[1] While marriage and coupling practices seem to correspond with obvious biological and social necessities, a more targeted question might include: Why do they choose to couple or marry with the people that they do? And, what happens when they marry someone who is perceived as different from themselves?

Admittedly, such overgeneralized questions are, of course, accompanied by the underpinning assumption that the modern, Western social practice of marriage is largely accepted as a contract between two individuals based on both their free will and their affection for or commitment to one another. However, the cultural normative characterizations of both marital practices and courtship rituals show great variability in different historical contexts, and as Stephanie Coontz shows in her work, *Marriage, a History: From Obedience to Intimacy or How Love Conquered Marriage*, marriage as an emotion-based, state-sanctioned union is a relatively recent social invention.[2] This leaves the task of defining marriage a difficult one. Over time, courtship and marital practices have taken many forms. In some contexts, to marry was a privilege, in others a necessity. Even in the present time, the tension between its dual meaning—both as a legal contract and as an emotional relationship—persists, and academic definitions vary. Anthropologist, Edmund Leach, for example, defines marriage as "a set of legal rules" that largely determines inheritance between generations.[3] Coontz, by contrast, notes the limitations of this definition and goes further to define it instead as a social practice that "determines rights and obligations connected to sexuality, gender roles, relationships with in-laws, and the legitimacy of children."[4] However, no matter the changing legal or social characterizations, the practice of marriage has always, at its core, represented the connectedness of individuals—connectedness between participants, between families, between larger kinship and social networks, and even between societies. The marriages that make up the subject of this work transcended national, cultural, and linguistic boundaries and connected individuals across the Atlantic.

While mixed marriages (in their many forms) are not a new phenomenon[5]—the practice of marriage long pre-dated many of the borders that it would come to cross—the concept of *transnational marriage* presents for the historian a unique methodological opportunity to move further beyond the analytical frameworks of national histories that have long caged them, as they continue their search for new categories of analysis that place the human experience into broader, more global perspectives.[6] In this context, the social practices of courtship and marriage become mechanisms through which borders were crossed and new cultural spaces were created, and they represent important elements of transnational entanglements. Because marriage is a microcosm of larger cultural and social values, examining how and why marriages occurred between two societies reveals the broader, complex cross-cultural encounters from which couples emerged. Moreover, examining how and why observable patterns of transnational marriage and coupling emerged between the same two societies and changed over time reveals broader shifts in the global currents of that interconnectedness.

Here, the entangled past of France and the United States provides an intriguing case study. Since their emergence as modern nation-states within the transatlantic system of trade and migration, the two nations shared a wistful and sometimes turbulent cultural and diplomatic relationship. The continued occurrence of clear patterns of Franco-American marriages during the nineteenth and twentieth centuries, therefore, provokes interesting questions about these transnational micro-dynamics. Two of those patterns are examined here: the first, when wealthy American heiresses married French aristocrats during the second half of the nineteenth century—a period marked by relatively free transatlantic circulation and mobility—and the second, when borders were far more solidified—during the world wars when American soldiers entered into matrimonial contracts with French women. The time frame selected is an important one as it represents a critical global moment that can be characterized by the culmination of the national project. This examination, therefore, situates transnational marriage practices within the context of the broader shift from nineteenth-century nation making to early and mid twentieth-century hyper-nationalism. In these different contexts, the continued occurrence of transnational marriages forces the researcher to reconsider the ways in which one thinks not only about coupling and family formation, but also about the permeability of national borders during these different stages of the national project.

Defining Transnational Marriage, Coupling and Courtship

Like the object of study, *transnational marriage* as an academic concept is also not entirely new. During the last two decades, overlapping terms such as mixed marriage, intermarriage, binational marriage, international marriage, global marriage, cross-border marriage, and transnational marriage have all made their way into the corpuses of various social scientific disciplines; however, the establishment of any kind of topical field remains both fragmented and underdeveloped. For the historian, a general lack of conceptual themes and methods creates two notable analytical problems: The first is defining transnational marriage as a *historical* concept, and the second is identifying appropriate categories of analysis through which to examine marriages of the past as a subject of inquiry.

Because the practice of marriage was rarely a private matter, the histories of modern marriage have often been written as the histories of the laws or external structures that shaped and regulated them.[7] The same has often been the case for the histories of marriages that crossed national borders.[8] With the rise of the modern nation-state, the practice of marriage came to serve an important function in the formation of national cultures. As Nancy Cott shows in her work, *Public Vows: A History of Marriage and the Nation*, marriage was an essential aspect in the making of the nation-state by underlining national belonging, establishing cohesion and setting national moral standards.[9] Therefore, both state and national apparatuses often attempted to shape relationships according to these national agendas by defining what were or were not acceptable practices of family formation.[10] When families constructed themselves beyond that national project, they failed to fit into national narratives of a long-standing past and unified culture surrounded by concrete boundaries, and state intervention in instances of transnational-marriage practices typically came in the form of laws that regulated marriage-related migration. While the examinations of legal restrictions tell us much about the state's role in family formation practices, these perspectives provide an incomplete picture of the past for a couple of reasons. First, they fail to explain how and why marriages that spanned national borders formed in the first place. Second, even from binational or comparative perspectives, historical examinations of state regulations remain inherently limited by national frameworks of analysis,[11] as they largely view the state(s), rather than marriage participants, as agents of historical change. Moreover, by narrowly defining marriage as a legal agreement that only begins at contractualization, these studies overwhelmingly neglect the transnational processes of coupling and courtship, which also served as an important source of intimate cross-border connections. Defining transnational marriage as a historical concept must, therefore, coincide with questions of the making of the nation-state, but it must be further investigated the extent to which marriage participants actually saw themselves as crossing borders and to what degree.

For these reasons, in this historical analysis, I employ the term transnational marriage over alternatives such as binational or international marriage—two terms that largely connote legal or diplomatic perspectives—and I draw on the intersecting methodologies of transnational history, cultural history, and emotions history. Here, rather than an active historical agent, the state is considered a non-static component of a larger global structure in which the historical actors—the marriage participants—had to navigate. Rather than viewing marriage simply as a legal agreement that begins at contractualization, this project places notable focus on the transnational spaces of extramarital coupling and courtship out of which transnational marriages emerged. Because the global/transnational turn led to the rethinking of the spatial dimension of history, I draw on the analytical concept of transnational space, which further allows researchers to move beyond national frameworks of history. An examination of these spaces remains important because they were spaces of both transnational sociability and cross-cultural negotiation. I, therefore, adopt and assess as a working definition of the concept of transnational marriage that of sociologists, Wen-Shan Yang and Melody Chia-Wen Lu, who in their work, *Asian Cross-Border Marriage Migration: Demographic Patterns and Social Issues*, maintain that the concept of transnational marriage situates more general cross-border marriages—in which geographical, national, racial, class, gender, or cultural borders are unspecified—into a context of wider transnational processes, networks, and spaces created by the actors themselves.[12]

Transnational Spaces of Marriage and Courtship

While British sociologist, Katharine Charsley, correctly notes in the edited volume, *Transnational Marriage: New Perspectives from Europe and Beyond*, that one of the key themes in the literature on transnational marriage is the degree to which marriages can be understood as a strategically motivated practice,[13] this analytical focus has often led researchers to reduce strategic motivation to socioeconomic circumstance. I contend that such explanations are simply too narrow and largely remain embedded in restrictive national perspectives. For example, if the researcher begins with the question, why did wealthy American heiresses marry French nobility during the nineteenth century, the focus largely rests of the question of what was happening in New York that made American women seek out Frenchmen. As such, the location of inquiry is inherently positioned on one side or the other and results in "push-pull" explanations largely based on socioeconomic factors. Therefore, rather than simply asking, how does one explain instances of marriages that transcended national boundaries in the past, based on the definition above, this work instead seeks to examine the ways in which patterns of transnational marriage emerged out of cross-cultural encounters. This question repositions the location of inquiry from the perspective of one culture or another to the liminal space between them—transnational spaces and social networks out of which marriage emerged.

Here, the concept of *space* is defined not as a geographical space but as a cultural space that is created through varied human practices interlaced with arrays of social meaning.[14] When these cultural spaces are created in transnational contexts beyond the limits of national boundaries, the notion that culture is tied to geographical places is called into question. Further, while transnationalism has been broadly defined as ties and interactions linking people across borders, the social spaces of transnationality that produced transnational marriages go beyond mere spaces occupied by each group that were comprised of a cultural mélange. In this way, the concept of transnational space can be further distinguished from postcolonial concepts of "hybrid" spaces.[15] Instead, transnational space is a negotiated space, within which the actors produced their own tastes, codes, and norms rather than simply combining them.

The following questions, therefore, frame the categories of analysis employed here: How does the historian locate and map transnational spaces of marriage and courtship? What are the cultural and emotional dimensions of those spaces? And finally, how did marriage participants conceptualize the spaces they occupied and the boundaries they crossed?

In order to map and analyze transnational spaces that produced marriages during the nineteenth and twentieth centuries, this work draws on descriptions of social events found in French and American press, travel literature, personal papers and accounts, and guest lists. By examining where and how couples met and courted one another, these sources provide an important glimpse into transnational social networks and their cultural rituals as well as how marriage participants perceived, experienced, and interpreted these spaces. Through a deeper reading of these descriptions and cultural rituals, I seek to further uncover the complex diversity of intimate cultural and emotional experiences that coincide with the practices of courtship and marriage—experiences that are even more multifaceted in this transnational context.

Emotional Evolution of Marriage and Courtship

The cultural and emotional dimensions of the spaces that produced transnational marriage are significant because prior to the second half of the nineteenth century, the practice of marriage had already begun to undergo a transformative evolution from marriage as an economic or political agreement to marriage as a personal or emotion-based engagement. While the period under analysis here is not long enough to provide a comprehensive study of changing cultural understandings of marriage as a multisided, multidimensional social phenomenon or of the making of emotions such as "romantic love,"[16] an examination of nineteenth- and twentieth-century transnational marriages must, nonetheless, be placed within the broader shift of changing emotional standards as they relate to the practice of marriage.

According to its most traditional religious definition, marriage was both monogamous and indissoluble—two qualities that have been traced back to Jewish and Greco-Roman law.[17] In addition, prior to the eighteenth century, marriage also served an important institutional function in early modern societies.[18] As Coontz explains: "For centuries marriage did much of the work that markets and governments do today. It organized the production and distribution of goods and people. It set up political, economic, and military alliances. It coordinated the division of labor … [and] orchestrated people's rights and obligations."[19] Thus, marriage existed as both an economic and a political institution in which cooperative networks expanded beyond the immediate family, and it was used to not only increase one's familial labor force but also consolidate and maintain wealth through subsequent generations. This strategically motivated institution also served important political functions that allowed European monarchs to merge resources and forge political alliances. In this way, the practice of marriage was considered a major investment, and great care was often taken in the arrangement of matches by the ruling class.[20] After these early political and economic unions were contracted, each party rarely occupied the same intimate familial spaces and often went their separate ways as they engaged in everyday rituals.

However, between the fourteenth and nineteenth centuries, marriage practices gradually underwent fundamental changes as understandings of emotion-based coupling began to infiltrate marriage practices; although, it should be noted that this evolution was neither linear nor was it marked by clear watershed moments in the past. The earliest origins of these cultural notions of emotion-based coupling can be found in medieval France. As William Reddy shows in his work, *The Making of Romantic Love: Longing and Sexuality in Europe, South Asia, and Japan*, the "courtly love of the troubadours" likely developed in opposition to Christian doctrine, which defined physical or sexual desire as sinful.[21] As the social and cultural relationships with the Church continued to change through sixteenth- and seventeenth-century reforms, a variety of values and coupling practices developed in Western Europe. However, as both Reddy and Coontz note, these earliest sentiments of courtly love were more often reserved for mistresses rather than for wives.[22]

According to Coontz, the most rapid and observable shifts from what had been economically and politically motivated marriage practices to marriages based on notions of what would come to be described as "romantic love" and "happiness" occurred during the eighteenth century—a shift which she attributes to not only the rise of the market economy and wage labor but also the dissolution of absolutism during the Age of Revolutions.[23] According to her, the economic shift to wage labor meant that men were no longer required to wait to inherit land or business, and with alternatives to domestic service, women were no longer required to live in the home of domestic masters.[24] Entangled with the permeation of enlightened thinking, these economic shifts led to the championing of individualism and the insistence that social relationships be based on reason and justice rather than force. In this way, she explains, marriage as an institution became viewed more and more as a "private agreement" that centered on emotional needs or emotional gratification of both participants—albeit, still having "public consequences."[25] By the end of the eighteenth century, she concludes that "people had begun to adopt the radical idea that love should be the most fundamental reason for marriage and that young people should be free to choose their marriage partners on the basis of love."[26] The broader implications of this emotional shift meant that public forms of coupling and courtship rituals become essential additions to marital practices. It should also be noted, however, that emotion-based marriage did not equate to egalitarian partnerships. Contrarily, the permeation of notions of romantic love into marital partnerships further forced marriage participants into stricter gender roles, and the husbands' control and protection over their wives was reaffirmed.[27]

Yvonne Rieker, in her work, "Love Crossing Borders: Changing Patterns of Courtship and Gender Relations among Italian Migrants in Germany," likewise recognizes these emotional shifts; however, she dates the most fundamental changes across all social segments of society in the beginning of the nineteenth century. Before this, she argues, forms of courtly love remained limited to members of the nobility and intellectual elite. She explains: "To pursue the ideal of romantic love in one's life implied leisure and educational and financial resources as well as integration into urban society or the possibility of traveling to augment the circle of candidates for one's affection and passion."[28] However, Roderick Philips notes in his work,

Untying the Knot: A Short History of Divorce, that these fundamental changes were more indicative of late eighteenth- rather than nineteenth-century shifts. Here, he points to one study by Margaret Darrow, who found that prior to the 1770s, only nine percent of those cited in petitions for dispensations from the Catholic Church in Montauban, France, argued that a marriage should be based on emotional attachment, but after the 1770s, forty-one percent thought so.[29] Contrary to Rieker's claim of elite exclusivity, Philips also remarks that what was most notable about this pattern was that it was representative across all social classes—peasants, bourgeoisie, and nobility.

While Coontz admits that marrying for political and economic advantage largely remained the norm until the end of the eighteenth century, secular and enlightened understanding of marriage as emotion based had, by that time, largely become a social or cultural *ideal*, and personal choice of partners had largely replaced more traditional forms of arranged marriages.[30] Kimberly Schutte in her work, *Women, Rank, and Marriage in the British Aristocracy, 1485–2000: An Open Elite?*, also agrees that by the nineteenth century, overtly arranged marriages among European aristocratic families were no longer seen as socially acceptable and that emotional aspects of potential unions were of great concern to aristocratic mothers.[31] However, that was not to say that socioeconomic factors were discounted entirely. The maintenance of social position continued to be important among the elite classes, and individuals still largely married within their social echelons.

While the tension between emotional and economic motivations remains prevalent in historical examinations of marriage, this dichotomy can sometimes be counterproductive. When examining transnational marriage motivations of the nineteenth and twentieth centuries, socioeconomic and emotional considerations should not be viewed as mutually exclusive.[32] In fact, when one married within their own social class, these socioeconomic and emotional considerations did not even necessarily exist in opposition to one another. That means that one could marry someone who was considered to be a "good match" and still have expectations that the marriage would be based on "love" and "happiness"—even if those notions of love and happiness differed from their current cultural conceptions.

Culture and Emotions as Categories of Analysis

Following the cultural turn, research interests shifted to other aspects of human experience that had previously been perceived as fixed and ahistorical; this included emotions. In order to trace and analyze the changing norms of feelings in the past, historians of emotions have drawn on debates in sociology, anthropology, psychology, and psychoanalysis to show that emotions not only were shaped by public and personal realities but also had larger social and cultural implications.[33] This social constructionist theory of emotions establishes that emotions such as romantic love and happiness were shaped by the societies in which they were embedded.[34] Despite criticisms that constructionist theories lend the risk of emotions becoming an unstable signifier onto which ever-proliferating meanings can be inscribed, viewing the past through the prism of emotions yields important new narratives. Yet, employing emotions as a useful category of analysis within transnational perspectives requires that the relationship between culture and emotions be more closely considered. Rather than a comparative, *longe durée* study of changing cultural understandings of marriage as a practice or the making of romantic love, such as those that William Reddy and Stephanie Coontz have produced,[35] this work is concerned instead with the emotional dimensions of different transnational spaces in the past, or more specifically, the ways in which emotional standards shaped interactions among groups across national and cultural borders. I, therefore, pose the following questions: If emotions are constructed, how do emotions like love and longing differ within transnational and transcultural spaces? Also, within this spatial analysis, to what extent can transnational sociability be considered a site of emotion?

In this work, emotions are employed as a category of analysis rather than simply a narrative device in order to show how complex cultural meanings within transnational spaces were experienced on personal levels among transnational-marriage participants. Because emotions manifested in both encounter and representations of the "other," I also propose for further consideration the extent to which *othering* can be considered as not only a cultural process but also an emotional one. In this way, I also seek to untangle the cultural and emotional processes in which the "other" was constructed in a way that made them desirable. In order to overcome the analytical constraints of the term *romantic love* and conceptualize this wider range of emotions, I adopt William Reddy's concept of *longing for association*—a term that overcomes the dichotomies created when the socially constructed emotion of romantic love is set against notions of more physiological feeling of desire—and, by placing in the transnational context, expand it to *longing for association with the "other."*[36]

For the historian, using emotions as a category of analysis in examining personal and intimate relationships is not without methodological limitations. This is especially the case when examining nineteenth-century elite transnational communities in which most contemporary subjects often saw outward displays of public emotion as contrary to proper behavior. Therefore, because personal accounts about intimate couple and family lives are scarce, the researcher is required to engage in a rereading of very select memoirs, which provide an important glimpse into transnational elite courtship practices, emotions, personal choice, and individual agency even if it cannot be considered representative of all cases of titled marriage during that time.

Conversely, the emotional dimensions of transnational spaces that were manifested in both encounter and representation are far more accessible. The evidence of the cultural and emotional processes of encounter and courting in transnational spaces is best noted in ways in which marriage participants from the two societies described one another in varied forms of media. An examination of these discourses found in the press, French and American literary works, travel literature, and personal accounts demonstrates not only how notions of difference were marked but also how these perceived differences provoked certain emotional responses.

Finally, the personal accounts of courtship and marriage processes during the world wars are far more numerous as transnational-marriage participants spoke far more openly about intimate experiences and relationship, especially in the context of war. These stories of wartime encounter, courtship, and marriage have been captured in unpublished memoirs, self-published memoirs, letters, and interviews collected by contemporary journalists and detailed in the invaluable oral histories that have preceded this work. Because the wars forced to the forefront a discourse of new emotional dimensions, these numerous personal accounts from both men and women allow the historian to push the theory of emotions further than nineteenth-century sources allow.

Organization

What follows is, therefore, a temporal comparison of two distinct historical contexts largely based on distinct sets of historical sources. Despite these and other differences, however, a story of similarity emerges. For the purpose of the comparison, the two types of transnational marriages are separated topically; although, it should be noted that they overlapped chronologically. Further, while changing social definitions of marriage over time have led to the social recognition of a variety of coupling practices (cohabitating without marriage, polyamorous relationships, and same-sex marriage, e.g.), the legal and social contexts of the nineteenth and twentieth centuries have left researchers with few sources on these other types of unions. This study, therefore, recognizes that not all couples had equal access to marriage and, for this reason, is mostly concerned with heterosexual couples of two that were contracted between French and American citizens who were involved in legally, religiously, or socially recognized relationships. This work also centers on the examination of noticeable transnational-marriage patterns between France and the United States, to which exceptions existed. In order to maintain the methodological focus of the temporal comparison, those exceptions have largely been excluded. The patterns examined here are also gender specific. This gender imbalance is not a categorical selection but was instead the result of various external structures that facilitated movement in the past and is largely representative of those patterns. These structures will be further addressed in the chapters that follow.

Because historians have generally treated these two patterns of marriage separately, each part is opened with an introductory section that situates the proposed analytical categories of transnational space, culture, and emotion within its existing historiography. Each of these historiographical frames is then followed by two chapters—one, which maps the transnational spaces and communities that produced marriage and one, which further examines the cultural and emotional dimensions of these transnational spaces of encounter and courtship. In both parts, I seek to examine the ways in which marriages emerged out of cross-cultural encounter by illuminating how notions of cultural difference were marked and how these perceived differences provoked certain emotional responses that shaped the marital, familial, and social experiences of transnational-marriage participants. In my analysis, I further place those cross-cultural encounters within three broader global contexts: (1) the shift from nineteenth-century nation making to twentieth-century hyper-nationalism, (2) the changing cultural relations between France and the United States, and (3) the changing emotional standards as they relate to the practices of marriage and courtship.

In the first part on titled marriages, I specifically challenge existing notions that marriages between wealthy American heiresses and French nobility were purely the result of strategic socioeconomic calculations on the part of American women and their families. By examining the making of elite transnational communities in the context of both nineteenth-century economic development and transatlantic mobility, I argue in the first chapter that these marriages were instead the result of social interaction within elite transnational social networks and spaces that existed between the United States and Europe, among those with largely unrestricted transatlantic mobility and who chiefly identified with others of similar economic and social status rather than national origin. Here, I will show how elite transnational social events such as costume balls and dinners came to serve as both a stage for Franco-American cross-cultural encounters and a cultural mechanism for elite coupling. In this chapter, I adopt the term *transnational high society* to describe those members of an elite social group who lived privileged lives not limited by national borders and who occupied elite, transnational social spaces in the Atlantic world. These social networks largely included wealthy Americans from urban centers such as New York, Boston, and Philadelphia; royalty, nobility, and aristocracy from around Europe; as well as diplomatic elites. To avoid replacing a national frame with a binational one, it should be noted that while this work is an examination of Franco-American marriages, this transnational high society was not limited to French and American members, and therefore at times, I also draw on the writings and words of members who resided in other important urban centers such as London.

In the second chapter, I go further to examine the cultural and emotional dimensions of the transnational spaces that produced elite, titled marriages by examining cultural othering as an emotional process. Here, I argue that at the intersection of encounter, elite class-consciousness and transnational coupling stood a profoundly emotional experience, and because that experience was so intertwined with cross-cultural interaction, the marriages that emerged from these spaces can be, in many respects, characterized as even more (rather than less) emotional than their elite, national counterparts. Within the transnational context, Franco-American cultural interactions, exchange, and the process of what I call *positive othering* facilitated sentiments of longing among marriage participants.

The second part on marriages in the context of the world wars continues with the application of the analytical categories of transnational space, culture, and emotion to the changing contexts of the twentieth century, and I argue that despite increasingly seeing their own identities through national lenses and despite changing cultural relationships between France and the United States, notions of perceived difference remained the driving force of transnational coupling. The third chapter begins by contextualizing the broader temporal comparison of nineteenth-century elite marriages and twentieth-century wartime marriages by examining some of the wider global changes brought on by the world wars. These changes shifted the context in which wartime encounter took place by producing a situation in which marriage participants would not only come from the working and middle classes but would also have an increased tendency to self-describe through national frameworks. In this setting, notions of difference were further heightened and the varied cultural projections that resulted from processes of othering shifted from those of the previous century. For American soldiers, rather than the elite high cultural forms of the nineteenth century such as food, dress, and art, cultural fascination with the French was laced instead with notions of romance, sex, and pleasure. These notions were subsequently transcribed onto French women. For French women, emotions of war such as fear, uncertainty, and the longing for stability under German invasion and occupation during World War II were soon contrasted by the overwhelming excitement and euphoria of liberation. This drastic emotional shift along with what was perceived as a striking and curious difference of American soldiers led young French women to actively engage American soldiers in their courting customs.

The fourth chapter shifts from wartime othering as an emotional process to a spatial analysis of transnational courtship and marriage and attempts to reconcile the relative absence of a transnational community or social network among these marriage participants by locating and defining new transnational spaces that were created during the world wars and examining how those transnational spaces of courtship and marriage existed in opposition to national spaces. One of the most important of those transnational spaces, I argue, was Red Cross dances, where other forms of mediated cultural cues associated with dancing not only compensated for lack of common language among participants but also became important cultural devices for transnational coupling and courting rituals.

This final chapter also goes further to contextualize wartime Franco-American marriages within broader themes of sexualization and emotionalization of marriage as a social practice. While the emotional evolution of marriage was not entirely linear, by the mid-twentieth century, that marriage was recognized as both an emotionally based union and a free and individual choice can no longer be doubted in either French or American societies. Further, in context of both wars, both societies experienced a temporary relaxation of moral and patriarchal standards as they had previously been enforced. Therefore, new dimensions of wartime encounter led to numerous intimate and sexual relationships that provide another interesting layer to cross-cultural encounter. According to one Army report produced in 1922, seventy-one percent of American soldiers claimed to have had sexual relationships with French women while serving in the American Expeditionary Forces, but only a fraction of these intimate encounters resulted in marriage.[37] Therefore, in this chapter, I also ask what conditions needed to be present for a Franco-American couple involved in an intimate relationship to take matrimonial vows.

In the end, I conclude that even though marriage participants from each of the two patterns conceived of the national and cultural boundaries that separated them in very different ways, notions of and attraction to difference largely remained the driving force of marriage and coupling processes in both contexts. Here, by participating in a transnational marriage, one bound oneself permanently not only to one's spouse but also to the culture of that spouse. Motivations for transnational marriage in these contexts were therefore strategic and based on preconceived notions of what they believed the other culture to be.

Notes

1 Jean Claude Bologne, *Histoire du couple* (Paris: Perrin, 2016), 7 reminds us that researchers too often examine the social processes of coupling through the prism of marriage, leaving out a variety of important relationships.
2 Stephanie Coontz, *Marriage, a History: From Obedience to Intimacy or How Love Conquered Marriage* (New York: Viking, 2005), 2.
3 Edmund Leach, "The Social Anthropology of Marriage and Mating," in *Mating and Marriage*, ed. Vernon Reynolds and John Kellett (Oxford; New York: Oxford University Press, 1991), 93.
4 Coontz, *Marriage, a History*, 34.
5 Jose Moya, "The Historical Emergence and Massification of International Families in Europe and Its Diaspora," in *Transregional and Transnational Families in Europe and Beyond: Experiences Since the Middle Ages*, ed. Christopher H. Johnson et al. (New York: Berghahn Books, 2011), 23 shows that people have been constructing families across borders as long as people have been mobile.
6 Daniel Rodgers, *Atlantic Crossings: Social Politics in a Progressive Age* (Cambridge, MA: Belknap Press of Harvard University Press, 1998), 2.
7 Margot Canaday, *The Straight State: Sexuality and Citizenship in Twentieth-Century America* (Princeton, NJ: Princeton University Press, 2009); Nancy F. Cott, *Public Vows: A History of Marriage and the Nation* (Cambridge, MA: Harvard University Press, 2000); John R. Gillis, *For Better, for Worse: British Marriages, 1600 to the Present* (New York: Oxford University Press, 1985); Silvana Seidel Menchi, Emlyn Eisenach, and Charles Donahue, *Marriage in Europe, 1400–1800* (Toronto: University of Toronto Press, 2016).
8 Candice Lewis Bredbenner, *A Nationality of Her Own Women, Marriage, and the Law of Citizenship* (Berkeley: University of California Press, 1998); Francisco Muñoz-Perez Tribalat, Michèle, "Mariages d'étrangers et mariages mixtes en France: Évolution depuis la Première Guerre," *Population (French Edition)* 39, no. 3 (1984): 427–62; Gérard Neyrand et al., *Mariages mixtes et nationalité française: les Français par mariage et leurs conjoints* (Paris: Ed. l'Harmattan, 1995); Ann Marie Nicolosi, "'We Do Not Want Our Girls to Marry Foreigners': Gender, Race, and American Citizenship," *NWSA Journal* 13, no. 3 Gender and Social Policy: Local to Global (2001): 1–21; Jessica Mai Sims and Runnymede Trust, *Mixed Heritage: Identity, Policy and Practice* (London: Runnymede Trust, 2007); Mika Toyota, "Editorial Introduction: International Marriage, Rights and the State in East and Southeast Asia," *Citizenship Studies* 12, no. 1 (2008): 1–7; Lucy Williams, *Global Marriage: Cross-Border Marriage Migration in Global Context* (Basingstoke; New York: Palgrave Macmillan, 2010); Helena Wray, *Regulating Marriage Migration into the UK: A Stranger in the Home* (Farnham, Surrey, England; Burlington, VT: Ashgate, 2011).
9 Cott, *Public Vows*, 5.
10 Williams, *Global Marriage*, 7.
11 Micol Seigel, "Beyond Compare: Comparative Method after the Transnational Turn," *Radical History Review* 2005, no. 91 (December 21, 2005): 62–90; Ian R. Tyrrell, *Transnational Nation: United States History in Global Perspective Since 1789* (New York: Palgrave Macmillan, 2015).
12 Wen-Shan Yang and Melody Chia-Wen Lu, *Asian Cross-Border Marriage Migration: Demographic Patterns and Social Issues* (Amsterdam: Amsterdam University Press, 2010). This definition was also adopted in the recent sociological edited volume, Katharine Charsley, *Transnational Marriage: New Perspectives from Europe and Beyond* (New York:

Routledge, 2012), 7, in which British sociologist, Katharine Charsley attempted to standardize some of the relevant concepts as they pertained to the emerging but still interdisciplinary and fragmented field of transnational marriage.
13 Katharine Charsley, ed., *Transnational Marriage: New Perspectives from Europe and Beyond* (New York: Routledge, 2012), 7.
14 Margrit Pernau, "Space and Emotion: Building to Feel," *History Compass* 12, no. 7 (2014): 542.
15 Homi K. Bhabha, *The Location of Culture* (London; New York: Routledge, 1994).
16 Coontz, *Marriage, a History*; William M Reddy, *The Making of Romantic Love: Longing and Sexuality in Europe, South Asia, and Japan, 900–1200 CE* (Chicago: University of Chicago Press, 2012).
17 Seidel Menchi, Eisenach, and Donahue, *Marriage in Europe*, 33–34.
18 For a region-specific analysis of marriage practices and the laws regulating them in various European societies from a comparative perspective, see Seidel Menchi, Eisenach, and Donahue, *Marriage in Europe*.
19 Coontz, *Marriage, a History*, 9.
20 Kimberly Schutte, *Women, Rank, and Marriage in the British Aristocracy, 1485–2000: An Open Elite?* (Basingstoke: Palgrave Macmillan, 2014), 88.
21 Reddy, *The Making of Romantic Love*, 5.
22 Coontz, *Marriage, a History*, 128.
23 Coontz, *Marriage, a History*, 7, 148.
24 Coontz, *Marriage, a History*, 146.
25 Coontz, *Marriage, a History*, 148.
26 Coontz, *Marriage, a History*, 5.
27 Reddy, *The Making of Romantic Love*, 21.
28 Yvonne Rieker, "Love Crossing Borders: Changing Patterns of Courtship and Gender Relations among Italian Migrants in Germany," in *Intimacy and Italian Migration: Gender and Domestic Lives in a Mobile World* (New York: Fordham University Press, 2011), 123.
29 Roderick Phillips, *Untying the Knot: A Short History of Divorce* (Cambridge: Cambridge University Press, 1991), 108.
30 Coontz, *Marriage, a History*, 7.
31 Schutte, *Women, Rank, and Marriage in the British Aristocracy*, 103–4.
32 Alison Shaw and Katharine Charsely, "Rishtas: Adding Emotion to Strategy in Understanding British Pakistani Transnational Marriages," *Global Networks* 6, no. 4 (2006): 405–21. In their examination of British Pakistani marriages, Shaw and Charsley go even further to argue that even traditionally arranged marriages were not void of emotion. They argue that marriages were, in fact, arranged in order to safeguard happiness.
33 Susan J. Matt and Peter N. Stearns, *Doing Emotions History* (Urbana: University of Illinois Press, 2014), 1.
34 Alain Corbin and Pascal Ory, *Une histoire des sens* (Paris: Robert Laffont, 2016); Anne-Emmanuelle Demartini et al., *Émotions contemporaines: XIXe-XXIe siècles* (Paris: A. Colin, 2014); Matt and Stearns, *Doing Emotions History*; William M. Reddy, *The Navigation of Feeling a Framework for the History of Emotions* (Cambridge, UK; New York: Cambridge University Press, 2001).
35 Reddy, *The Making of Romantic Love*; Coontz, *Marriage, a History*.
36 Reddy, *The Making of Romantic Love*, 6.
37 George Walker, *Venereal Disease in the American Expeditionary Forces* (Baltimore: Medical Standard Book Co., 1922), 101.

Part I

"TRADING TITLES FOR TREASURE?": ELITE MARRIAGES DURING THE NINETEENTH CENTURY[1]

As long as the modern nation-states of France and the United States have existed, people have constructed families across their borders. For example, in 1782, Elizabeth Livingston of New York married the Comte de Mosloy, attaché to the French Minister. During the French Revolution, Edmond-Charles Genêt, French ambassador to the United States, married Cornelia Clinton, the daughter of New York Governor George Clinton (1794), and soon after, Betsy Patterson of Baltimore married Jérôme Bonaparte, brother of Emperor Napoleon I (1803). In the early nineteenth century, Maria Bingham of Philadelphia first married Jacques Alexandre, Comte de Tilly and later wed the Marquis de Blaizel (1826); whereas Prince Napoleon Lucien Charles Murat married Caroline Georgina Fraser of Charleston (1831).[2] While these early marriages likely occurred by chance and in relatively small numbers, as the nineteenth century continued—a century marked by growing nationalism and heightened boundary-making—a noticeable pattern of transnational marriages began to emerge between wealthy American women and European aristocrats. According to contemporary American commentator Gustavus Meyers, by 1909, five hundred American heiresses had married titled nobility and had taken nearly $220 million out of the United States to Europe.[3] While these women entered into matrimonial contracts with nobility from all over Europe, an overwhelming majority of these marriage contracts were established with men from Great Britain and France.

Even though these mixed marriages were not entirely exceptional, they remained (and in many ways continue to remain) exceptional in public discourse as contemporaries and historians struggled to explain their occurrence. For example, in January of 1887 the American newspaper *Town Topics: Journal of Society* published the following story:

> Direct from the banks of the Seine: M. le Duc de Charenton is a nobleman of the type common in the palmy days of the Second Empire. Paris laughed at his eccentricities then, and Paris is laughing still [...] This gay old dog of Napoleon's court has been living for years "au troisième," apparently dead broke, in a slum at Montmartre. He has been seen at odd intervals late at night on the Boulevards, evidently on the prowl: but he has always dodged old acquaintances and was generally written off by society as a bad debt. What, then, was the surprise of the strollers in the Bois the other day, when M. de Charenton resurrected himself in a brand new chariot, exquisitely horsed, and accompanied by a charming blond, whose accents were suggestive of Chicago. It seems the M. le Duc has courted and has been successfully courted by one of those ladies who tried for a title in London last year [...] must be a relief to all her friends who know how much she wanted it.[4]

Likewise, in 1895, American novelist William H. Chambliss made the following claims about these titled European husbands:

> A Chinese exclusion act we already have. What we need now is a European exclusion act [...] The general exclusion act should contain an article specially designed for the unconditional exclusion of penniless princes, lords, barons, counts, and all other cheap-titled adventurers who, like Prince Andre Poniatowski and Count de Castellane, are likely to be sent over here in the future by the same board of matrimonial brokers that sent these two sweet-scented "noblemen" to marry rich parvenuesses on percentage [...] The Chinaman who goes to the market to purchase a wife always gets more for his money than does the American heiress who goes shopping for a titled husband [...] In the name of common sense, will our novel-reading girls never learn that a foreign title amounts to nothing more than the paper it's written on.[5]

Even French novelist Victorien du Saussay created a similar image of these Franco-American marriages in his novel, *La traite des blancs : mariages franco-américains : roman de passion*:

> Et comme elle a mis au Mont-de-Piété ses derniers joyaux, la noblesse vend le diadème au plus offrant. Elle se livre, comme une catin. Et à qui ? A qui la noblesse s'allie-t-elle et se vend-elle ? A tout ce qu'il

y a de douteux sur terre. L'Amérique ; refuge de la lie de l'humanité, productrice de milliardaires aux origines inavouables, fils et petits-fils de voleurs, d'assassins, de déclassés impunis, achète pour quelques poignées d'or infâme les plus fières couronnés du vieux monde.

Pourquoi [...] les jolies riches américaines croient-elles nécessaire de se faire épouser par les gentils hommes de la vieille Europe, au lieu de rester Américaines ? [...] Ici, une jeune fille riche [...] dit "je vaux tant de rentes" ; et, immédiatement, de toutes parts, on lui fait la cour, on se bat pour la conquérir ; elle n'a que l'embarras du choix [...]⁶

[And since it has put its last jewels at the Mont-de-Piété, the nobility sells the coronet to the highest bidder. It surrenders itself like a whore. And to whom? To whom does the nobility ally and sell itself? To all that is questionable on earth. America—refuge of the dregs of humanity, producer of billionaires with unspeakable origins, sons and grandsons of thieves, of assassins, wretched, unchastened criminals—buys for a few handfuls of infamous gold the proudest crowned of the old world.

Why [...] do pretty, rich American women believe it necessary to marry gentlemen of old Europe rather than remaining American? Here a young wealthy lady says, "I am worth a lot of money," and immediately, from everywhere, they all want to court her, they all battle to conquer her, and she only has to choose from among them [...]]⁷

Given the nature of these passages, it is little wonder that the few historians who have taken on the subject of nineteenth-century titled marriages (focusing often on Anglo-American cases) have come to describe them as little more than socioeconomic arrangements, in which European titles were exchanged for American dollars through marital contracts.⁸ Frederic Cople Jaher, for example, in his 1975 work, *The Rich, the Wellborn, and the Powerful: Elites and Upper Classes in History*, argues that these marriages, which he describes as a caricature of the shaky pretensions of fashionable New York, were impelled by status anxieties of the *nouveaux riches* and were, therefore, arranged with European nobility in order to "fortify mediocre genealogies."⁹ Likewise and more recently, transnational historian Thomas Adam agrees, labeling such unions the "result of purely economic and social calculations" in his 2009 work, *Buying Respectability: Philanthropy and Urban Society in Transnational Perspective, 1840s to 1930s.*¹⁰ According to Adam, these women married impoverished nobility to whom they promised financial support in exchange for social honor in an artificial New York high society, which had been founded on social prestige and exclusion rather than on more tangible political or economic power.

Upon closer examination, however, one quickly finds that these socioeconomic explanations are limited for several reasons. First, the title-for-treasure-exchange paradigm is based largely on problematic contemporary sources such as the popular American press, which often attempted to capitalize on the most scandalous tales. These articles, such as the one quoted above from *Town Topics*, employed popular gendered classifications of men as emotionless and in search of only money rather than companionship and women as having little else besides money, lending to a need for a husband, thereby perpetuating the notion of these marriages as title-for-dollar exchanges. Other accounts of these marriages were largely based on the views of contemporary nonparticipants, like Gustavus Meyers and William H. Chambliss, who remained outside of the internal, private space of these marriages and whose critiques largely rested on the juxtaposition of American republican ideals with European monarchy and aristocracy.

There are further limitations to the titles themselves. In these marriages, very large sums of money were exchanged for little in return. The American publication *Titled Americans: A List of American Ladies Who Have Married Foreigners of Titled Americans: A List of American Ladies Who Have Married Foreigners of Rank*, issued in March 1890, warned American girls seeking noble titles through marriage of the following: "These honorific distinctions are, however, not officially recognized in this country, and their use is not in accordance with the democratic institutions and social systems of the United States."[11] Because these titles were neither recognized in the United States nor did they extend to the rest of the women's family, obtaining European titles did not translate into any additional political or economic power for American women or their families.

Additionally, when compared with their British counterparts, French titles in particular were problematic. Both feudalism and titles of nobility had been explicitly abolished in 1790 by decree of the National Assembly. Even though in 1804 Napoleon reinstated the system and began creating his own titles, neither feudalism nor the judicial status of a privileged *noblesse* were ever restored, and postrevolutionary France became marked by a long tradition of well-articulated, anti-aristocratic sentiment and discourse. Although viewed by many as markers of an elite and privileged social class, by 1835 French titles had become completely separated from landed claims and continued to exist merely as hereditary appendages to a family name. When the July Monarchy was overthrown in 1848, titles were again abolished, and then again restored in 1852 by Napoleon III during the period of the Second Empire, but again without prerevolutionary legal privilege or precedence. Finally, upon the establishment of the Third Republic in 1870, the French state allowed for the continued existence of titles of nobility as an appendage of a legal name—a status that continues to remain in effect.[12]

Nancy Green argues in her recent work, *The Other Americans in Paris*, that even though the economic and political power of French titles had been waning by the nineteenth century, it was their symbolic power within French society that persisted and provided incentives for transnational marriages.[13] Here, she points to the work of Arno J. Mayer, *The Persistence of the Old Regime*, which argues that in the years leading to World War I, European post-feudal nobility held great power and influence over both civil society and foreign affairs.[14] However, others have questioned to what extent Mayer's argument could be applied to all of Europe at the time. While Edward R. Tannenbaum, for example, largely agrees with Mayer's assessment, he suggests that it appears more convincing in the cases of Central Europe and Great Britain since the landed aristocracy in these territories retained its influence through landed privilege as well as cultural and social prestige and political skill despite changing economic structures. However, in the case of France, he claims that Mayer's arguments of aristocratic persistence are less convincing.[15] James J. Sheehan also disagrees with Mayer and argues that French aristocratic power in foreign and internal affairs was minimal.[16] The late nineteenth-century French count, Boniface (Boni) de Castellane seems to have offered confirmation of the latter arguments. In his turn-of-the-century memoir he complained:

> French society has undergone many changes [...] and through not understanding the necessity for judicious selection, it developed into the Capernaum of today [...] It is the same in the country as well as in the capital; old tastes and pursuits have no place in modern life [...] A château is often another name for a hotel, its original purpose has disappeared, and our peasants have either become indifferent to us or have openly declared themselves our enemies [...] Our former prestige has suffered terrible loss.[17]

Green claims that the political position of nobility in France did not impact the fascination of Americans with French titles.[18] Therefore, one would assume, as Jaher and Adam have, that for American women, the attraction to French titles took the form of social and cultural capital.[19] While the purpose of this chapter is not to minimize the social symbolism involved in the obtaining of noble titles by Americans, I do maintain that the American perceptions of French titles, in particular, must be further questioned. Similar to the complaints of Boni de Castellane, many American visitors and residents in France remarked on the declining social position of the French aristocracy.

Harriett Beecher Stowe, for example, claimed in 1854 on her tour through imperial France that "no country has been swept cleaner of aristocratic institutions, and the old bastilles and prisons of tyranny."[20] Likewise elite, American novelist and established member of Parisian high society, Edith Wharton later confirmed that "if in those days any authentic member of the Faubourg Saint-Germain had been asked what really constituted Paris society, the answer would undoubtedly have been: There is no Paris society any longer—there is just a welter of people from heaven knows where [...] The old social conventions [of Paris] were tottering or already demolished."[21] Further, because of the various nineteenth-century regime changes in France—each accompanied by the creation of its own titles— Americans considered the status that accompanied French titles to be less stable in comparison to their English counterparts, whose holders seemed to maintain more cultural and social prestige, as Tannenbaum has suggested. Therefore, while marriages to British nobility, like that of Consuela Vanderbilt to the Duke of Marlborough, were admired and portrayed as storybook romances, marriages to French nobility were often looked at with suspicion and contempt.[22]

American women hoping to find a noble husband would not have been unaware of this perception of French titles. *Titled Americans*, which also published a section that was comprised of "a carefully compiled list of Peers who are supposed to be eager to lay their coronets, and incidentally their hearts, at the feet of the all-conquering American girl," warned of the untrustworthiness of French titles:

> In France, titles at the present moment are somewhat at a discount. While on the one hand there are the representatives of those grand old families, which formerly constituted the very kernel of European "noblesse," there are on the other hand thousands of persons who have, without the slightest authority, adopted titles and names to which they have no right. It is true that there is a law in France which ordains that no one shall adopt a nobiliary title or even adorn his button-hole with a foreign order without having previously obtained a permit in due form to do so from the Grande Chancellerie of the Order of the Legion of Honor [...] But since the overthrow of the empire and the abolition of monarchy in France, no steps have been taken by the government to enforce the law, and people ornament their names with any title which suit their fancy.[23]

Contrarily, it boasted: "English titles enjoy greater consideration, both at home and abroad, than those conferred by any other State."[24] Similarly to the claims made in *Titled Americans*, Richard Harding Davis, American journalist and novelist, also warned in his work, *About Paris*, that French titles should not be sought after:

> There are, as a matter of fact, only a very few titles worth buying, and in selecting the choice should always lie between one of England and one of Germany. An English earl is the best the American heiress can reasonably hope for, and after him a husband with a German title is very desirable. These might be rated as "sure" and "safe" investments. But these French titles created by Napoleon or [...] created by the Papal Court [...] are not really worthwhile. Theirs are not titles, as someone has said, they are epitaphs.[25]

Yet, in 1892 the *Social Register of New York* listed thirty-one titled American women, and of those, twenty-one of them were married to Frenchmen.[26] Given this seeming knowledge on the part of American ladies, it is hard to place the majority of these Franco-American marriages within the title-for-treasure exchange paradigm.

Further, these socioeconomic explanations have failed to account for changes in emotional standards over time, thereby resulting in the reductionist treatment of the practice of marriage. Emotions, often excluded from the study of history because they are hard to capture, played a significant role in the experiences of transnational-marriage participants and provided an essential motivating factor. While marital practices show great variability in different historical contexts, by the second half of the nineteenth century, many Westerners had come to idealize love-based marriage—so much so that the absence of love even justified the dissolution of marriage, leaving divorce rates a valuable indicator of emotional expectations.[27] In his memoir written after his divorce from Anna Gould, Boni de Castellane insists numerous times that he did indeed love her and that they both had entered into the marriage with the expectation that it would be based on love and happiness.[28] Whether or not he actually loved her, only he could have truly known; however, his insistence is evidence that he recognized the social norms of love-based marriages even among elite classes. However, just as it would be a mistake to reduce marriage to a quest for socioeconomic well-being, so to would it be a mistake to reduce the emotional dimensions of marriage to *romantic love* alone. Therefore, in this work I suggest the need to further uncover the complex diversity of intimate emotional experiences that coincide with the practice of marriage—emotional experiences that are even more multifaceted once placed within the transnational context.

Finally, while these socioeconomic explanations have successfully expanded the concept of social class formation developed by E.P. Thompson by applying it to the case of the American bourgeoisie from a compelling transnational perspective,[29] I argue that they still fail to fully escape the "analytical cage of the nation-state"[30] as they largely attempt to explain the marriages from the perspective of one culture or the other rather than from the spaces out of which they emerged—transnational communities located liminally between the two. By drawing on the concept of *transnational marriage*, which situates cross-border marriages within a context of wider transnational processes and which places focus on the transnational networks and space created by the actors themselves,[31] the following two chapters suggest instead the ways in which intersecting methodologies of transnational history, cultural history, and the history of emotions might compliment these socioeconomic explanations in order to provide us with a more complete picture of mixed marriages in the past. Therefore, in an attempt to reposition the space of inquiry to the transcultural spaces that produced the marriages, the next two chapters address the following question: How do patterns of transnational marriage emerge out of cross-cultural encounters, and to what extent did larger Franco-American cultural relations facilitate marriages in the context of the nineteenth century?

By placing emotions in broader transnational and cultural frameworks, I show how complex cultural meanings within transnational spaces were experienced on personal levels among marriage participants and highlight what they hoped to gain in addition to their foreign spouse. Descriptions of elite social events found in the French and American press, travel literature, personal papers, and guest lists provide an important glimpse into these transnational communities and their cultural rituals. Further, by focusing on these spaces of transnationality we are able to highlight a series of cross-cultural relationships and experiences otherwise unavailable.[32] Through an analysis of these elite social events and other social spaces, I argue that these nineteenth-century, Franco-American titled unions emerged out of transnational communities and spaces that existed parallel to national spaces, and resulted from the interplay of social compatibility (rather than social anxiety) among elite European and American participants on one hand, and, on the other, mutual fascination and what I call *cultural infatuation*—an affection for perceived culture itself.

Such an undertaking is not without limitations and deficiencies. The first is the problem of quantifying the number of these titled marriages. While the work of Gustavus Meyers, who claimed that by 1909 five hundred American heiresses had entered into transnational marriages with titled nobility, and the lists generated by *Titled Americans: A List of American Ladies Who*

Have Married Foreigners of Rank provide valuable indicators, obtaining precise, nationally categorized numbers is difficult, and no complete list exists.[33] During the course of this project, I encountered mention of approximately one hundred French-American titled marriages in the French and American press and other sources—the earliest of which occurred in 1782 and the latest in 1993. This also points to the problem of periodization. The topic of titled marriages between Americans and Europeans seems to have peaked in the last two decades of the nineteenth century. As its novelty wore off, fewer mentions in the press make later marriages far less visible to the historian. Therefore, the analytical focus on titled marriages for the purpose of this work rests within the nineteenth century. Finally, because the purpose of this part is to compliment other socioeconomic explanations of marriage motivations, the analytical focus also rests on the broader cultural and emotional dynamics of transnational sociability and cross-cultural interaction rather than intimate in-depth biographical portraits of individual couples and their post-marriage lives—as interesting and scandalous as they sometimes were.

Notes

1 P. Harvey Middleton, "Dukedoms for Ducrats: Europe Is $900,000,000 Ahead of America in Trading of Titles for Treasure," *Omaha World Herald*, May 30, 1909.

2 Elizabeth Eliot, *Heiresses and Coronets* (New York: McDowell, 1959), 14; William Thomas Roberts Saffell, *The Bonaparte-Patterson Marriage in 1803, and the Secret Correspondence on the Subject Never Before Made Public* (Philadelphia: The Proprietor, 1873), v; Comte Alexandre de Tilly, *Mémoires du comte Alexandre de Tilly, pour servir à l'histoire des moeurs de la fin du 18me siècle* (Paris: Chez les Marchands de Nouveautés, 1828), 247.

3 Gustavus Myers, *History of the Great American Fortunes*, vol. 3 (New York: The Modern Library, 1909); Gabriel A. Almond, *Plutocracy and Politics in New York City* (Boulder, Colo.: Westview Press, 1998), 116.

4 "Saunterings," *Town Topics: Journal of Society*, January 27, 1887, New York Genealogical and Biographical Society Collection, New York Public Library.

5 William H. Chambliss and Laura E. Foster, *Chambliss Diary, Or, Society as It Really Is* (New York: Chambliss & Co., 1895), 15.

6 Victorien Du Saussay, *La traite des blancs: mariages franco-américains: roman de passion* (Paris: Librairie des pubications modernes, 1900), 17.

7 Unless otherwise noted, all translations are my own.

8 Ruth Brandon, *The Dollar Princesses* (London: Weidenfeld and Nicolson, 1980); Dana Cooper, *Informal Ambassadors: American Women, Transatlantic Marriages, and Anglo-American Relations, 1865–1945* (Kent State University Press, 2014); Nancy L. Green, *The Other Americans in Paris: Businessmen, Countesses, Wayward Youth, 1880–1941* (Chicago: The University of Chicago Press, 2014); Elisabeth Kehoe, *The Titled Americans: Three American Sisters and the British Aristocratic World into Which They Married* (New York: Atlantic Monthly Press, 2004); Gail MacColl and Carol Wallace, *To Marry an English Lord* (New York: Workman Pub., 1989); Frances McNeil, *Sisters of Fortune*

(Sutton: Severn House, 2007); Maureen E Montgomery, *"Gilded Prostitution": Status, Money, and Transatlantic Marriages, 1870–1914* (London; New York: Routledge, 1989).
9 Frederic Cople Jaher, "Style and Status: High Society in Late-Nineteenth-Century New York," in *The Rich, the Wellborn, and the Powerful: Elites and Upper Classes in History*, ed. Frederic Cople Jaher (Secaucus, N.J.: Citadel Press, 1975), 258–84.
10 Thomas Adam, *Buying Respectability: Philanthropy and Urban Society in Transnational Perspective, 1840s to 1930s* (Bloomington: Indiana University Press, 2009), 94.
11 *Titled Americans. A List of American Ladies Who Have Married Foreigners of Rank* (New York: Street & Smith, 1890), 11.
12 For more on the history of the French nobility see: Philippe du Puy de Clinchamps and Patrice du Puy de Clinchamps, *La noblesse* (Paris: L'Intermédiaire des chercheurs et curieux, 1996); Alain Texier, *Qu'est-ce que la noblesse?* (Paris: Le Grand livre du mois, 2000); Jean Tulard, *Napoléon et la noblesse d'Empire: avec la liste des membres de la noblesse impériale, 1808–1815* (Paris: Tallandier, 2003).
13 Green, *The Other Americans in Paris*, 89.
14 Arno J. Mayer, *La persistance de l'ancien regime : L'europe de 1848 a la grande guerre* (Paris: Flammarion, 1983).
15 Edward R. Tannenbaum, "Reviewed Work: *The Persistence of the Old Régime. Europe to the Great War* by Arno J. Mayer," *The American Historical Review* 87, no. 2 (April 1982): 439–40.
16 James J. Sheehan, "Reviewed Work: *The Persistence of the Old Régime. Europe to the Great War* by Arno J. Mayer," *Social History* 8, no. 1 (January 1983): 111–12.
17 Boni de Castellane, *How I Discovered America* (New York: Alfred A. Knopf, 1924), 107–8.
18 Green, *The Other Americans in Paris*, 89.
19 Pierre Bourdieu, *Distinction: A Social Critique of the Judgment of Taste* (London: Routledge & Kegan Paul, 1986); Pierre Bourdieu, *The Field of Cultural Production*, ed. Randal Johnson, 1st edition (New York: Columbia University Press, 1993).
20 Harriet Beecher Stowe, *Sunny Memories of Foreign Lands*, vol. 2 (Boston: Phillips, Sampson, 1854), 410.
21 Edith Wharton, *A Backward Glance* (New York; London: D. Appleton-Century Co., 1934), 259.
22 Harvey A. Levenstein, *Seductive Journey: American Tourists in France from Jefferson to the Jazz Age* (Chicago: University of Chicago Press, 1998), 193.
23 *Titled Americans*, 21–22.
24 Ibid., 24.
25 Richard Harding Davis, *About Paris* (New York: Harper & Brothers, 1895), 201–202.
26 *Social Register of New York*, 1892 (New York: Social Register Association, 1891); Cited in Almond, *Plutocracy and Politics in New York City*, 116.
27 Bologne, *Histoire du couple*; Coontz, *Marriage, a History*; Matt and Stearns, *Doing Emotions History*, 2; Phillips, *Untying the Knot*; Reddy, *The Making of Romantic Love*.
28 Boni Castellane, *Comment j'ai découvert l'Amérique : mémoires*. (Paris: G. Crès et cie, 1924).
29 E. P. Thompson, *The Making of the English Working Class* (New York: Pantheon Books, 1964).
30 Rodgers, *Atlantic Crossings*, 2.
31 Charsley, *Transnational Marriage*, 2012, 19.
32 Peter Jackson, Phil Crang, and Claire Dwyer, *Transnational Spaces* (London; New York: Routledge, 2004), 3.
33 Myers, *History of the Great American Fortunes*, 1909; *Titled Americans*.

Chapter 1

THE MAKING OF A TRANSNATIONAL HIGH SOCIETY

This chapter is divided into four parts: In the first, I examine the making of elite transnational communities in the context of both nineteenth-century economic development and transatlantic mobility. By adopting Thorstein Veblen's concept of the American leisure class and applying it to a transnational context, I argue that a transnational high society developed as wealthy American travelers began to keep company with the aristocratic and diplomatic echelons of Europe, whose lifestyles appeared to resemble their own. The second part goes further to examine the cultural dimensions of this elite social network by examining the cultural rituals of their social events. Here, I argue that elite transnational social events such as costume balls and dinners came to serve as both a stage for Franco-American cross-cultural encounters and a cultural mechanism for elite coupling. The third part examines the ways in which American women saw their own place within these elite transnational social networks. Through an examination of assertions of common socioeconomic belonging, I argue that rather than American social or status anxieties driving these marriages, it was instead a sense of social confidence or a confident assertion of elite position among members of elite transnational communities that facilitated them. Finally, the fourth part examines how legal questions around marriage and citizenship affected the extent to which participants saw themselves as marrying across national lines. Here, I conclude that a relative absence of nineteenth-century legal barriers further facilitated not only elite high society's transnational existence but also cross-border coupling.

Emerging Transnational Communities

The emergence of the pattern of Franco-American titled marriages in the second half of the nietieth century coincided with two interconnected developments that facilitated both movement and encounter: First, technological developments of the Industrial Revolution made transoceanic steam travel between Europe and America safer, more comfortable, more rapid, and more frequent.[1] The second was the development of what Thorstein Veblen calls the American *leisure class*.[2] Identifying and associating with only those whose economic and social positions afforded them similar lifestyles, this leisure class was characterized by conspicuous consumption of luxury goods, increased leisure time, and travel for no other reason than to mark their prestige. That meant, for wealthy Americans, extended leisurely trips to Europe became synonymous with upper-class tastes and social distinction.[3] As Maureen Montgomery explains: "By the 1870's, visiting Europe had become an integral part of a broader pattern of American consumption, alongside of, inter alia, the decoration of houses, residential segregation, food, dress, education, religion, social activities and leisure."[4]

While many members of America's leisure class traveled widely throughout Europe during the second half of the nineteenth century, as one contemporary writer put it, Paris became their "Mecca."[5] The French city attracted them not only with traditions of friendship but also promises of art and beauty. For them, he explained: "London was a duty, but Paris was a joy."[6] The journal of elite American traveler George Frederic Jones also demonstrates this attraction. During a European tour with his wife in 1847–1848, he wrote that he was "more disgusted than ever with London […] [and] decidedly disgusted with Milan." He found the smell of the canals in Amsterdam to be unbearable, and the unrefined dinners in Berlin to be nothing but "hard eating, hard drinking, and loud talking." He was, however, "always glad to be back in France." For him France was "more agreeable than any other place."[7] Similarly, Emery A. Storrs, after having spent ninety days in Europe, claimed in his address at the Central Music Hall of Chicago in 1882 that "Paris [was] the most beautiful city in all the world" and that "there [was] something marvelously attractive about Frenchmen."[8] Even after World War I, a writer for the *Paris Comet* declared, it was in Paris "that America begins, not at New York."[9] The cultural prestige of Paris further attracted many wealthy Americans not only for leisurely travel but oftentimes, as an ideal place for extended residency as well.

For Veblen, however, the concept of the leisure class was an American one. Yet, transatlantic steam liners carried passengers in both directions, and just as more and more affluent Americans made their way to Europe, so too did European aristocrats and plutocrats, intrigued by rise of American economy, travel increasingly to places like New York and Boston.[10] Mixing industrial and commercial wealth with old privilege on both sides of the Atlantic, the American leisure class began to fraternize with the elite echelons of Europe, whose lifestyles appeared to resemble their own. And through webs of established connections and systematic patterns of introduction, elite transnational communities and social spaces formed. Linked by the urban centers around the North Atlantic, these elite networks came to occupy unique social spaces in which transnational ties and sociability were continuously interweaving and expanding. Therefore, Veblen's theory, when applied to transnational contexts, provides an important foundation for the concept of an elite *transnational high society*—social networks that existed within transnational spaces between Europe and the United States and among those who identified with shared economic and social status rather than national or ethnic origin.[11] As economic historian Sven Beckert shows, despite their diverse national origins, these various members of transnational high society often spoke the same languages, shared common values, read similar literature, and participated in similar cultural rituals.[12] Further, it was within these transnational high society communities that marriages such as that of the Napoleon III's first equerry, Baron Pierre, to Miss Thorne of New York emerged.[13]

Transnational high society in the court of Napoleon III

Contemporary discussions around the court of Napoleon III provide the most obvious demonstration of that process, as it is here that the extravagant character of transnational high society expressly took form as Napoleon III famously and eagerly welcomed cosmopolitan elites to the Tuileries. An article in *Figaro* explained: "The Emperor and Empress not infrequently take a great liking to persons accidently presented to them, and sometimes rousing a little jealousy by doing so among persons belonging to the court."[14] In a letter to her mother, Lillie Moulton (née Miss Lillie Greenough of Cambridge Massachusetts), wife of an American banker who resided in France, recounted the story of her "first [accidental] appearance in Parisian society" in 1863. She met the Emperor and Empress when she went ice-skating on the newly frozen lake in the *bois* near the home of her in-laws, who resided in the Chateau de Petit Val, an estate twelve miles from Paris. There, as she spoke to an acquaintance of her father-in-law, Prince Joachim Murat, the Emperor approached them, and Murat provided her with an introduction. Napoleon III complimented her on her skating ability and asked her to skate with him and the Empress, who then invited her to the Tuileries. In the letter, Moulton explained that normally there would have been a number of steps in which people were welcomed into the court—most typically through a series of introductions in the established patterns of the social network—but after extending a personal invitation to the Tuileries, the Empress informed her that such steps were no longer necessary, now that they were "personally acquainted."[15] Nonetheless, Moulton decided she would take the appropriate steps anyway. According to her, her in-laws had become so well-established in France that her father-in-law could have used the title "de Petite Val" had he so desired. Therefore, her mother-in-law accompanied her on these preliminary steps and presented her to the Empress's grand mistress. Upon arriving at the ball at the Tuileries, she received a message from the Empress expressing imperial delight at her presence. Moulton replied: "I am glad to be here, your Majesty; but I went through all of the preliminary steps all the same because my *belle-mère* insisted upon it."[16]

Other Americans such as Annie Fields entered the court in similar fashion. In a letter to her friend Sara, she explained how she was invited by another American to go hunting at Compiègne with the Emperor and Empress.[17] This visit, she explained, led to "a beautiful dinner in a beautiful house with all the French of the 'ancien régime.' It was in the Quartier St. Germain too, which has a mysterious interest for us from its old aristocratic reputation which is indeed wonderfully sustained."[18] Her reference to the *ancien régime* is an important one, as she attempted to highlight the perceived exclusivity of her new social acquaintances.

Exclusivity and social exclusion remained important markers of transnational high society, just as they had in more national elite circles of New York or London. Therefore, here it is important to distinguish members of the elite transnational community from other cosmopolitans who simply traveled on Grand Tours. Often labeled as *nouveaux riches*, these less established American travelers lacked the social connections and sometimes language skills to participate in dinners and balls at the Tuileries, and instead spent most of their time surrounded by their compatriots engaging in more superficial forms of tourism. The diaries of Americans Laura J. Libbey and Annie Bradley provide excellent examples. Much of what Laura Jean Libbey wrote can be characterized as scenic and historical descriptions. For example, she discussed at length the orderly fashion in which passengers are allowed on transport; how even at midnight, the sidewalks are full of people; and how the streets are lit by electricity.[19] Similarly, Annie Bradley described palaces and landmarks typical of those one would find in a travel guide in a short matter-of-fact manner. At times, however, she even expressed disappointment in visiting certain monuments, such as the Panthéon. Her writing, therefore, demonstrates dissonance between the reality of travel and her idealized expectations that had been shaped by travel literature and national stereotypes.[20] Neither of the women provided details of interaction with anyone beyond other American travelers or the occasional American resident in Paris. Such a superficial experience is characteristic of many Americans on their European tours—tours occupied by visits of monuments, cathedrals, and museums. Therefore, while transatlantic circulation provided a precondition for the formation of transnational high society, and while it provided opportunity for the transfer of cultural models that became imperative in transatlantic self-definition of high society, it did not allow one to secure his or her place within an elite transnational community that produced transnational marriages.

Generally speaking, their privileged position enabled members of transnational high society to move quite freely across and around the Atlantic during this period, and national borders mattered little in conducting of their day-to-day lives. As John Torpey shows in his work, *The Invention of the Passport: Surveillance, Citizenship, and the State*, over the course of the "long nineteenth century"—a period marked by economic liberalism, industrialization, and relative peace—many of Europe's existing state restrictions on entry and exit were either relaxed or in some cases allowed to lapse entirely.[21] While they traveled with a variety of identification papers, elite travelers rarely passed through passport checkpoints or immigration inspections and took extended residencies in places like Paris quite easily.

However, even though the period between 1815 and 1914 had been comparatively peaceful, brief conflicts did complicate this privileged free circulation. During the Franco-Prussian War for example, the American legation in Paris issued passports to 3,300 tourists or residents as well as "protection papers" for any property they might have had in their Parisian residences.[22] Similarly, in a letter to her mother, Lillie Moulton explained at length the difficulty she faced obtaining the necessary authorization and passport to leave Paris during this time:

> Mr. Moulton thought it better that I should leave Paris. But to leave Paris one must have a passport from the Prefect of Police. He consulted Mr. Washburn [the American Minister] about it, who not only consented to give me a card of introduction to Raoul Rigault (whom he knew personally), but offered to send me to the prefecture in his own carriage [...] I don't know how many times I had to pull out my "billet de circulation" before we reached the prefecture [...] I must have gone through at least seven rooms before I reached the sanctuary in which Monsieur Raoul Rigault held his "audience."

It is noteworthy that she was obliged to obtain the necessary documents from French rather than American authorities. However, as Torpey explains, not only was there no global standard for passport issuances at this time, but formal citizenship was also not necessarily the foundation upon which to claim a passport for travel. As in the case of Moulton, some states issued passports simply for interstate travel and some issued them to noncitizen nationals, resident aliens, or noncitizen population over which the state held domination.[23]

In her description of her difficulties, Moulton, emotionally attached to the idea of the monarchy and its court, displays an interesting antagonism to the French Republican official, Monsieur Raoul Rigault, with whom she was obliged to communicate in order to obtain her passport. She writes:

> This autocrat, whom the republicans (to their eternal shame be it said) had placed in power after the 4th of September, is (and was then) the most successful specimen of a scamp that the human race has ever produced. At this moment Rigault has more power than anyone else in Paris [...] "Monsieur, I have come to procure a passport, and here is Mr. Washburn's card to tell you who I am." [...] "Does the citoyenne wish to leave Paris? Pourquoi?" [...] At this moment I confess I began to feel dreadfully nervous, seeing the powerless situation in which I was placed [...] I fancy Raoul Rigault had never been in the society of a lady (perhaps he had never seen one), and his innate coarseness seemed to make him gloat over the present situation, and as a true republican, whose motto is "Égalité, Fraternité, Liberté," he flattered himself he was on an equality with me, therefore he could take any amount of liberty. He took advantage of the unavoidable questions that belong to the making out of a passport and showed a diabolical pleasure in tormenting "la citoyenne" who stood helplessly before him.[24]

While her social connections to the Emperor and Empress mattered little in that moment, those to the American Minister did, and she was able to secure a passport to leave Paris in August of 1870.

Moulton explained the hastiness of her departure: "We left Petit Val rather precipitately, leaving everything behind us, clothes in wardrobes and letters in commodes." But she added: "We shall not be gone more than a month." Clara Jerome (sister of Jennie Jerome who married Lord Randolph Churchill) had also occupied for years a place in the court of Tuileries, and like Lillie Moulton, she frequently stayed with the Emperor and Empress at Compiègne, in the north of France. But with the outbreak of the war, she, along with her mother and sister, abandoned Paris for London. Elizabeth Eliot, in her work *Heiresses and Coronets*, argues that with the fall of the Second Empire, Americans like Clara Jerome shifted both their travel and social interests to London. "Paris without the emperor and empress and without the royal court was," according to Eliot, "not at all what it had been."[25] Likewise, upon Moulton's return in 1871, she recounted: "Everything was terribly changed. All the chateaux we passed are utterly abandoned, some quite in ruins; one can see, for instance, right through beautiful Grand Val, bereft of windows and doors [...] I could have cried when I saw the Tuileries [...] As we drove by I thought of the famous ball given [there] last May (le bal de Plébiscite) [...] And now! The Tuileries deserted, empty, the Emperor a prisoner, the Empress a fugitive! All France demoralized! All prestige gone! One wonders how such things could be!"[26]

Elite Social Events as Transnational Spaces

Even though the Franco-Prussian War was demoralizing for those like Moulton, and even though it effectively ended the lavish social events at the Tuileries, transnational high society continued to thrive and socialize in Paris in many of the same excessive ways as new elite social spaces formed. The American legation under Levi P. Morton was one of these transnational spaces. Morton, the founder of the banking firm, LP Morton and Co., served as American Minister to France from 1881 to 1885. Because Morton felt that the previous site of legation failed to exemplify the "grandeur and prosperity of the United States," he spent much of his own money to convert a hotel at the Place de la Bitche in Paris into both his private residence and a place for diplomatic and social gatherings. One newspaper clipping called the new legation an "American palace," explaining that it "was furnished in the style of Louis XVI and could accommodate 1500 guests."[27]

The French press was quite fond of both Mr. and Mrs. Morton, at least according to the French editions of American newspapers of which there were many in Paris at the time. One French version of a Boston newspaper called Morton "a gentleman of elegant address, pleasing manners, and distinguished for his social habits"—all "qualities the French admire."[28] Likewise, an article in the *Figaro* expressed: "[M]arié à une femme charmante qui parle français comme une Parisienne, le nouvel ambassadeur se propose, dit-on, de donner de nombreuses fêtes l'hiver prochain."[29] (Married to a charming woman who speaks French like a Parisian, the new ambassador offers, they say, to host plenty of social engagements next winter.) He, along with his wife, were the first formal diplomatic representatives to turn the American legation into a popular center for elite social events, and it came to serve as a gathering place for members of transnational high society.

Similar to those in New York and London, Morton's numerous *fêtes* were both highly publicized and intricately described in both the French and American press. As the following excerpt from the *New York Tribune* shows, these descriptions are useful to the historian because they can be used to map the expansion of social networks within transnational communities: "Mr. and Mrs. Morton had their first formal reception in Paris a fortnight ago, opening for the purpose the magnificent hotel now occupied by the legation [...] a very large number, of not only Americans, but also of the most distinguished representatives of Parisian and foreign society, were in attendance [...] The reception established at once the influence of Mr. and Mrs. Morton as leaders in American social life in Paris."[30] A closer examination of his papers reveals that Morton's guest lists, which can be described as a representative sample of transnational high society, included not only elite Americans, but also foreign ambassadors, diplomats, and state heads, titled and untitled French elites, as well as Spanish, British, Russian, German, and Austrian nobility.[31] The American newspaper, the *Boston Post*, also confirmed: "It is [...] at the American legation alone in all of Paris that republicans, legitimists, Orléanists, Bonapartists, ultra-monarchs and Gallicans can meet and mingle."[32]

More importantly, these descriptions also provide important insight into the personal encounters between American women and French aristocrats that occurred at Morton's dinners. The same *Boston Post* article, for example, boasted that it was at Morton's many elaborate *soirées* at the legation where young American ladies were able to find a wide selection of eligible nobility.[33] In its discussion of an earlier dinner in May of 1884, another newspaper reported on one such encounter. It claimed that "a young lady expressed to the Minister her wish to be acquainted with the Comte de Paris, and Mr. Morton conveyed to him her desire. Instead of advancing toward her [...] [the Comte] imitated that he would feel much pleasure in allowing her to be presented. Accordingly, Mr. Morton went back to her and said, 'The Comte de Paris permits me to introduce you to him'."[34] This particular introduction ended in scandal and near diplomatic crisis for the American Minister. According to the rumors in the press, Morton had not only introduced the Comte to the young lady as either "royal highness" or the "future King of France,"[35] but earlier when the Comte de Paris had arrived to the dinner, it was also reported that "the American minister and his wife descended to receive him as he alighted from his carriage, in imitation of the etiquette observed by foreign Ministers when receiving foreign royalty."[36] The real scandal had little to do with meeting American ladies who may or may not have been looking for a noble husband, but instead whether or not anything was done or said by the American Minister on the occasion not in keeping with the friendly relations existing between the American government and the established republican government of France.[37] Nonetheless, when examining the motivations of Franco-American titled marriage, the descriptions of Morton's *soirées* demonstrate that cross-cultural interaction at such elite social events should not be underestimated as a facilitator.[38] In this way, what was intended to serve as a national space both created and encouraged transnationalism, and Morton's breach of etiquette with the Comte de Paris may be seen as part of a pattern to further his own transnational social connections.

Figure 1.1 La Sortie du bal en 1902, Escalier de l'Hôtel du Marquis de Vogüé, Raymond, Fournier-Sarlovèze Joseph. CC⌀ Bibliothèque de l'Institut d'Histoire de l'Art.

At the end of the nineteenth century, elite balls and dinners like those at the American legation in Paris were some the most important cultural forms of the transnational leisure class throughout the Atlantic's urban centers.[39] They were used to not only publicly display wealth and social prestige but also as a cultural mechanism for elite coupling. In her examination of British aristocratic marriage patterns over the course of five centuries, Kimberly Schutte explains that by the nineteenth century, "overtly arranged marriages" were no longer viewed as culturally appropriate. Therefore, members of British high society used exclusive social events such as balls, where the guest lists could be controlled and young women could be well chaperoned, to promote "appropriate social interaction."[40] In this way, elite balls took on the quality of what she calls "marriage markets." Likewise, historian, Eric Homberger explains in his examination of social elites in New York that this was the case for Americans as well. According to him at these events, "[t]he etiquette of the ballroom was designed to ensure the social decorum was maintained."[41] Such was also the case for transnational high society; however, it should be reinforced that these elite social spaces, like those at the American legation in Paris, were not national spaces; they were occupied by elites from around the North Atlantic. Therefore, the pool of potential partners in their "marriage markets" was transnationally comprised, and transnational marriages were a result of those cross-border social interactions.

Dinners and balls of transnational high society not only provided an opportunity for social interaction between potential partners but also regulated that interaction through strict cultural codes. For example, Lady St. Helier of London explained in her memoir that an "unwritten law of etiquette and conduct enjoyed that no one should dance more than once with the same partner. Under certain circumstances to dance twice was permissible, but after that the girl was considered fast, and held up as a warning to well-brought-up and well-conducted young ladies."[42] The cultural codes of the ballroom also demonstrate the role of other members of high society to participate in the arrangement of potential matches. Along with its list of eligible nobility, *Titled Americans* also provides a lengthy description of what it called "The Great Ball." Attended by members of New York high society as well as European nobility and diplomatic elites, this ball took place on the evening of January 2, 1890, at the Metropolitan Opera House in New York.[43] It further explained that while the committee was dining, "there was a succession of dances downstairs. It was the intention of the committee to give the young folks every chance to amuse themselves in this fashion" before the formal cotillion.[44] Regarding the cotillion, it then noted:

All knew that the chief event of the evening was to take place. The ninety-six chosen whose presence in the quadrille d'honneur was because of their indisputable right to claim the respect of their fellows, were to go through the stately measures of Sir Roger de Coverley [...] The formation of the sets was calculated to give something more than ordinary ceremonial to the quadrille d'honneur. The debutantes were assigned to the first set, and here was a veritable garland of buds. It was a distinction of no small significance to make one's first bow to society at the New Year's ball, and so the prizes, but twenty-four in all, were eagerly disputed. The arrangement of the four sets was based upon a somewhat poetical idea of Mr. McAllister. He was desirous that social prominence should be hemmed in by beauty; that weight of dignity, that a combination of millions and ancestry, should dance with flankings of the prettiest women that New York could muster.[45]

This description demonstrates not only role of dancing as an important cultural mechanism in coupling but also the role of other members of high society in the arrangement of potential matches. At transnational social events, the term "arranging a match" sometimes took the form of simply providing an introduction. For example, one of Morton's attachés, Jules Brulatour of New Orleans "engineered the match" between one of Isaac Singer's daughters, Isabelle-Blanch, and Jean Elie Octave Louis-Sèvére Amanieu Decazes, the third Duc Elies Decazes at game of billiards for her brothers. The couple was married in 1888, and among the guests were Queen Isabelle of Spain, Duc and Duchesse de la Rochefoucauld, the Comtesse de Trobriand, also an American woman (née Jones) of New York, the Prince de Polignac, and Miss Fanny Reed, an American resident of Paris, who would later "engineer" the match between Anna Gould and Boni de Castellane.[46] In addition to those fashioned in the ball room, many other titled Franco-American unions were facilitated by well-established and continuously expanding transnational social and familial ties. Anna Gould was not the only member of her family to marry a French citizen. Her youngest brother, Frank J. Gould, also married a French woman named Florence Lacaze, with whom he lived in Juan-les-Pins.[47] Further, in addition to Boni de Castellane, three other members of the Talleyrand-Perigord family married American women.[48] One of Ambassador Morton's daughters, Helen, married the Duc de Valeccay (formerly Comte Boson de Talleyrand-Perigord) in 1901; although, that marriage ended in divorce shortly after.[49] Three members of the Sauvan d'Aramon family—Bertrand, Paul, and Jacques—each married American women.[50] The hotel heiress, Minnie Stevens (née Mary Fiske Stevens, daughter of Mr. Parah Stevens) who was a relation of Miss Fanny Reed and also a social acquaintance of Boni de Castellane and

Anna Gould was meant to marry the Duc de Guiche, the son of the Duc de Grammont. The marriage, however, never took place, and she later married prominent Englishman, Arthur Henery Fitzroy Paget, grandson of the first Marquis of Anglesey in 1902 but continued to reside in Paris.[51]

Social Comparability between American and European Members

But did American women like Helen Morton and Anna Gould really need titles of nobility in order to position themselves within the ranks of this transnational high society? It is important to once again note that not all American cosmopolitans traveling on Grand Tours found their way into exclusive transnational social circles. As historian Harvey Levenstein convincingly shows, it is unlikely that many of those who were considered to be *nouveaux riches* in the United States would have had the social connections necessary to participate in the elite social events and marriage networks like those previously mentioned.[52] Instead, they more often engaged in more superficial forms of tourism and travel with fellow Americans rather than keeping company with French nobility or diplomatic elite.[53] However, researchers should resist the temptation to define transnational high society too closely according to the contemporary American concept of "old" and "new" money. Instead, nineteenth-century transnational high society was defined by broader, albeit still exclusive, elite social connections that transcended national borders among those who possessed a self-conscious sense of shared identity and superiority. Further, those who did make their way into elite transnational social circles, like Helen Morton and Anna Gould, often took their place with ease. In 1895, the respected French news publication *Le Gaulois*, often considered the journal of high society, wrote of the American ladies there: "Toutes se sont assimilées avec une souplesse et une rare intelligence aux habitudes françaises et sont devenues des ornements gracieux de la sociétés paroissienne, se distinguant d'une façon toute particulière par les bienfaits qu'elles répandent autour d'elles."[54] (All have assimilated with a flexibility and a rare intelligence to French habits and have become graceful ornaments of parish society, distinguishing themselves in a very particular way by the benefits they spread around them.) Further, as one member of the transnational community living in London explained, wealthy American women often saw themselves as equal to their noble European counterparts:

> The one thing that gave her a foothold in [European] Society was perhaps the one thing about her which is most distinctly American—her sense of equality. [...] She was, and she felt herself, the social equal

of those whom she met, and her bearing was such that others perceived it instantly [...] So she glided into this brilliant company, and took her place as if it had always belonged to her, and she kept it with ease [...] without effort and without timidity [...] There are differences of all kinds: of wealth, of intellect, of distinction in public life, of superior virtue, as well as rank. But the meeting of all these various excellences becomes possible only when all agree to meet for social purposes on equal terms. We perfectly understand that in America, to suppose a different state of things here merely because there are degrees of rank is absurd. The best proof of the absurdity is the fact that rank alone gives no one social distinction, and that some of those whose position in society is highest are of the lowest rank.[55]

Another example of this assertion of social equality can be found in the memoir of Boni de Castellane, who described his American wife's self-awareness: "[Anna] was utterly unimpressed by rank. She disregarded it completely [...]. [This lack of] proper consideration for rank came less from the indifference which she felt toward rank in general than from her infernal pride which made her believe she was superior to everybody."[56] One time she remarked: "Oh dear, what a stupid Princess! You force me to curtsy her, but she isn't in the same street as an American like myself."[57] Such statements signify that even though New York's "artificial" and "arbitrary" elite were often juxtaposed against European nobility, which was viewed as "natural" and "constant,"[58] the concept of a transnational high society levels this differentiation between community members. One might even go so far as to argue that given the turbulent political history of nineteenth-century France, along with its well-articulated anti-aristocratic, post-revolutionary discourse, New York's "social aristocracy" as Eric Homberger has called it,[59] was not all that different from that which had been created by Napoleon III. Nonetheless, we can conclude that rather than social or status anxieties of the American nouveaux riches driving these marriages, it was instead a sense of social confidence or, at least, a confident assertion of elite position among members of elite transnational communities that facilitated them. In other words, nineteenth-century elites continued the practice of marrying within their own socioeconomic echelons; however, those echelons were not defined by national boundaries, but rather by self-proclaimed social ones.

Conceptions of National Borders and Public Criticisms

While this work is better understood as a cultural examination of the spaces and process that produced transnational marriage, the legal questions regarding the connection between marriage and citizenship remain important ones in determining the extent to which participants saw themselves as marrying across national lines. The relatively unrestricted movement of members of the elite between different urban centers such as New York, London, and Paris along with the assumption of common socioeconomic belonging between elite Americans and elite Europeans, meant that for nineteenth-century Franco-American titled marriage participants, their marital unions often emerged out of spaces that were not entirely defined by national boundaries. Their tenuous conception of being bound by national limits was further confirmed as legal questions of American citizenship were rarely raised for those taking up extended, and sometimes lifelong, residence in places such as Paris. While the American Expatriation Act of 1868 did grant the right of a naturalized American citizen to "divest himself from former allegiance," I-Mien Tsiang explains in his work, *The Question of Expatriation in America Prior to 1907*, that "congress did not, in the legislation of 1868, or in any until 1907 provide conditions under which an American citizen might be deemed" to have lost citizenship. "The failure of the legislators to cover this phase of the question in 1868 was," according to him, "due to the fear that a provision on the matter of losing American citizenship would in effect weaken the American position."[60] He also notes that taking extended residence in places such as Paris between 1868 and 1907, as many members of transnational high society did, was also "not regarded by the American State Department or by the courts as a decisive factor in expatriation."[61] Here, he cites the 1869 Court of Claims case 571, *Brown vs United States*, which proclaimed the following: "We cannot accept the idea that the matter of domicile affects that fact of citizenship not that a mere foreign residence of itself can work a forfeiture of political rights."[62] Recognizing the lack of legal restrictions on extended residencies is important when examining the privileged position and transnational existence afforded to elite members of high society who occupied social spaces beyond national borders.

Similarly, the coupling processes that accompanied this transnational existence were further facilitated by the ability to contract such unions across national borders relatively easily. When *Titled Americans* published its "carefully compiled list of Peers who are supposed to be eager to lay their coronets, and incidentally their hearts, at the feet of the all-conquering American girl," it did so for the explicit purpose of "arous[ing] the ambition of the American Girl with the prospect of other worlds to conquer" and without any mention of national citizenship and marriage laws.[63] The marriage of Anna Gould and Boni de Castellane, at least, to the extent that the historian understands it according to Castellanes's memoir, also shows that nineteenth-century marriage participants faced few international or legal hurdles in contracting their cross-border marriages. This marriage, which took place in New York in March of 1895, was first celebrated in a civil ceremony at the Gould home officiated by New York Mayor William Lafayette Strong. It was then followed by a Catholic ceremony on the following Monday, which was performed by Archbishop Michael Corrigan.[64] Neither Castellane's memoir nor the numerous American newspaper articles covering the wedding mentioned any additional administrative steps that the couple was required to undertake before the transnational union could take place. Castellane also did not discuss any international legal issues that burdened their wedding planning. One article from the *Pittsburg Press*, entitled "American wives of French Husbands" explained in 1900 that both the United States and France recognized marriages contracted in the other country as long as the marriage was celebrated according to the laws of the country in which it took place and conformed with the regulations on marrying age, prior marriage, parental consent, and consent of both parties.[65] One year later, French law student, Albert Cauwes, noted in his doctoral dissertation entitled "Des rapports du mariage avec la nationalité" that while issues surrounding the topic of marriage had been thought through in national law, very few international laws or bilateral agreements between nation-states dealt with the subject of "mixed marriages."[66]

The question of loss of citizenship (or expatriation) becomes an important one, but only at the turn of the twentieth century. According to the Article 19 of France's 1804 *Code Civil*, it had long been established that "la femme française qui épouse un étranger, suit la condition de son mari" (the French woman who marries a foreigner, assumes the status of her husband). This condition was reaffirmed by the loi du 26 juin 1889.[67] Under the same logic, according to Article 12 of the *Code Civil*, "l'étrangère qui aura épousé un Français, suivra la condition de son mari" (the foreigner who marries a French man will acquire her husband' status).[68] Therefore, an American woman married to a French man in the nineteenth century would have been granted French citizenship, as would their children have; however, in the United States she faced different legal circumstances. Even though an 1855 law allowed a foreign woman who migrated the United States to become American as the result of a marriage to a U.S. citizen, with regards to the loss of citizenship of natural-born American women, as Cauwes noted that in 1901, the United States "refuse encore à permettre à la femme indigène qui épouse un étranger de perdre la nationalité américaine" (still refuses to provide a means for the native-born woman who marries a foreigner to lose her American nationality).[69] Martha Gardener, in her work, *The Qualities of a Citizen Women, Immigration, and Citizenship, 1870–1965*, also confirms that "the law remained mute on the status of American women who married alien men until 1907."[70] In that year, American Congress became more and more concerned with the increasing numbers of naturalized citizens returning to their countries of origin.[71] The 1907 American Expatriation Law legislated that any American citizen who resided in a foreign state for five years "without intent to return" would be expatriated. Further, conceived under the same logic as laws of coverture that prevented women from voting, it also included a provision that American women who married foreigners would be stripped of their American citizenship and would take the nationality of her husband, even if they lived in the United States.[72]

The 1907 Expatriation Law did not mean, however, that all American women who took French husbands were destined to remain in France and never return to the United States. Section 3 of the law stipulated: "At the termination of the marital relation she may resume her American citizenship, if abroad, by registering as an American citizen within one year with a consul of the United States, or by returning to reside in the United States, or, if residing in the United States at the termination of the marital relation, by continuing to reside therein."[73] Therefore, while some women such as Anna Gould did remain in France even after divorcing their French husbands, others, such as Helen Morton, returned to the United States, and some contracted subsequent marital unions with other European members of transnational high society. The 1907 Expatriation Law also made it possible for extended residents to "overcome the presumption of expatriation by competent evidence produced to a diplomatic or consular officer of the United States" by simply proving that their stay was for reasons such as commerce, health, or education and that they intended, in good faith, to return to the United States.[74] According to the Expatriation Law of 1907, Anna Gould's 1908 second marriage to Boni's cousin Hélie de Talleyrand-Périgord, Duc de Sagan should have stripped her of her American citizenship, even though a prior *New York Times* article already claimed she was a citizen of France.[75] However, this did not stop her from returning to the United States to live on her father's estate in 1939 for a period of time; though, she later died in Paris.

The 1907 Expatriation Law as it applied to the nationality of married women was upheld during the 1915 case *Mackenzie v. Hare*, which involved an American woman who had married a British citizen. However, once American women were granted the right to vote they began to argue that their citizenship should no longer be dependent upon that of their husbands'. The 1922 Married Women's Independent Citizenship Act (also known as the Cable Act) reversed the 1907 law. However, its implications remained racialized, as it only provided that a married American woman was entitled to keep her American citizenship as long as she married a man who would be *eligible* for American citizenship—a category that included only those legally defined as "white" or "of African descent."

Just as citizenship and expatriation laws such as that of 1907 affirmed national borders in the establishment of cross-border marital contracts, the questions surrounding nineteenth-century elite conceptions of these boundaries should also be placed within the context of public critiques of these unions. As shown in the introduction of this section, contemporary public discourse painted a picture of these matrimonial unions as desperate and sometimes ridiculous and described them as attempts to exchange European titles and the social honor that accompanied them for large amounts of American money. These title-for-treasure caricatures were a commonplace in nineteenth-century literature such as in the novels of Edith Wharton, who mocked American nouveaux riches as crass and uncultured, and in the 1898 play *Les Transatlantiques* by Abel Hermant, which depicts a rich American father's arrangement of his daughter's marriage to a French marquis.[76] The notion of elite American women as "title hunters" was even further perpetuated by the American press. During the Morton-Comte de Paris scandal, for example, the American publication *Truth* referred to those present at the dinner as ladies who "quite unworthy of their great country, set up to be the leaders of society here, because they have large fortunes and have married idle Frenchmen of more or less dubious nobility." It continued: "These ladies regard all untitled Europeans as mean whites and have come to fancy that a nation without nobility is like a garden without flowers."[77] For example, according to the *New York Times*, Americans scorned Anna Gould's second marriage to Boni de Castellane's cousin, Hélie de Talleyrand-Périgord, even more than they had her first. "Seldom, indeed," it explained, "has any of one of these so-called international marriages taken place that has excited such general and outspoken condemnation on the part of the people on this side of the Atlantic."[78] It should also be noted, however, that not all of the noble husbands were subject to their opprobrium. *Town Topics* claimed that the name of Winaretta Singer's first husband the Prince de Scey-Montbéliard was "well known in circles of upper French aristocracy. The family is one of the oldest and most exclusive in France."[79] Likewise, the *Pittsburg Press* reported that the husband of Helen Morton was a "well-known figure in Paris Society, where he has to a large extent taken the place of his father who for a quarter century was known as the Prince de la Mode."[80] However, after their divorce the *New York Times* called him "one of the most unpopular figures in French life."[81]

These national critiques more often stemmed from American, rather than French, public discourse. To this, Boni de Castellane remarked: "America alone is responsible for the outcry which invariably occurred whenever an heiress of the country married a foreigner, and the unfortunate man was at once described as a fortune hunter, whose sole aim was to restore the tarnished glories of his escutcheon."[82] And, like William H. Chambliss's call for a titled European exclusion act, most critiques largely rested on the juxtaposition of American republican ideals with European monarchy and aristocracy, rather than simply shaming American women for marrying foreigners. The problem was not in their eyes that American women married French men, but that these French men were members of the nobility.

The other problem, of course, was that even though some marriages like that of Mattie Mitchell of Portland Oregon to the Duc de la Rouchefoucauld were celebrated in the press as "love matches," most of these marriages were viewed as mere exchanges of American money for social status and little else.[83] Here, the dichotomy created in these criticisms—where one either married for love and happiness or for money and status—tells us much about changing emotional standards regarding the practice of marriage. When a union was criticized as being motivated purely by financial arrangements, the criticism was, for the most part, an attempt to render it as illegitimate or at least less legitimate than the alternative. The assumptive basis of such a reproach then rests on the notion that an ideal contemporary marriage was, therefore, an emotional one, rather than an economic one.

In charging that American heiresses were entering into emotionless unions, one contemporary commentator, Richard Harding Davis, pointed out: "It may be, after all, that she married for love in spite of the title, and not on account of it. But if these are love-matches, it would surely sometimes happen that the American men, in their turn would fall in love with foreign women of title, and that we would hear of impecunious princesses and countesses hunting though the States for rich brokers and wheat-dealers."[84] Despite Davis's claim, such gendered exceptions did indeed exist. For example, wealthy American businessman, Isaac Singer married Duchesse Isabella Eugenie Boyer; Thérèse Mayer of New York had an American father and French mother; and Frank J. Gould, the youngest brother of Anna Gould, married a French woman, Florence Lacaze. Nonetheless, the gendered nature of the majority of these nineteenth-century elite marriages remains a characteristic worthy of further consideration. Nancy Green addresses this imbalance by suggesting that it was more acceptable for French aristocratic families to accept American money when the American was female because welcoming wealthy American women allowed for the continuation of the family name.[85] Her claim is echoed from Henry James's 1877 novel *The American*, which depicts the failed marriage attempt of the main character, Christopher Newman, a wealthy American businessman, to Claire de Cintré, the daughter of a noble family, the Bellegardes.[86] In the novel, Claire's mother and brother sabotage the union because they cannot "reconcile [themselves] to a commercial person" of inferior background and instead favor an alternative match with an "old family."[87] Like those of Edith Wharton, James's novels play on the larger themes of misconceptions in old and new world encounters, often reminiscent of his own cross-cultural experiences during his stay in France. However, it should be noted that unlike Wharton, James remained largely outside the upper echelons of high society.[88] Further this argument about the force of familial obligation and pressure not only leaves contemporary marriage participants without agency, but it also remains inherently unilateral as it attempts to explain the gendered nature of the marriages from the perspective of only one of the two cultures. Because marriage scholars have observed gender imbalances in many global patterns of transnational or mixed marriage,[89] one might instead consider broader transatlantic travel patterns—more specifically the feminization of American tourism to France—as well as the gendered roles in which elite leisure time was spent, such as the female domination of balls and other social events.

In the earlier part of the nineteenth century, Americans viewed Germany as a feminine place for artists, and they often described France by invoking its masculine, fear-inducing military. By the second half of the century, however, this changed as tourism in France increasingly became feminized and associated with women as young American men took extended residencies in places such as Germany or London. In a 1909 poem, Henry van Dyke proclaimed: "Oh London is a man's town, there's power in the air; And Paris is a woman's town with flowers in her hair."[90] Likewise, Sinclair Lewis in his book, *Dodsworth*, (1929) also called Paris a "feminine and flirtatious refuge from reality."[91] Levenstein explains: "In large part this was because [high] culture—still its chief desideratum for the genteel class—remained feminized in the public mind."[92] Therefore, because cultural improvement was the goal, it was common that mothers and daughters maintained extended residencies in places like Paris. Contemporary sources support this conclusion. In their work, *Pairs Is a Woman's Town*, two American travelers explained:

> Through diplomatic connections wealthy American fathers are sometimes able [...] to place their daughters in distinguished French families where [...] they have entrée into the most cultivated French society and make contacts which would be impossible under any other circumstances [...] For a young unmarried woman, a household with sons dominated by a clever, socially inclined mother is to be recommended.[93]

Further evidence can be found in the Morton Family Papers. The American Minister's personal correspondence includes countless invitation responses from various "Mrs. and Misses" to his numerous transnational social events.[94] Morton's papers also include many letters of introduction or letters requesting introduction for young American ladies.[95] For example, one correspondent wrote:

> Dear Sir,
> I have a young friend in Paris, Mrs. Louis N. Thibault, of whom I think a great deal. She was a belle in San Francisco until about a year ago when she married a gentleman from Bordeaux and has gone to live in France. She cannot give up her love of America, though in the gay city of Paris and she asks me to send her a letter of introduction to the American Minister there […] I recommend her to your kind attention and ask for her such consideration as you always give to the young, good and beautiful of our country-women.[96]

Because there were far more American women such as this belle from California going to Paris than American men, and far more Americans going to France than French coming to America, the gendered character of this particular marriage pattern can be considered unsurprising if not predictable. It is also important to remember that the transnational spaces out of which nineteenth-century elite transnational marriages emerged were spaces largely created by and dominated by women.[97]

What is even more interesting about Davis' critique is that he poses the question of motivation in a way that can only be explained by either love *or* money and titles as if they were the only possible desires to be satisfied by transnational unions. However, the institution of marriage in transnational context evoked emotions and satisfied desires far more complex and varied than simply one's personal affection for another person or their own economic well-being. Therefore, historians must also consider the array of other emotions involved—emotions that were far more complex once intertwined with transnational, cross-cultural encounter.

Notes

1. For more on transatlantic travel see: Stephen Russell Fox, *The Ocean Railway: Isambard Kingdom Brunel, Samuel Cunard, and the Revolutionary World of the Great Atlantic Steamships* (London: Harper Perennial, 2004); Mark Rennella, *The Boston Cosmopolitans: International Travel and American Arts and Letters*, 1st ed. (New York: Palgrave Macmillan, 2008).
2. Thorstein Veblen, *The Theory of the Leisure Class. 1899*; Reprint, New York: A. M. Kelley, Bookseller, 1965).
3. Levenstein, *Seductive Journey*, 93.

4 Maureen E. Montgomery, "'Natural Distinction': The American Bourgeois Search for Distinctive Signs in Europe," in *The American Bourgeoisie: Distinction and Identity in the Nineteenth Century*, ed. Sven Beckert and Julia B Rosenbaum (New York: Palgrave Macmillan, 2010), 27.
5 John Joseph Conway, *Footprints of Famous Americans in Paris* (London; New York: John Lane; John Lane Co., 1912), 66.
6 Conway, *Footprints of Famous Americans in Paris*, xii.
7 Quoted in Wharton, *A Backward Glance*, iii.
8 Emery Storrs, "Ninety Days in Europe," *Chicago Tribune*, October 24, 1882, 3.
9 "Why I Like Paris," *Paris Comet: Anglo-American Fortnightly Magazine*, October 10, 1927, 14.
10 David Cannadine, *The Decline and Fall of the British Aristocracy* (London: Penguin, 2005), 375.
11 Sven Beckert and Julia B. Rosenbaum, *The American Bourgeoisie: Distinction and Identity in the Nineteenth Century* (New York: Palgrave Macmillan, 2010).
12 Sven Beckert, "Die Kultur Des Kapitals: Bürgerliche Kultur in New York Und Hamburg Im 19. Jahrhundert," in *Vorträge Aus Dem Warburg-Haus*, ed. Warburg-Haus (Berlin: Akademie, 2000), 4: 143–75.
13 Washington Irving et al., *The Journals of Washington Irving*, vol. 3 (Boston: Bibliophile Society, 1919), 213; *Titled Americans: A List of American Ladies Who Have Married Foreigners of Rank*, 100.
14 L. de Hegermann-Lindencrone, *In the Courts of Memory 1858–1875: From Contemporary Letters* (New York: Harper & Bros., 1912), 51.
15 Hegermann-Lindencrone, *In the Courts of Memory 1858–1875*, 25.
16 Hegermann-Lindencrone, *In the Courts of Memory 1858–1875*, 28.
17 Annie Fields to Sara, November 30, 1859, Annie Fields Papers, Massachusetts Historical Society.
18 Annie Fields to Boylston, December 22, 1859, Annie Fields Papers, Massachusetts Historical Society.
19 Laura Libbey, "Laura Jean Libbey Journals," vol. 3 Visit to Europe, 1892, Manuscript and Archives Division, New York Public Library.
20 Annie J. Bradely, "Annie J Bradley Diary" 1872–1874, Manuscript and Archives Division, New York Public Library.
21 John Torpey, *The Invention of the Passport: Surveillance, Citizenship, and the State* (Cambridge; New York: Cambridge University Press, 2000), 91–92.
22 Green, *The Other Americans in Paris*, 52.
23 Torpey, *The Invention of the Passport*, 161.
24 Hegermann-Lindencrone, *In the Courts of Memory 1858–1875*, 511–25.
25 Elizabeth Eliot, *Heiresses and Coronets*, 64.
26 Hegermann-Lindencrone, *In the Courts of Memory 1858–1875*, 276.
27 "Newspaper Clipping, Title Unknown," June 1882, Levi P. Morton Papers, Series VII Scrapbook, vol. 5, 64, New York Public Library.
28 "Newspaper Clipping, Title Unknown," *Boston ___ Nouvelles*, May 4, 1881, Levi P. Morton Papers, Series VII Scrapbook, vol. 4A, 53, New York Public Library.
29 "Newspaper Clipping, Title Unknown," *Figaro*, 1881, Levi P. Morton Papers, Series VII Scrapbook, vol. 4A, 53, New York Public Library.
30 "Newspaper Clipping, Title Unknown," *New York Tribune*, January 1882, Levi P. Morton Papers, Series VII Scrapbook, vol. 5, 31, New York Public Library.

31 "Americans in Europe," newspaper clipping, 1882, Levi P Morton Papers Series VII Scrapbook vol. 5, 60, New York Public Library.
32 "Levi P. Morton: A Review of His Career as Minister to France," *Boston Post*, December 16, 1884, Levi P. Morton Papers, Series VII Scrapbook, vol. 6, 95, New York Public Library.
33 "Levi P. Morton: A Review of His Career as Minister to France," 95.
34 "The Levy-Morton Incident," *Truth*, May 29, 1884, Levi P. Morton Papers, Series VII Scrapbook, vol. 5, 133, New York Public Library.
35 "Minister and Pretender," newspaper clipping, June 15, 1884, Levi P. Morton Papers, Series VII Scrapbook, vol. 5, 137, New York Public Library. Based on the selected sources left by Morton, one can only speculate what was actually said during the event. "Newspaper Clipping, Title Unknown," *Morning News*, May 30, 1884, Levi P. Morton Papers, Series VII Scrapbook, vol. 5, 130, New York Public Library. This article, which quoted the author of the *Truth* article, claimed that not only was the dinner not given in honor of the Comte de Paris but that it never even took place. "Le Comte de Paris Chez M. Morton," *Matin*, n.d., Levi P. Morton Papers, Series VII Scrapbook, vol. 5, 130, New York Public Library states that he was only invited but did not attend any dinner at the American legation; *Figaro*, May 30, 1884, Levi P. Morton Papers, Series VII Scrapbook, vol. 5, 130, New York Public Library says that he was not even invited to a dinner; "The American Minister and the French Royalty," May 31, 1884, Levi P. Morton Papers, Series VII Scrapbook, vol. 5, 132, New York Public Library declared that he was "informally invited on the day previous to a small after-dinner dancing party composed mainly of Americans." However, despite numerous attempts following the scandal by both French and American press to declare otherwise, the Comte de Paris was most likely in attendance as confirmed by the following: Comte de Paris, "Telegram from the Comte de Paris to Levi P. Morton," May 14, 1884, Levi P. Morton Papers, Box 2, Folder "Correspondence 1884 May," New York Public Library, which stated, "*I accept with pleasure your kind invitation and I shall be glad to that opportunity to pay my respects to this evening to Mrs. Morton. With your leave, I shall bring with me M. Aubry-Vitet who presently accompanies me. Don't take the trouble to call here today.*" Also, given the transnational nature of the social events, he was also most likely introduced to young, American women.
36 "The American Minister and the French Royalty," May 31, 1884, Levi P. Morton Papers, Series VII Scrapbook, vol. 5, 132, New York Public Library.
37 "The American Minister and the French Royalty."
38 "The Levy-Morton Incident"; "Levi P. Morton: A Review of His Career as Minister to France."
39 See Figure 1 Raymond, *La Sortie Du Bal En 1902, Escalier de l'Hôtel Du Marquis de Vogué*, Raymond, Fournier-Sarlovèze Joseph, Estampes et photographie, Collections Jacques Doucet, NUM OC 52, Bibliothèque de l'Institut National d'Histoire de l'Art. Domaine public CCØ http://bibliotheque-numerique.inha.fr/idurl/1/25679
40 Schutte, *Women, Rank, and Marriage in the British Aristocracy, 1485-2000: An Open Elite?*, 91–92.
41 Eric Homberger, *Mrs. Astor's New York: Money and Social Power in a Gilded Age* (New Haven: Yale University Press, 2002), 120.
42 Susan Mary Elizabeth Stewart-Mackenzie Jeune, *Memories of Fifty Years* (London: E. Arnold, 1909), 67.
43 *Titled Americans. A List of American Ladies Who Have Married Foreigners of Rank* (New York: Street & Smith, 1890), 194.

44 *Titled Americans*, 214.
45 *Titled Americans*, 206–8.
46 "American Society: The Singers," *Town Topics*, May 11, 1916, New York Genealogical and Biographical Society Collection, New York Public Library.
47 "Persistent Curse of the Gould Millions," *Milwaukee Journal Sentinel*, June 16, 1929.
48 "Three French Dukedoms and a Prussian Principality Belong to the Talleyrand-Perigords: Historic House Which Has Already Formed Three American Alliances," *New York Times*, July 12, 1908.
49 *San Francisco Call*, November 22, 1905.
50 Green, *The Other Americans in Paris*, 88.
51 Castellane, *How I Discovered America*, 176.
52 Levenstein, *Seductive Journey*, 178.
53 Bradely, "Annie J Bradley Diary"; Libbey, "Laura Jean Libbey Journals."
54 "Bloc-Notes Parisien : Un Milliard Américain en Europe," *Le Gaulois*, May 14, 1895.
55 G. W. S., "American Girl Abroad," *New York Daily Tribune: War Ships Sunk in Samoa, Library of Tribune Extras*, 1, no. 7 (July 1889): 83.
56 Castellane, *How I Discovered America*, 128.
57 Castellane, *How I Discovered America*, 168.
58 Ralph Pulitzer, *New York Society on Parade* (New York; London: Harper & Bros., 1910), 3 argued, "Instead of having an aristocracy whose caste is beyond question and beyond change and whose mutual hospitalities constitute Society, New York has an 'Aristocracy' whose elevation is largely artificial, whose membership is largely arbitrary, and whose existence vitally depends upon those activities which are known as social functions. In other words, while in Europe the mutual entertainments of an inherently stable upper class create Society, in New York the constant contortions of Society are indispensable to create and maintain a precarious upper class; while in Europe the pleasures of Society are among the prerogatives of rank, in New York the pleasure of 'rank' is the inducement to Society."
59 Homberger, *Mrs. Astor's New York*, 1.
60 Tsiang I-Mien, *The Question of Expatriation in America Prior to 1907*, The Johns Hopkins University Studies in Historical and Political Science, LX 3 (Baltimore: The Johns Hopkins Press, 1942), 94. He also notes on pages 88-89 that the passing of the Expatriation Act of 1868 was followed by a series of naturalization treaties in 1860s and 1870s, which accorded that naturalization along with five years uninterrupted residence in one nation was reciprocally accompanied by expatriation of the other. Those treaties were enacted with the North Germany Confederation, Belgium, Norway, Sweden, Great Britain, Denmark, Mexico, and Ecuador. However, no such reciprocal treaty existed with France.
61 I-Mien, *The Question of Expatriation in America Prior to* 1907, 103.
62 Quoted in ibid. Original citation: Court of Claims 571 (1869). Cf. U.S. v. Wong Kim Ark, 169 U.S. 704 (1898).
63 *Titled Americans*, 157.
64 "For the Gould Wedding: All Arrangements Have Been Practically Made," *New York Times*, February 26, 1895.
65 "American Wives of French Husbands," *The Pittsburg Press*, January 20, 1900.
66 Albert Cauwes, *Des rapports du mariage avec la nationalité*. (Paris: L. Larose & Farcel, 1901), viii–ix.
67 Albert Cauwes, *Des rapports du mariage avec la nationalité*, 60.

68 Albert Cauwes, *Des rapports du mariage avec la nationalité*, 41.
69 Albert Cauwes, *Des rapports du mariage avec la nationalité*, xi.
70 Martha Gardner, *The Qualities of a Citizen : Women, Immigration, and Citizenship, 1870–1965. (Computer File, 2009) [WorldCat.Org]* (Princeton: Princeton University Press, 2009), 14, https://www.worldcat.org/title/qualities-of-a-citizen-women-immigration-and-citizenship-1870-1965/oclc/1165606929&referer=brief_results.
71 I-Mien, "The Question of Expatriation in America Prior to 1907," 71.
72 For an analysis of the 1907 Expatriation Act from a gendered theoretical perspective, see Nicolosi, "'We Do Not Want Our Girls to Marry Foreigners': Gender, Race, and American Citizenship."
73 "An Act in Reference to the Expatriation of Citizens and Their Protection Abroad," *The American Journal of International Law*, 1907, 258, https://archive.org/stream/jstor-2212395/2212395_djvu.txt.
74 Quoted in I-Mien, "The Question of Expatriation in America Prior to 1907," 106.
75 "Mme. Gould to Wed the Prince in Paris: Ill in Consequence of Family Opposition, She Decides to Return to France," *New York Times*, April 1, 1908.
76 Edith Wharton, *The Custom of the Country* (New York: Charles Scribner's Sons, 1913); Abel Hermant, *Les transatlantiques* (Paris: Michel, 1927).
77 "Newspaper Clipping, Title Unknown," May 30, 1884. Levi P. Morton Papers, Series VII Scrapbook, vol. 5, 130.
78 "Three French Dukedoms and a Prussian Principality Belong to the Talleyrand-Perigords: Historic House Which Has Already Formed Three American Alliances."
79 "Saunerings," *Town Topics: Journal of Society*, July 14, 1887, New York Genealogical and Biographical Society Collection, New York Public Library.
80 *Pittsburg Press*, October 5, 1901.
81 "Three French Dukedoms and a Prussian Principality Belong to the Talleyrand-Perigords: Historic House Which Has Already Formed Three American Alliances."
82 Castellane, *How I Discovered America*, 132.
83 "American Girls Who Married Titles: Mattie Mitchell Becomes the Duchesse de La Rouchefoucauld," *The Pittsburgh Press*, August 22, 1915, sec. The Sunday Press Illustrated Magazine Section, 48 labelled the marriage Mitchell-Rouchefoucauld a "purely love match" in which "money played no part."
84 Davis, *About Paris*, 201.
85 Green, *The Other Americans in Paris*, 89.
86 Henry James, *The American* (London: Macmillan and Co., 1878), 39–40.
87 James, *The American*, 239.
88 Jeanne Delbaere-Garant, "Paris," in *Henry James : The Vision of France*, Bibliothèque de La Faculté de Philosophie et Lettres de l'université de Liège (Liège: Presses universitaires de Liège, 1970), 3–21, http://books.openedition.org/pulg/906.
89 "Concluding Roundtable" (International Conference on Intermarriage and Mixedness: New Research Challenges on Intermarriage and Mixedness in Europe and Beyond, Sorbonne, Maison de la Recherche, Paris, France, 2015) found that most patterns of transnational or mixed marriages during the nineteenth and twentieth centuries were characterized by gender imbalances.
90 Henry Van Dyke, *America for Me - Van Dyke*, 1909.
91 Quoted in Green, *The Other Americans in Paris*.
92 Levenstein, *Seductive Journey*, 183.

93 Helen Josephy and Mary Margaret McBride, *Paris Is a Woman's Town* (New York: Coward-McCann, Inc., 1929), 136–40.
94 "RSVP," n.d., Levi P. Morton Papers, Box 7 Social Correspondence, Folder "Accepts and Regrets, Ball 1884 April 24," New York Public Library.
95 "Correspondence," n.d., Levi P. Morton Papers, Box 2, Folder "Correspondence 1883 Jan-1888 Dec," New York Public Library.
96 Stephen Fi___ to Levi P. Morton, January 26, 1882, Levi P. Morton Papers, Box 1, Folder "Correspondence 1882 Jan," New York Public Library.
97 Anja Werner, *The Transatlantic World of Higher Education: Americans at German Universities, 1776–1914*, European Studies in American History, vol. 4 (New York: Berghahn Books, 2013).

Chapter 2

EMOTIONAL DIMENSIONS OF ELITE TRANSNATIONAL SPACES

In Chapter 1, I argued that rather than attempts of nouveaux riches Americans to gain social status by participating in title-for-dollar exchanges, titled Franco-American marriages in the nineteenth century were instead the result of social interaction within elite transnational spaces that existed between the United States and Europe and among those who identified with others of similar economic and social status rather than national origin. What follows is a continued attempt to move beyond limited explanations of these elite marriages as mere socioeconomic arrangements by more closely examining the cultural and emotional dimensions of those spaces. Here, I argue that at the intersection of encounter, elite class-consciousness and transnational coupling stood a profoundly emotional experience, and because that experience was so intertwined with cross-cultural interaction, the marriages that emerged from these spaces can be, in many respects, characterized as even more (rather than less) emotional than their national counterparts.

This chapter is divided into four parts: In the first, I demonstrate how perceived notions of cultural difference within elite transnational social circles were the driving force of transnational elite marriages. As members of transnational high society encountered one another, perceived cultural stereotypes as well as processes of othering led to what I call *cultural infatuation*—affection not (only) for another person but for the perceived culture to which they belonged. This long-standing, mutual fascination between French and American members of high society created for many marriage participants a *longing for the perceived "other."* In this section, I also examine the role that the perception of one's own otherness in these spaces played into marriage motivation and the extent to which this too was a profoundly emotional issue. Thereafter, the second and third parts of the chapter go further to contextualize these marriages within broader emotional and cultural shifts in European and American societies as they pertained to marriage practices. Here, I examine elite cultural rituals of transnational courting and divorce patterns in order to demonstrate how their details confirm that the emotionalization of marriage practices—a process that had begun over the previous centuries—was already deeply rooted in elite society by the nineteenth century. In this section, I argue that personal happiness and mutual affection were as much the aim of transnational marital unions as was material and social circumstance. Finally, I conclude the chapter by examining the decline of the titled-marriage pattern between France and the United States. Here, I argue that while the coming of World War I and the global economic crisis that followed did not end the pattern of titled marriages—as they continued well into the twentieth century—it did effectively end the domination of the transnational space that existed in between France and the United States by the upper echelons of society, thereby allowing for new transnational-marriage patterns to emerge.

Cultural Othering in Transnational Spaces

While the analytical concept of an elite transnational social community levels socioeconomic and national distinctions between American and European elites, it is important to note that as elite Americans and Europeans encountered one another in transnational spaces, processes of cultural differentiation still took place. These notions of perceived difference were sometimes marked simply by nuanced and overlapping cultural characteristics. For example, in her work *French Ways and Their Meanings*, American novelist and distinguished member of elite society, Edith Wharton, justified the use of the terms "Latin" and "Anglo-Saxon" as "a loose way of drawing the division between the people who drink spirits and those who drink wine."[1] Other times, notions of difference were labeled more strikingly. In 1882, one French journalist observed: "Les américains, établis à Paris, conservent un vif attachement pour leur pays; parmi nous ils gardent leurs mœurs, leurs habitudes, et cela sert à s'imaginer qu'ils sont encore de l'autre côté de l'océan."[2] (Americans, established in Paris, keep a strong attachment to their country; among us they keep their customs, their habits, and this allows them to imagine themselves on the other side of the ocean.) Indeed, these notions of difference within transnational high society, whether constructed or assumed, played a central role in elite Franco-American marriage motivation. The role of difference in transnational marriages, therefore, presents for the researcher a unique opportunity for further exploring the concept of *othering*, its theoretical framework, and its applications in spaces of transnationality such as these.

The theoretical framework of othering has its roots in the work of German philosopher, Georg Wilhelm Friedrich Hegel, and proposes that the juxtaposition of the *other* is crucial to constituting the *self*.³ This theory has been most fruitfully employed in postcolonial and feminist scholarship. Notable examples include the works of Edward Saïd, who examined the "imagined geography," in which the Orient is constructed as the "other,"⁴ and Simone de Beauvoir's *The Second Sex*, in which she describes men as the "self" and women as the "other."⁵ Gayatri Chakravorty Spivak was, however, the first to use the concept in a systematic way in her 1985 work, "The Rani of Simur," in which she examines the ways in which British colonial authorities constructed an Indian colonial "other."⁶ Like those of Said and de Beauvoir, Spivak's "other" is constructed as inferior through a political process of unequal power relations.

While the concept has not been systematically applied to the context of the nineteenth-century Atlantic elite, the notion of becoming the "self" in opposition to the "other" during encounter has, to some extent, been explored by Maureen Montgomery in "'Natural Distinction': The American Bourgeois Search for Distinctive Signs in Europe." Although it is not the central focus of her examination of the cultural work of class formation through elite American travel to Europe—and although she does not employ these terms—she concludes that such travel contributed to the making of a "national identity" as American travelers sought to define and differentiate themselves during their European stays.⁷ In addition, this structuralist understanding of othering as a process of identity formation among nineteenth-century Atlantic elites has perhaps been most fruitfully explored by literary theorists' examinations of the works of transnational high society member Edith Wharton. Publishing nearly one novel each year between 1897 and 1937, Wharton often depicted events, characters, and settings that were derived from her own cross-cultural experiences with the French. As a biographer and litterateur, Hermonie Lee explains: "In almost every one, there is a cultural comparison, a conflict, a journey or a displacement, a sharp eye cast across national characteristics."⁸ Literary theorist Maria Strääf further argues that these cultural conflicts or encounters with Europeans produced for Wharton a hyper-state of national awareness as she and other elite Americans were forced to question, modify, abandon, or affirm their own cultural values. According to Strääf, the Franco-American encounters that played out in Wharton's novels demonstrate a "process through which contemporary French and Americans were made aware of their own and others' distinguishing qualities."⁹ Literary scholar Millicent Bell reaches similar conclusions. She argues that the longer Wharton stayed in France, the more American she *became*.¹⁰ Embedded in the context of nineteenth-century nation-making, this process of othering as identity formation takes the form of becoming a "national" self.¹¹

But othering as identity formation and postcolonial and feminist othering as a political process through which unequal power structures are created and reinforced seem to offer an incomplete picture in the context of the Atlantic elite. Further, the extent to which cultural othering is an emotional process has also yet to be fully explored. Examining othering as an emotional response to encounter reveals the intimate nature of the relationships between not only French and American elites but also between them and the transnational spaces that they created.

When Americans encountered Europeans in elite transnational spaces, despite identifying with them socially and economically, subsequent self/other *distantiation* still took place and, more importantly, sentiments for the "other" were created in the process. However, unlike feminist and postcolonial othering, this was neither a political process nor did it result from (or create) unequal power distribution. On the contrary, a perceived sense of socioeconomic uniformity between European and American members of transnational high society more often characterized these elite social spaces. Further, unlike Said's or de Beauvoir's othering, these processes were *positive* in that they often isolated desirable cultural traits and produced a fascination with the perceived "other." *Positive othering*—the process in which the "other" is constructed as desirable and fascinating through perceived cultural forms—I argue, is distinct from concepts such as the "colonial gaze" and "exoticism" of postcolonial theory,[12] as these concepts are still largely embedded in an unequal power distribution. In this case, attraction to difference implies only difference and not superiority of the "other" or the "self," merely difference. In elite transnational communities, these othering processes were accompanied by preconditioned *cultural infatuation*—affection for the perceived culture itself—that was deeply embedded in national and gendered stereotypes. In the context of transnational marriages, this mutual cultural infatuation then produced in cross-cultural encounters more personal sentiments of longing for the "other" that were, for many, at the root of cross-border marriage motivation.

Evidence of these processes is best observed in ways in which members of transnational high society described one another in varied forms of media. An examination of these elite discourses demonstrates not only how notions of difference were marked but also how these perceived differences provoked certain emotional responses. Further, elite social events such as dinners and balls are of particular interest as they provided the stage on which many of these processes played out. Therefore, their descriptions found in both the press and the writings and papers of hosts, like American Minister to Paris, Levi P. Morton, as well as those of attendees provide an important glimpse into the ways in which elite transnational social spaces themselves were perceived and interpreted and how these cultural systems of meaning were translated into processes of cultural othering and the production of sentiments for the perceived "other."

For the French, the gendered and extravagant nature of transnational social spaces, such as the dinners and balls hosted by Morton and his wife at the American legation in Paris, facilitated the creation of an enchanting image of the American "other" with young, elite women and their wealth at the center. One French journalist writing for *Le Gaulois* tried to capture this allure. While covering one of Morton's dinners, he wrote: "Et des beautés et des élégances, et des jeunesses américaines, à foison ! Quelle admirable race, et quelle grâce ardente elle déploie à la valse!"[13] (And beautiful, elegant, youthful American ladies, galore! What an admirable race, and what ardent grace she displays dancing the waltz!) On the subject of a separate social event at the American legation, another French journalist for *La Patrie* wrote:

> On sait qu'il n'y a plus guère, en effet, de fêtes à Paris sans que les ravissantes Américaines y apportent l'attrait d'une beauté idéale et d'une gaieté française. Les Américains sont un peuple en qui fleurissent la santé—virilité intellectuelle et force chez l'homme et la grâce—sérénité de la beauté—chez la femme. Aussi, le monde américain est-il depuis quelques années fort recherché à Paris, où les salons français se complètent, quand, pourvus déjà de l'élément gaulois, ils s'agrémentent du type délicieux de la femme américaine [...] A ce compte, la légation des Etats Unis à Paris était, hier, un véritable 'keapside', où éclatait la vivacité de la grâce parisienne à côté de la charmeresse beauté américaine. Avec cela, et comme cadre, l'originalité de toilettes la plus sui generis, c'est-à-dire [...] américaine, rehaussée de ce je ne sais quoi plein d'un bon goût dont on se plaît partout à emprunter le ton et le tact aux modèles parisiens.[14]
>
> [It's well known that there are few festive occasions in Paris any more, without the delightful Americans bringing the attraction of ideal beauty and [...] cheerfulness. The Americans are a people in which health flourishes –intellectual virility and force in the men and grace, serenity of beauty in the women. Also, the American world has for a number of years been much sought after in Paris, where French salons already provided with the Gallic element are completed when combined with the delightful type of the American woman. On this account the Legation of the United States in Paris was, yesterday, a real "keapside" [sic], where the vivacity of Parisian grace burst forth beside the charming American beauty. With that, and as a frame, the originality of the garments the most sui generis, that is to say [...] American, enhanced by the tone and tact of good taste borrowed from Parisian models.]

Both excerpts show how notions of beauty, grace, and elegance that were transcribed onto American women were rooted in their perceived difference. Further, because elite social events like dinners and balls were used as elaborate displays of wealth and refinement, the process of positive othering and the fascination that it produced were linked directly to the spaces of encounter themselves. For example, when the recently widowed Mrs. "Plus" Moore, née Miss Kate Robinson of Philadelphia, moved to Paris in the 1880s, she quickly made her way into a prominent position in transnational high society.[15] Her private residence, where the social events were held, like those of the American legation, became an important gathering place for Atlantic elite, and as Boni de Castellane explained, "certain political men" of France were especially "attracted by the topsy turvy love peculiar to the house."[16] This "topsy turvy love" was rooted in the elaborate cultural rituals of Mrs. Moore's social events and others like them, and the passage further demonstrates how the spaces themselves were endowed with emotional forces of attraction and fascination.

But how was the image of the othered American woman fashioned into an attractive potential wife in ways that went beyond the sum of wealth that would be brought into the marriage? Juliette Adam, a French woman, wrote a piece for the *North American Review* in an attempt to offer a "European stand-point on [the attraction to] the young American girl in Europe." She admitted that while she had never been to the United States, she knew America "by its history, its literature, and [by] important facts of its daily life" and that she knew its women by observing those who had been residing in France. She then went on to adorn them by writing:

> The young American girl in France, even though she should reside there a long time, still remains a peculiar being, disturbing the men and a source of uneasiness to the women [...] She is beautiful with perfect beauty, or endowed with a triumphal grace [...] The Young girl is the aristocracy, the luxury, the art, the crown of American society, as the Epicurean was of ancient society. She alone enjoys and profits from her leisure. It is for her that man bends with such fury beneath the weight of the labor for his betrothed or his daughter [...] She never looks like a shopkeeper's daughter [...] They may be charged with what we call in France airs de coquettes, but not one of them looks like a tradeswoman [...] The American girl has a science of pleasing which captivates even the old-world Don Juan's unawareness. She seems to us exceptional, intelligent, putting for all her talent to attain the final end, which is trapping, often for his own good, a titled husband.[17]

Like the writers for *La Patrie* and *Le Gaulois*, Adams transcribed the American woman's otherness as captivating, graceful, luxurious, beautiful, and notably exceptional. For her, it was for these reasons that they so easily attracted titled husbands. Interestingly, her observation that such an arrangement was "for his own good" indicates a favorable judgment of such transnational unions, unlike the writers examined in the first chapter.

Other contemporary commentators also attempted to further explain the European attraction to American women as suitable wives—an attraction that was fervently rooted in her perceived difference. One member of transnational high society, writing from London speculated: "The reason which underlies all the others is social [...] American women were seen as far more social and less timid," he explained. "Men like variety [...] Her intelligence, quickness, freshness, animation, fullness of character, often her brilliancy, always her individuality were perfectly novel to him and perfectly delightful."[18] Likewise, French citizen and good friend to Edith Wharton, Louis Simonin confirmed during his visit to New York that American women possessed an "exaggerated love of pleasure." He wrote:

> There are [...] in New York many young ladies who are, as they say, a little fast [...] [and] they astonish Europe with their carelessness of conversational restraints [...] Many persons accustomed to our usages would not choose these young ladies for wives. They are right and they are wrong; it matters little: the truth is, that these young Americans, on their introduction to society so frivolous, and sometimes—to speak plainly—compromised by grave acts, make in the end good wives and excellent mothers.[19]

In elite Franco-American encounter, processes of cultural othering occurred bilaterally. However, for Americans, positive othering and longing for the French "other" was heavily rooted in perceived cultural infatuation. As Nancy Green explains: "Many Americans were in Paris for the love of the French, literally." The idea of "being swept off one's feet by a French nobleman remained the most visible image of the French-American marriages in the early part of the twentieth century."[20] In the 1920s book *Paris Is a Woman's Town*, the two young female authors explained: "No more diverting and fascinating male exists than the aristocratic Parisian."[21] They added that "to be perfectly frank, we were much more interested in the male human element than the female in Paris."[22] But for American women, the attraction to French otherness went a little deeper than the men with whom they wished to partner. They often found a love affair with France and French culture just as appealing. For many of these elite women, France had become synonymous with social luxuries in ways that Britain and Germany had not, and marriage was a way to permanently insert themselves into it. To fully understand this, an examination of the development of America's elite social class and the ways in which it put culture to use is necessary.

By the second half of the nineteenth century, America's growing economic development had begun to produce a wealthy population that flocked to fashionable New York. While elite cultural forms such as the dress, architecture, and gastronomy of places like Boston or Philadelphia were determined by historical customs; New York's elite began to construct their own high society based on European, and largely French, cultural models. As Thorstein Veblen in *Theory of the Leisure Class* first showed in 1899, New York's emulation of European aristocracy was a central element in the commerce and culture of luxury.[23] In order to more fully understand the meanings that New York high society attributed to the cultural forms taken from European aristocracy, we must carefully examine how this fascination was materialized within their cultural rituals.

The social ambitions of Ward McAllister provide an excellent example. He went to New York determined to create a high society and did so with French aristocracy in mind. As a young man, he had traveled widely in Europe. Overwhelmed with the hustle and bustle of Paris, he took residence in Pau, a small village overlooking the French Pyrénées where he spent most of his time with French aristocrats, learned about Bordeaux wines, and perfected his etiquette.[24] He wrote: "There I learned how to give dinners; to esteem and to value the *coq de Bruyère* of the *Pyrénées* and the *Pie de Mars*."[25] He began hosting one to two dinners a week in France, and they were so successful that he resolved to host a ball himself when he returned to New York from Paris based on this model.[26]

New York's high society also replicated European nobles' style of life through architecture and art. Multimillion-dollar, French-style *chateaux* were constructed on Fifth Avenue and at Newport. Mr. Rutherfurd-Stuyvestant (Stuyvesant Rutherford) built the first "French flat"—reproducing customs found in Paris, in which a concierge guarded the entrance. All suites were rented by young couples of New York society, and this model quickly dominated the modern city. In these lavish homes, extravagant collections of French antiques and art became "necessary expenditures."[27] The art collection of William H. Vanderbilt featured many French artists. While he always had a taste for art, when he came into his fortune, he turned his nose on American art, as his tastes could only be satisfied by "the best and most costly in the world."[28] Likewise, for American women, the best corsets were French.[29] From France they got dresses, gowns, cloaks, fans, jeweled combs, gold hairnets, and head ornaments. As American author and critic

Lloyd R. Morris wrote: "[Ladies] had to send to Paris for everything, and the tyranny of Monsieur Worth—intransigent and perdurable—began."[30] This cultural fascination also materialized in dinners and costume balls in New York. Mrs. William Colford Schermerhorn, for example, invited 600 guests to a magnificent *affair de luxe*. All the guests were asked to dress in costume of the period of Louis XV; however, according to Ward McAllister, many of the men preferred the imperial style of Napoleon III. The house itself was completely redecorated and refurnished in the style.[31] The servants were dressed in uniforms and wigs of Versailles. McAllister remembered: "It was intended to be the greatest affair New Yorkers had ever seen [...] The men, as well as the women, vied with each other in getting up as handsome costumes as were ever worn at that luxurious court."[32] The use of French words here is also interesting. Mrs. Schermerhorn's invitations did not request the pleasure of her guests' company but instead simply announced a *bal paré*.

Here, like in other instances of intercultural transfers, modification and adaptions were made and the replication of French models was often less than precise. Menus at every dinner event were written in French, and the food was prepared by a French chef. However, on his American tour, M. Simonin wrote:

> The *cuisine* is neither good nor suitably prepared. Meals are served in the American fashion—all the dishes at once, and every variety of condiment is placed upon the table for seasoning the viands according to the taste of the guest. The head-cook is a Frenchman, but he is obliged to renounce good traditions by modifying his practice to suit the requirements of his employers. He is paid like a minister of state, receiving frequently four hundred dollars a month.[33]

Likewise, when transnational-marriage participant Boni de Castellane visited New York, he came across a chef who had previously worked for his grandmother. In their discussion, the chef warned him that he would not like the cooking and asked that he should not judge him too harshly as he was forced "to please [the Americans]."[34] One can therefore conclude that it was not necessarily the case that elite Americans preferred superiority of French cuisine, but instead the idea or representation that it was *French* made it a mark of elite status despite the fact that it was far from authentic. These kinds of replications are a crucial element of the emotion of cultural infatuation. American elites had been seasoned and enabled by cultural institutions of the transnational community, and there was a self-conscious sense of how their cultural images were produced. How they placed themselves in this imaginary world via the performance of their balls and social events is especially interesting. The historical researcher should not consider this mere imitation because the prestige came from the performance of French culture. Transnational marriage in this context gave further prestige to that performance, as the performance further give prestige to the marriages.

Finally, because cultural imagery creates emotions, one must also question how marriage participants saw themselves as subjects through its lens. Therefore, by examining the ways in which actors thought of their own flourishing in the context of their transnational community, we might consider the satisfaction that one receives from being the subject of *positive othering* or the emotional enjoyment that one's own otherness provided. The following example from contemporary American novelist, Booth Tarkingon, provides the foundation for such an inquiry. He wrote: "Half a dozen Americans stand at one end of an aisle of Notre Dame in Paris, another half dozen at the other end. The two parties exchange glances of hostility at first sight. Says a lady of the first half dozen: 'The place is spoiled. One can never come here without finding a lot of *Americans*.' Says a lady of the second half dozen: 'Let us go. Here come a lot of Americans!'"[35] If we adopt Martha Nussbaum's concept of emotions as forms of evaluative judgment,[36] then by maintaining one's own otherness and their affection for this otherness, they attempted to distinguish themselves from the growing number of American tourists. This, therefore, can also be considered as one of the emotional goals of marriage participants.

Courting Practices and Emotions

A continued attempt to move beyond more limited explanations of transnational elite marriage unions as mere socioeconomic transactions requires that they be contextualized within broader emotional shifts that pertained to courtship and marital practices in European and American societies. As marriage and emotions historians have shown, by the nineteenth century, the cultural notion of love-based marriage had become firmly rooted as a cultural ideal in both societies.[37] Further, while material and economic circumstance remained important for elite participants, marriage was, nonetheless, a profoundly emotional issue for both men and women. In her examination of the marriage practices of British nobility over three centuries, Kimberly Schutte draws similar conclusions arguing that by the nineteenth century, the ultimate aim of elite courting for women "was to fall in love with a man whom their family would also consider fitting."[38] Further, while family pressure to "marry well" occurred consistently within elite families in both Europe and America, marriage participants still exercised a great deal of agency in partner selection. And for them, personal happiness was as much an aim of transnational marital unions as was material and social circumstance.

Miss Mattie Mitchell, of Portland Oregon, for example, was the daughter of American Sectator John H. Mitchell. Like many of her peers, she went to France to be educated and found her place easily within the elite transnational community residing in Paris. In 1886, she attended a dinner and dance hosted by a French general, where she met Duc François Alfred Gaston de la Rouchefoucauld. In recounting the story of their marriage, the *Pittsburgh Press* quoted their meeting as "love at first sight."[39] The article went on to say: "The day following the dinner, a picnic was given at St. Germain, to which the duke and Miss Mitchell were asked, and from that date the young Frenchman [...] never ceased his attentions and devotions" and proposed within the year. In an attempt to further distinguish this "love match" from other marriages that had been labeled title-for-treasure exchanges, the publication described Duc de la Rouchefoucauld as the "heir to one of the oldest and most historic families in France" and insisted that "he was not a fortune hunter" and that "money played no part in [their] love affair." Both his mother and her father objected to the union, each insisting on what they considered more suitable matches. Despite being separated for several years, however, "the two lovers" continued to correspond. And when Miss Mitchell accompanied her mother on a trip to Royat, they were reunited. There, he is reported to have said: "There is no use waiting any longer for consent. My mother refuses and your father also. We will be married without consent." According to the article, his mother did eventually accept the union and embraced her new daughter-in-law as she gifted her the family lace, which Miss Mitchell wore when the two were married in 1892. They continued to reside in France where, according to a later *New York Times* article, she "gained the love and admiration of the entire Faubourg and the old nobility."[40]

For the historian, using emotions as a category of analysis in examining personal and intimate relationships in nineteenth-century elite transnational communities is not without methodological limitations. The story of the Duc and Duchesse de la Rouchefoucauld, for example, is only told as a second-hand account in the American press. Lack of first-hand accounts are likely tied to the fact that most contemporary subjects often considered outward displays of public emotion to be contrary to proper behavior. As one 1882 etiquette manual advised: "It is a mark of good breeding to suppress undue emotion, whether of disappointment, of mortification, or laughter, of anger, or of selfishness in any form."[41] Therefore, because very few openly discussed the emotional dimensions of their own personal relationships in an overt way, the few sources that do provide such descriptions are especially invaluable (albeit perhaps not representative) windows into emotions of the past. One example of such a first-hand account is the memoir of Boni de Castellane. Therefore, a reexamination of the events leading to his marriage Anna Gould—one that has been labeled as the most notorious and scandalous example of a fortune-hunting arrangement[42]—provides a further glimpse into transnational elite courtship practices, emotions, personal choice, and individual agency.

While little historical work has been done on courting practices in nineteenth-century transnational communities, comparative conclusions can, nonetheless, be drawn from those undertaken in national frameworks. In both the United States and France, elite courting was a semipublic affair. Its practices often adhered to strict cultural decorum, and potential matches involved not only families but also chaperones and sometimes other members of high society during costume balls, which came to often serve as quasi marriage markets and public theater of elite courtship. As Schutte has also shown, because by the nineteenth century overtly arranged marriages were seen as in poor taste, balls along with the ridged social exclusion that defined their guest lists were used to ensure that only appropriate social interaction was promoted among those hoping to marry.[43] Further, while the role of mothers in their daughters' (and sons') partner selection was an important one, Schutte argues that for them, "the emotional aspects of a proposed match remained a deep concern."[44] In the case of transnational courting practices, the role of the mother was not always an essential one. As one American member of transnational high society residing in London explained: "The American girl asks little or no help from her mother in choosing a partner for life. The English girl has always been dependent upon her mother for a husband [...] She has toiled, schemed, and intrigued to find husbands for her girls [...] Perhaps the very men she has fixed on for her own offspring have married Americans."[45] Such agency seems to have also been the case for Anna Gould.

Anna Gould was the daughter of Jay Gould, the American railroad tycoon, who, by the age of forty-five possessed more than 100 million dollars, had a yacht Atlanta, and owned "a massive brownstone at the northeast corner of fifth and forty-seventh, in the heart of the aristocratic section [of New York City]."[46] When he died in 1892 at age fifty-six, unlike the Astors, Gould did not transmit the bulk of his wealth to his eldest son, but instead divided it among all his children.

Like many elite women, Anna Gould traveled often to Europe and was especially fond of France. In the spring of 1894, she arrived in Paris to take extended residence with Miss Fanny Reed, a relation of Minnie Paget (née Stevens). According to Castellane, upon her arrival, there had been much gossip around Paris regarding both her reputable wealth and her matrimonial future, and many in Parisian high society flocked to see her.[47] Like the others,

Castellane was impelled by curiosity. And although Reed, who was meant to chaperone Anna during her stay, did not care for him, she nonetheless introduced the two of them. According to Castellane, Gould was unimpressed by both his name and rank, but she was happy to find a Frenchman who spoke English. Of his attraction to her, Castellane insists, it was her unusual personality—one that was both shy and childish but charming—that fascinated him the most rather than her wealth, which "played only a secondary part in her attraction."[48] It is important to note that he was writing in the period after their divorce and that he published his memoir in both English and French for the explicit purpose of "telling his side" of what became a rather scandalous separation. The public had been especially critical of their marriage and often classified it as the epitome of a fortune-hunting marriage. Here, however, he insisted numerous times that her fortune was not his primary motivation for pursuing her and that, in fact, he had really loved her. His repeated insistence of that love and affection is central to the examination of broader emotional shifts as they applied to elite marriage practices. In interpreting his claims, one can assume that either (1) he was telling the truth and that they both had mutual feelings of affection for one another and entered into the marriage with expectations of love and happiness or (2) one could consider the possibility that he was lying and that his memoir was merely an attempt to curtail a fairly prominent scandal surrounding the termination of an economically motivated marriage. However, if in fact he was lying, his very insistence itself is evidence that he, nonetheless, recognized the evolving social norms of love-based marriages as a cultural ideal. Therefore, we can conclude that in claiming that his marriage to Gould was in fact a love-based marriage, he was attempting to defend its legitimacy against critiques that viewed economically based marriages as less legitimate than their emotionally based counterparts.

From what the researcher can presume from Castellane's account, Gould exercised tremendous agency and personal choice in the coupling courtship process. According to him, she needed to be convinced of both him and his affection for her, and in embarking on a courtship process he explained that he was "determined to carry the warfare of love into the enemy's camp."[49] He wrote to her several times, passed under her window on horseback, and sent her a Persian lilac—each action a courtship ritual that would denote genuine or at least presumed affection and unnecessary in a mere economic arrangement.[50] Further, after her return to the United States, Castellane followed her in order to "complete his conquest of this charming daughter of the new world."[51] He called his trip an "amorous adventure" and said even though he knew he would encounter "many difficulties and much opposition," he left at once to "win" her.[52]

Figure 2.1 Portrait de Boni de Castellane et Anna Gould, Davis & Sanford. CC0 Paris Musées / Musée Carnavalet—Histoire de Paris.

According to him, their interactions during their courtship period were rife with flirtation and teasing. He wrote: "Like most women who play with fire, she found it an exciting habit, and one excessively difficult to drop."[53] In hopes of winning her over, he also tried purposefully on occasion to make her jealous by holding a dinner for her and other charming high society girls. "I was not to allow her to retain the idea that foreigners were not sympathetic to other American beauties." He subsequently explained that she was furious, but it worked. "The display of the temper told me that I was now regarded by her as her especial property, and little by little, I prepared the way for my ultimate proposal," which he carried out during their visit to Quebec.[54]

His depiction of his marriage proposal was also laced with mentions of romanticized emotions. He explained that during a mass at the cathedral, he "felt that the exquisite harmonies of color and sound, by which [he and Gould] were encompassed, were fraught with some subtle meaning." He reminisced further in his memoir: "I listened to my beloved mother tongue, I was one with the indissoluble Spirit of France, and I was at peace. And as I looked at my companion, I thought that I could wish for no better fate than to share my life with this young girl, and to awaken love in her heart." According to him, after they left mass, he "unveiled [his] inmost soul" to her and asked her to become his wife.[55] Likewise, regarding their wedding, he recalled: "I was carried away by varying emotions... I visualized the possibilities of my chosen road, its brilliance, its romance, and I thrilled at the prospect. I dreamt of happiness for my wife; and for myself—success in everything that appertained to my tastes, my country, and my faith."[56]

Divorce and Emotions

Boni de Castellane and Anna Gould were married for eleven years before the marriage ended in divorce.[57] Some historians, such as Elizabeth Eliot, have claimed divorce in the case of transnational elite marriages may be evidence of post-marriage disillusionment with pre-marital cultural expectations.[58] This may have been the case for some like Levi P. Morton's daughter Helen, who returned to the United States after her short marriage to the Duc de Valeccay with the majority of her fortune.[59] However, that some of these women remained in France and married other Frenchmen shows that perhaps it was with their husbands rather than their husbands' culture that they became disillusioned. Daisy Foster, for example, remained in France after her divorce from her first husband in order to marry her second, Pierre Alyn, who was well known as a singer and composer. According to *Town Topics*, regarding the decision not to return to the United States, "she professed to loathe the restrictions and conventions of her native heath."[60] Anna Gould also stayed. Her second marriage even remained within the established familial and social networks from which the first had emerged. After her divorce from Castellane, she married his cousin, Hélie de Talleyrand-Périgord, Duc de Sagan. Likewise, Castellane also continued to surround himself with American women, claiming this was because they were livelier and more independent than their French counterparts.[61]

While instances of divorce may or may not indicate cross-cultural disillusion, they can instead serve as a more important indication of emotional expectations. As Stephanie Coontz shows in her examination of marriage practices over the centuries, increased instances of divorce coincided with the rise of love-based marriage cultural ideals. She explains: "No sooner had the ideal of the love match and lifelong intimacy taken hold than people began to demand the right to divorce."[62] For Gould a successful marriage meant one that was based on happiness, and for her the absence of happiness provided a valid reason for the marriage to be dissolved. When Castellane proposed marriage to Gould, she had accepted without hesitation but with the disclaimer that she refused to become Catholic. "I will never become a Catholic," she explained, "because if I were to do so I should not be able to divorce you, and if I were not happy I would not remain your wife for a moment longer than necessary."[63] The use of *happiness* in her own valuation of successful marriage was also reiterated in their annulment proceedings, when one of Castellane's witnesses, Catherine Cameron, testified that Anna had told her that "it was the custom of American girls to divorce husbands who did not make them happy."[64] Therefore, because the absence of happiness justified the dissolution of marriage, increasing divorce rates not only call into question the notion of these nineteenth-century transnational marriages as strictly economic arrangements, but also become a valuable indicator of emotional expectations among marriage participants in both national and transnational circumstances.

The United States Census Bureau already recognized in 1909 that American divorce rates had been steadily increasing. Between 1887 and 1906, divorce rates had increased at an approximate rate of 30 percent every five years. Thus, the divorce rate was almost three times as great in 1905 as it had been in 1870. Based on total population, the annual divorce rate in 1870 had been 28 divorces per 100,000-person population sample. In 1900, it had increased to 73 divorces per 100,000 people. Further, when they limited their analysis to only the married population, they found that in 1870 approximately 1 out of 625 marriages ended in divorce annually, and in 1900, approximately 1 out of 250 American marriages ended in divorce.[65]

So how do these rates compare with those in France? As American heiresses entered into matrimonial unions with Europeans, divorce became part of a broader cross-cultural negotiation within transnational-marriage spaces. In the dedication of his 1893 novel, *L'Américaine*, French writer Jules Claretie called divorce an "American importation." "With you, divorces are obtained with prodigious facility," he criticized. "We have not yet reached the same condition of things France."[66] Likewise, Boni de Castellane claimed that in the United States divorce was "a household word." "Women take more than one husband, and men several wives," he boasted.[67] As Gould had noted in her refusal to convert to Catholicism when she accepted his marriage proposal, Protestant tradition rendered Americans relatively strong proponents of loose divorce laws, a quality on which Coontz also remarked in her cross-cultural marriage study.[68] Despite these claims, however, France also saw a rise in divorce rates during this period.

Dating back to the period of the *ancien régime*, French Catholics often held strict views of marriage as indissoluble. However, this view later eroded during the Revolution, when the French State recognized religious pluralism and became secular. In this process, marriage was detached from religious sacrament and became a civil contract. This, therefore, meant that divorce also had to be recognized as an individual liberty, and the 1792 *Loi de floréal an II* legalized divorce on the grounds of incompatibility.[69] However, in 1816, as the Catholic religion became once again the religion of the State under the Restoration, these liberal divorce laws were repealed. It was not until 1884 that the right of divorce was reestablished under the Third Republic by the *loi Naquet*.[70]

The aforementioned U.S. census report on marriage and divorce in 1909 also examined foreign statistics, and those obtained from the French *Annuaire Statistique* noted that the general tendency in France from 1887 to 1905 also showed a steady increase in the divorce rates. In 1887, there were 10 divorces reported to every 100,000-person population sample, and in 1905, it was 26 to every 100,000-person population sample.[71] While these records, unfortunately, do not include an analysis limited to the married population like the American records, we can nevertheless conclude that even though there were greater instances of divorce in the United States, French divorce rate also showed a similar rate of increase of nearly 30 percent every five years during approximately the same period. Like in the United States, it was also nearly three times greater in 1905 than it had been in 1880s.

Because both France and the United States officially recognized marriages that had been contracted by the other State, they also recognized the divorces that had been granted in the other as well. Further, as the aforementioned census demonstrated, it was possible to dissolve a marriage in one country that had been contracted in the other. The specific divorce and annulment rates among the transnational-marriage participants are difficult to ascertain with any real accuracy. We do know that the number of divorces granted in the United States for marriages that had been contracted in France between 1887 and 1906 was 282.[72] It is unclear however, how many of these were titled marriages or how many were even between French and American citizens. The sample of elite Franco-American marriages during the nineteenth century that I collected through mentions in the French and American press—which cannot, because of this limitation, be claimed as comprehensive—included nearly one hundred marriages; of them, I found mentions of ten of them ending in divorce (leaving a sample divorce rate of about 1 out of 10). Therefore, the more significant conclusion that can be drawn is that elite transnational couples during the nineteenth century both contracted and terminated marital unions beyond national borders relatively easily.

Rather than national borders, it was perhaps religious boundaries that proved to be more difficult to cross. When the Court of the Rota at Rome allowed for the annulment of Castellane and Gould's marriage, it subsequently and inadvertently gave the public the impression that the Catholic Church was also weakening its stand on the indissolubility of marriage. The case still remained rather scandalous among Catholics however, and in order to reaffirm the Church's position, one expert at the time responded that it "might be made harder [in the future] for Catholics and non-Catholics to marry."[73]

Decline of Titled Marriage Pattern

An effort to temporalize the pattern of elite Franco-American titled marriages and their decline is not without limitations. What was at the end of the nineteenth century a subject of much interest and gossip in both the French and American press soon lost its novelty, and references of titled marriages in the publications like *Town Topics* began to wane during the first decades of the twentieth century. Further, while the coming of the Great War temporarily halted their occurrence as transatlantic travel became not only dangerous but also difficult due to food and fuel shortages, new passport regulations, and travel restrictions, it did not end such marriages entirely. Notable twentieth-century Franco-American examples include the Comte de Janzé's early 1920s marriage to Alice Silverthorne of Chicago, who notoriously shot her English lover in the *Gare du Nord* in an attempted murder suicide a couple of years later[74]; the marriage of Lela Emery of Cincinnati to the Marquis de Talleyrand-Perigord in 1938; Arnaud de Rosnay's marriage with Jenna Severson of California in 1981; and New York socialite Luanne Nadeau's 1993 marriage to Alexandre de Lesseps.[75] However, these twentieth-century examples remain limited, leaving the greatest numbers of titled marriages between French and America citizens in the second half of the nineteenth century.

The global economic crisis that followed World War I further strained the position of elite transnational high society. When the crisis made its way to France by May 1931, many wealthy members of the transnational community abandoned France for other, less expensive parts of Europe. Characteristic of this period is Scott Fitzgerald's short story "Babylon Revisited," in which the main character finds Paris nearly absent of Americans during the Depression, a stark contrast to what had been known as the city's "American Colony" during the second half of the nineteenth century.[76] Likewise, Gabriel-Louis Jaray also complained about the departure of elite Americans in the 1935 *Revue de Paris*. He wrote: "They were the best clients of the French resorts and the most faithful luxury lovers in France. How many bankruptcies of luxury establishments in Paris, in the spas, and the seaside, and high commerce have been caused by this exodus of resident Americans?"[77] American historian William G. Baily also confirmed: "By the end of the 1920s the American Colony in Paris looked more like a gigantic garage sale what with automobiles, mink coats, and antiques on the auction block."[78] Levenstein, however, cautions against such watershed periodization and argues that elite cosmopolitans in France may not have been as directly affected by the economic crisis as previously thought, and maintains that elite travel continued to revolve around social engagements in both Paris and luxury resorts in places such as Deauville or Nice well into the mid-century. Here, he points to the Parisian edition of the *New York Herald*, also referred to as the *Paris Herald*, which was founded in 1887 by American James Gordon Bennett Jr. Since its founding, the *Paris Harold* frequently reported on the elite social events of high society in France and continued to do so well into the late 1930s.[79] Further, Levenstein argues that new luxury ocean liners that catered to elite travelers, like the *Normandie*, a French liner built in 1935, still managed to turn profits.[80] Even on the eve of World War II, the *Paris Herald* reported on the social events at the Deauville, which "were filled with a brilliant crowd of international socialites," and listed barons, princes, duchesses, lords, and rich Americans in attendance.[81]

Nonetheless, the coming of the twentieth century brought with it important changes that contributed to the decline of Franco-American titled marriages—notably, as Nancy Green shows, the changing relationships between French aristocrats and the rest of the French population.[82] After World War I, conceptions of rank and national identity changed in France and Great Britain alike.[83] In France, the legal status of nobility had long been gone since the Revolution and was never completely recreated. French titles, however, which had been reinstated by the nineteenth-century monarchies, had not been entirely abolished by the subsequent republican governments, and continued to exist as part of a legal name, but without privilege or precedence. Moreover, long without a monarchy and an official aristocracy to support them, those who retained their titles into the twentieth century learned to be discreet about their backgrounds and melted into the various ranks of society. During the early 1930s, two titled Frenchmen were shocked to discover that the man carrying their bags in train station was also of rank, and in response, they created *l'Association d'entraide de la noblesse française* specifically to provide "financial, moral, and cultural support" to struggling titled families in France.[84] A simpler explanation of declining Franco-American titled marriages may also be that there were simply fewer French titles in existence. As French titles were no longer created after 1870, the number of titled families in France diminished steadily over the course of the twentieth century. A survey of directories shows that there were approximately 5,000 titled families in the early 1900s,[85] 3,500 in the 1970s,[86] and 2,300 by the end of the century.[87] These numbers seem even more minimal when compared to the 25,000 on the eve of the French Revolution.

More importantly, however, the coming of the twentieth century brought with it important transformations to the transnational cultural spaces that existed between France and the United States. The outbreak of war not only changed the dimensions of the broader cultural and power relations between the two countries, but it also led to the breakdown of many class barriers in both Europe and the United States. Therefore, World War I (and the global economic crisis of the 1930s) effectively put an end to the elite's domination of transnational spaces in the Atlantic world as it paved the way "for the invasion of the lower orders"[88] and gave rise to new marriage patterns—like that between American soldiers and local French women.

Notes

1 Edith Wharton, *French Ways and Their Meaning* (New York; London: D. Appleton and Company, 1919), viii.
2 "Newspaper Clipping, Title Unknown," June 1882 Levi P. Morton Papers, Series VII Scrapbook, vol. 5, 64, New York Public Library.
3 Georg Wilhelm Friedrich Hegel, Hans-Friedrich Wessels, and Heinrich Clairmont, *Phänomenologie des Geistes* (Hamburg: F. Meiner Verlag, 1988); Although Lajos Brons in Lajos L. Brons, "Othering, an Analysis," *Transcience* 6, no. 1 (2015): 69–90, argues that while the theoretical "roots of othering grew in Hegelian soil," his dialectic of self-other identification and distantiation in the "Master-Slave Dialectic" is more of a necessary, unavoidable aspect of social existence, rather than a construction of unequal opposition driven by psychological and/or other needs.
4 Edward W Said, *Orientalism* (New York: Vintage Books, 1979).

5 Simone de Beauvoir and H. M. Parshley, *The Second Sex* (New York: Alfred A. Knopf, 1993).
6 Gayatri Chakravorty Spivak, "The Rani of Sirmur: An Essay in Reading the Archives," *History and Theory* 24, no. 3 (1985): 247–72; Gayatri Chakravorty Spivak, "Can the Subaltern Speak?," in *Marxism and the Interpretation of Culture*, ed. Cary Nelson and Lawrence Grossberg (Urbana: University of Illinois Press, 1988), 271–313.
7 Montgomery, "'Natural Distinction': The American Bourgeois Search for Distinctive Signs in Europe."
8 Hermione Lee, *Edith Wharton* (New York: Alfred A. Knopf, 2007).
9 Maria Strääf, "In between Cultures: Franco-American Encounters in the Work of Edith Wharton" (Linköping University, Department of Culture and Communication, 2008), 3.
10 Millicent Bell, "Edith Wharton in France," in *Wretched Exotic: Essays on Edith Wharton in Europe*, ed. Katherine Joslin and Alan Price (New York: P. Lang, 1993), 64.
11 Brooke Lindy Blower, *Becoming Americans in Paris Transatlantic Politics and Culture between the World Wars* (Oxford; New York: Oxford University Press, 2011) examines similar processes in the later interwar period of the twentieth century. Here, she argues that through temporary yet extended stays in Paris, Americans intellectuals participated in process through which they defined themselves as Americans. She argues that Americans in Paris manifested an offshore extension of their national lives, projecting an image of the nation as something not rooted in fixed geographical space but made up of moveable social institutions and cultural parts. In this process, she explains, *Americanness* emerged as a transnational concept—one that cannot be completely explained by an introspective analysis.
12 Said, *Orientalism*; Charles Forsdick, "Travelling Concepts: Postcolonial Approaches to Exoticism and Diversity," in *Travel in Twentieth-Century French and Francophone Cultures: "The Persistence of Diversity"* (Oxford: Oxford University Press, 2010).
13 "Newspaper Clipping, Title Unknown," *Gaulois*, May 26, 1883, Levi P. Morton Papers, Series VII Scrapbook, vol. 5, 84, New York Public Library.
14 "Les Receptions de Mme Morton," *La Patrie*, June 19, 1882, Levi P. Morton Papers, Series VII Scrapbook, vol. 5, 59, New York Public Library.
15 "Society at Home and Abroad," *New York Times*, September 6, 1903.
16 Castellane, *How I Discovered America*, 106.
17 Juliette Adam, "Those American Girls in Europe," *The North American Review*, October 1, 1890, 404.
18 G. W. S., "American Girl Abroad," 82.
19 Louis Simonin, "A Frenchman in New York," *Appletons' Journal: A Magazine of General Literature*, April 3, 1875, 433.
20 Green, *The Other Americans in Paris*, 88.
21 Josephy and McBride, *Paris Is a Woman's Town*, 159.
22 Josephy and McBride, *Paris Is a Woman's Town*, 161.
23 Veblen, *The Theory of the Leisure Class*.
24 Homberger, *Mrs. Astor's New York*, 164.
25 Ward McAllister, *Society as I Have Found It* (New York: Cassell Pub. Co., 1890), 65.
26 McAllister, *Society as I Have Found It*, 69.
27 Jaher, "Style and Status: High Society in Late-Nineteenth-Century New York," 279.

28 W. A Croffut, *The Vanderbilts and the Story of Their Fortune* (London: Belford, Clarke, 1886), 164.
29 Homberger, *Mrs. Astor's New York*, 169.
30 Lloyd R. Morris, *Incredible New York; High Life and Low Life of the Last Hundred Years*. (New York: Random House, 1951), 25.
31 McAllister, *Society as I Have Found It*, 15.
32 McAllister, *Society as I Have Found It*, 15.
33 Simonin, "A Frenchman in New York," 432.
34 Castellane, *How I Discovered America*, 27.
35 Quoted in Levenstein, *Seductive Journey*, 177.
36 Martha Craven Nussbaum, *Upheavals of Thought: The Intelligence of Emotions* (Cambridge; New York: Cambridge University Press, 2001).
37 Bologne, *Histoire du couple*; Coontz, *Marriage, a History*; Matt and Stearns, *Doing Emotions History*; Reddy, *The Making of Romantic Love*.
38 Schutte, *Women, Rank, and Marriage in the British Aristocracy, 1485–2000: An Open Elite?*, 87.
39 "American Girls Who Married Titles: Mattie Mitchell Becomes The Duchesse De La Rouchefoucauld."
40 "What Is Doing in Society," *The New York Times*, May 19, 1899.
41 Walter Raleigh Houghton, *American Etiquette and Rules of Politeness* (Chicago: Rand, McNally, 1882), 214.
42 Eliot, *Heiresses and Coronets*, 165.
43 Homberger, *Mrs. Astor's New York*, 120; Schutte, *Women, Rank, and Marriage in the British Aristocracy*, 91–92.
44 Schutte, *Women, Rank, and Marriage in the British Aristocracy*, 104.
45 G. W. S., "American Girl Abroad," 82.
46 Gustavus Myers, *History of the Great American Fortunes* (New York: The Modern library, 1936), 89.
47 Castellane, *How I Discovered America*, 13.
48 Castellane, *How I Discovered America*, 15.
49 Castellane, *How I Discovered America*, 15.
50 Castellane, *How I Discovered America*, 15.
51 Castellane, *How I Discovered America*, 16.
52 Castellane, *How I Discovered America*, 37.
53 Castellane, *How I Discovered America*, 42.
54 Castellane, *How I Discovered America*, 42.
55 Castellane, *How I Discovered America*, 45.
56 Castellane, *How I Discovered America*, 48.
57 For more on their lives and marriage see: Laure Hillerin, *Pour le plaisir & pour le pire: la vie tumultueuse d'Anna Gould et Boni de Castellane* (Paris: Flammarion, 2019). See also Figure 2 Davis & Sanford, *Portrait de Boni de Castellane et Anna Gould*, Paris Musées / Musée Carnavalet – Histoire de Paris. Domaine public CC0 https://www.parismuseescollections.paris.fr/fr/palais-galliera/oeuvres/portrait-de-boni-de-castellane-et-anna-gould#infos-principales
58 Eliot, *Heiresses and Coronets*.
59 "Morton Suing Duke: Seeks to Recover Property Transferred before Daughter's Marriage," *New York* Times, March 7, 1905; *San Francisco Call*, November 22, 1905.
60 "Broadway Banter," *Town Topics*, 1919, New York Genealogical and Biographical Society Collection, New York Public Library.

61 Castellane, *How I Discovered America*, 86.
62 Coontz, *Marriage, a History*, 8.
63 Castellane, *How I Discovered America*, 45.
64 "Defends Church in Anna Gould Case," *New York Times*, December 18, 1913.
65 S. N. D. North, Director, *Special Reports : Marriage and Divorce, 1867–1906, Part One: Summary, Laws, Foreign Statistics* (Washington: U.S. Government Printing Office, 1909), 12–13.
66 Jules Claretie, *L'Américaine* (Chicago: W.B. Conkey, 1893), 3.
67 Castellane, *How I Discovered America*, 31.
68 Coontz, *Marriage, a History*, 181.
69 Jean-Paul Sardon, "L'évolution du divorce en France," *Population* 51, no. 3 (1996): 717.
70 Sardon, "L'évolution du divorce en France," 718.
71 S. N. D. North, Director, *Special Reports*, 436.
72 Joseph A. Hill, *Marriage and Divorce: 1887–1906*, ed. The United States Department of Commerce and Labor Bureau of the Census (Washington: Government Printing Office, 1908), 9.
73 "Defends Church in Anna Gould Case."
74 Paul Spicer, *The Temptress: The Scandalous Life of Alice De Janze and the Mysterious Death of Lord Erroll* (New York: St. Martin's Griffin, 2011).
75 These examples are limited to titled Franco-American marriages that took place during the twentieth century; however, countless other twentieth-century marriages between Americans and title holders from around Europe and the Middle East and can be found in various news sources.
76 F. Scott Fitzgerald, "Babylon Revisited," *Best Short Stories of … and the Yearbook of the American Short Story* (Boston: Houghton Mifflin Co., 1931) 122–42.
77 Gabriel-Louis Jaray, "La Crise Du Tourism Étranger En France," *Revue de Paris*, August 1935, 624.
78 William G Bailey, *Americans in Paris, 1900–1930: A Selected, Annotated Bibliography* (New York: Greenwood Press, 1989), 60.
79 Harvey A. Levenstein, *We'll Always Have Paris American Tourists in France Since 1930* (Chicago: University of Chicago Press, 2004), 22.
80 Ibid., 13–14.
81 *Paris Harold*, August 27, 1939.
82 Green, *The Other Americans in Paris*, 222.
83 Schutte, *Women, Rank, and Marriage in the British Aristocracy*, 7.
84 ANF, "L'Association d'Entraide de La Noblesse Française - L'association," accessed March 6, 2017, http://anf.asso.fr/fr/page/42/l-association. The story of the association's founding was also noted in an interview with its president Jacques de Crussel, the Duc d'Uzes in Hugh Schofield, "Why France's Aristocracy Hasn't Gone Away," *BBC News*, October 30, 2016.
85 F. de Saint-Simon and E. de Seréville, *Dictionnaire de La Noblesse Française: Supplément* (Paris: Éditions Contrepoint, 1977).
86 Régis Valette, *Catalogue de la noblesse française contemporaine* (Paris: R. Laffont, 1977).
87 ANF, "L'Association d'Entraide de La Noblesse Française - L'association."
88 Levenstein, *Seductive Journey*, Part 4.

Part II

"PARIS IS FREE—AND SO ARE ITS KISSES":[1] WARTIME MARRIAGES DURING THE TWENTIETH CENTURY

In the first part of this work, I examined the ways in which marriages emerged out of cross-cultural encounter within elite transnational communities during the nineteenth century and the extent to which the cultural and emotional dynamics of those communities facilitated those unions. In this second part, I examine twentieth-century Franco-American marriages that occurred when national borders were most solidified—during and between the world wars. Unlike those discussed in the first part, wartime-marriage participants were no longer members of an elite, transnational social network that effortlessly carved out an existence and moved freely beyond national boundaries but were instead local women restricted by the conflict around them and soldiers who acted as representatives of a nation-state and moved only insofar as the military regulations allowed. Yet, despite encountering one another during a period of heightened boundary-making and hyper-nationalism,[2] these men and women still managed to construct families that transcended those national limits in far greater numbers than the Franco-American marriages of the nineteenth century. In 1919, the *Literary Digest*, a weekly American magazine explained that "[s]o many of the American soldiers in France [had] married French girls that an official pamphlet [had to be] issued setting out the legal requirements governing marriage in that country."[3] Likewise, in a March 7, 1918 memo to the Adjutant General, one commanding general complained that 350 marriages to French women had taken place in his division alone in a period of only seven months.[4] At the war's end, American military newspaper *Stars and Stripes* estimated that 6,000 or more Franco-American marriages had been registered in town halls across France and speculated that many more went uncounted by authorities.[5] Just after

World War II, in a letter written to the President of France on January 8, 1947, the Ambassador to the United States Henri Bonnet estimated the number of French women who had followed their American husbands to the United States by that time was also about 6,000.[6] While official immigration numbers provide important indications, one also can assume that numerous marriages (and especially might-have-been marriages) went uncounted.[7]

In an effort to explain the occurrence of transnational marriage during wartime, many historians have linked the motives behind them to the demographic dilemma faced by local women following the military deaths of local men.[8] These demographic realities in war-torn France during each of the global conflicts were substantial and must be considered.[9] During World War I, France lost nearly 1.3 million of its men. It should be noted, however, that of this number, only 332,000 were classified as *hommes mariables* (not including those that left widows, who would have or could have remarried).[10] During World War II, military deaths were not the only factor that contributed to population disparities. As historian Mary Louis Roberts shows, by early 1944, two million French men had been sent to German labor or prison camps, and many others had gone into hiding or were engaged in the Resistance.[11] The observations of contemporary American soldiers confirm these disproportions. For example, one World-War-II soldier noted: "I was struck again, as I often was in France, by the absence of men. Only the very old were seen in any numbers."[12] This significant gender imbalance created by both World War I and World War II would not be fully reconciled in the French population until the 1970s. Nonetheless, such an explanation remains both oversimplified and limited as pointing to the lack of French men alone not only fails to consider the complex cultural and emotional dynamics involved in wartime interactions among American soldiers and French women but also leaves the intimate details of those interactions unexplained. Such rationalizations also fail to fully escape the analytical cage of the nation-state by explaining the occurrence of marriage from the perspective of only one society and largely ignoring the motivations of American soldiers for participating in transnational unions. Likewise, they fail to account for broader changes in emotional standards over time, thereby reducing the practice of marriage to socio-economic arrangement that, in this case, was only beneficial to one of the two marriage participants.

The story of the "war bride" is also one that has become firmly embedded into American immigration discourse by both contemporaries and historians, who have approached the topic from social or migration perspectives.[13] While their quantitative studies have told us much about the migration and post-marriage struggles of women in their new homes, they still leave us with an incomplete picture of transnational marriages of the past. Further, the official records of the American and European militaries, on which these studies are largely based, not only overemphasize the nation-state but also rarely detail the personal motivations or emotional expectations of marriage participants.

Therefore, while these matrimonial stories cannot be completely separated from the conflicts that facilitated them, what follows is not an account of war. It is instead an account of encounter. As in the first part, the central question rests on the cultural and emotional dimensions of Franco-American interaction; however, in the absence of elite transnational social networks like those that produced titled marriages during the previous century, this part seeks to locate new transnational spaces that were created by the war and map them accordingly. Within these new spaces, cross-cultural encounter took a very different form than it had in the nineteenth century, but it produced transnational marriages, nonetheless.

By again shifting the position of inquiry to the space between two cultures and using emotions as a category of analysis, I seek to compliment the stories told by official records and more systematically capture the ways in which marriages emerged out of cross-cultural, wartime encounter. While very few marriage participants remain to directly inform this study, their personal accounts have been captured in numerous unpublished memoirs, self-published memoirs, interviews collected by contemporary journalists who were fascinated with their marriages and migration stories and detailed in the invaluable oral histories that have preceded this work. By reading deeper into their recorded words, we are able to not only place ourselves within their cultural rituals—rituals that had been altered and reshaped by the conflict around them—but also further uncover the complex diversity of intimate emotional experiences that coincide with the practice of marriage—emotional experiences that are even more multi-faceted in this transnational context. While some of these sources are not without their own limitations—personal accounts are often filtered through years of one's recollections, memories and later experiences, and some of the later published letters or memoirs have been edited for enhanced literary prose or to reflect the natural modernization of language—I have little reason to believe that the "simplest and deepest emotions" of the texts have not been maintained as their authors and editors have claimed.[14] Further, as Paul Fussell shows, a great number of twentieth-century soldiers were not only literate but were "vigorously literary."[15] Their accounts have produced incredible volumes of literature during both conflicts. And though Fussell admits that much of this literary repertoire holds a special fictional quality, it still remains largely historical and therefore of great value to cultural and emotional perspectives. Because the wars forced to the forefront a discourse of new emotional dimensions, these numerous personal accounts from both men and women allow us to push the theory of emotions further than the previous section. Unlike their nineteenth-century counterparts, wartime participants were much more likely to discuss personal, sexual, and emotional experiences surrounding their personal relationships.

For the sake of the broader temporal comparison of Franco-American marriage patterns during the nineteenth and twentieth centuries, in the two chapters that follow I examine both World War I and World War II as one continuous period despite their different natures.[16] This analytical continuity is also justified because the cross-cultural interactions that had occurred during the first conflict effectively shaped encounter during the second. Separated only by a generation, World-War-II soldiers arrived in France with preconceived notions of French women that had been conditioned by the experiences of their fathers or grandfathers during World War I. Therefore, while I attempted to maintain chronological order, the following chapters are more thematically organized and when necessary, I make overlapping analyses and draw similar conclusions about the marriages that emerged out of both conflicts. I do, however, take great care in highlighting the differences when appropriate, and maintain their traditional titles in order to do so.

Notes

1 "Paris Is Free—and So Are Its Kisses," *Stars and Stripes*, August 28, 1944.
2 Ian Tyrrell, *Transnational Nation: United States History in Global Perspective Since 1789* (Basingstoke: Palgrave Macmillan, 2007).
3 "Cupid Has Had to Print a Set of Rules for the Doughboys in France," *Literary Digest*, July 12, 1919, 78.
4 Albert B Kellogg, *Marriage of Soldiers* (Washington, D.C.: Historical Section, Army War College, 1942), 5.
5 *Stars and Stripes*, June 6, 1919; John R. Ellinston, "Paths of a French War Bride Are Rocky: In American Men They Seldom Find Husbands Who Understand Their Racial Needs," *New York Times*, August 2, 1925, 10, which referenced records of the US Army, the YWCA, and the American Red Cross, put the number at only 5,000; however, its estimation likely reflected only the number of women who migrated to the United States with their husbands.
6 Quoted in Hilary Kaiser, *French War Brides in America: An Oral History* (Westport, CT: Praeger Publishers, 2008), xxxi.
7 It should also be noted that during World War I, what the American military considered a "marriage problem" was largely a *French* problem. However, during World War II, American soldiers married women from all over Europe and Asia. Based on a 1950 Committee on the Judiciary report entitled "Immigration and Naturalization Systems of the United States," Jenel Virden, *Good-Bye, Piccadilly: British War Brides in America* (Urbana: University of Illinois Press, 1996) estimates that a total of 115,000 war brides came to the United States during and after World War II. Of them, 70,000 were British and another 7,000 were from Australia or New Zealand.

8 Elisa Camiscioli, *Reproducing the French Race: Immigration, Intimacy, and Embodiment in the Early Twentieth Century* (Durham: Duke University Press, 2009); Bok-Lim C. Kim, "Asian Wives of U.S. Servicemen: Women in Shadows," *Amerasia Journal* 4, no. 1 (1977): 91–115; Susan R Grayzel, *Women's Identities at War: Gender, Motherhood, and Politics in Britain and France During the First World War* (Chapel Hill, NC: University of North Carolina Press, 1999); Mark Meigs, *Optimism at Armageddon: Voices of American Participants in the First World War* (Washington Square, NY: New York University Press, 1997), 134; Teresa K. Williams, "Marriage between Japanese Women and US. Servicemen since World War II," *Amerasia Journal* 17, no. 1 (1991): 135–54.
9 For more on the British case see: Virginia Nicholson, *Singled Out: How Two Million Women Survived Without Men After the First World War* (London: Viking, 2007).
10 Michel Huber, *La population de la France pendant la guerre, avec un appendice sur Les revenus avant et après la guerre* (Paris; New Haven: Les Presses universitaires de France; Yale University Press, 1931), 568. *Hommes mariables* were defined as unmarried men, ages 18–59.
11 Mary Louise Roberts, *What Soldiers Do: Sex and the American GI in World War II France* (Chicago: University of Chicago Press, 2014) 61.
12 Quoted in Roberts, *What Soldiers Do*, 61.
13 Kim, "Asian Wives of U.S. Servicemen"; Francisco Muñoz-Perez, "Mariages d'étrangers et mariages mixtes en France: Évolution depuis la Première Guerre," *Population* (French Edition) 39, no. 3 (1984): 427–62; Elfrieda Berthiaume Shukert and Barbara Smith Scibetta, *War Brides of World War II* (Novato, CA: Presidio Press, 1988); Williams, "Marriage between Japanese Women and US. Servicemen since World War II"; Susan Zeiger, *Entangling Alliances: Foreign War Brides and American Soldiers in the Twentieth Century* (New York: New York University Press, 2010).
14 Such claims have been made by the interviewees in Kaiser, *French War Brides in America*; Aramais Akob Hovsepian, *Your Son and Mine*. (New York: Duell, Sloan, and Pearce, 1950); Jacques Petit, *Au coeur de la bataille de Normandie: souvenirs d'un adolescent de Saint-Lô à Avranches : été 1944* (Louviers: Ed. Ysec, 2004) among others.
15 Paul Fussell, *The Great War and Modern Memory* (New York: Oxford University Press, 1975), 155–57.
16 While the notion of World War II as a direct extension of World War I is generally accepted among historians, Ian Kershaw, *To Hell and Back: Europe, 1914–1949* (London: Penguin Books, 2016) goes further to introduce the concept of the "Thirty Years War" of the twentieth century.

Chapter 3

LONGING FOR THE OTHER THROUGH THE WAR

In the last chapter of Part One, I proposed for consideration the extent to which cultural othering could be successfully analyzed as an emotional process. In this chapter, I apply this inquiry to the changing contexts of the twentieth century and the subsequent pattern of Franco-American marriages during the world wars. Here, I argue that despite increasingly seeing their own identities through national lenses and despite changing cultural relationships between France and the United States, notions of perceived *difference* remained the driving force of transnational coupling during the world wars.

This chapter is divided into four parts. The first part begins by contextualizing the broader temporal comparison of nineteenth-century elite marriages and twentieth-century wartime marriages by examining some of the broader global changes brought on by the world wars. These changes shifted the context in which a wartime encounter took place by producing conditions in which marriage participants not only came from the working and middle classes but self-described through more national frameworks. In this setting, notions of difference were therefore further heightened. The remainder of the chapter examines more extensively the extent to which encounter and othering could be considered an emotional process in the context of war. By examining the accounts of marriage participants as well as national news publications, I show not only how notions of difference were marked but also how these perceived differences provoked certain emotional responses. Even though mutual attraction developed among both French and American marriage participants, the processes of othering for each took very different forms and are examined separately. In the second section, I trace the othering of French women by American soldiers and argue that rather than the elite, high cultural forms of the nineteenth century, cultural fascination of the French (or what was perceived as French culture) during the World War I became laced with notions of romance, sex, and pleasure. These conceptions were subsequently transcribed onto French women and the notions of their perceived difference, thereby creating the contradictory construct of war as an opportunity for romance. The third and final section examines the ways in which fear, uncertainty, and the longing for stability under German invasion and occupation during World War II were contrasted with the overwhelming excitement and euphoria of liberation. This drastic emotional shift provided an important context in which Franco-American encounter and marriages manifested. Here, I argue that the combination of the euphoria of liberation along with what was perceived as a striking and curious difference led young French women to actively engage American soldiers in their courting customs.

Shifting Contexts of Encounter in the Early Twentieth Century

The coming of the war in the beginning of the twentieth century allowed for a geographic mobility that had previously only been afforded to the transnational leisure class during the nineteenth century, thereby, effectively ending its monopoly on both transatlantic travel and transnational marriage. In this context, wartime marriages did not emerge out of elite social networks like they had in the nineteenth century but rather were contracted throughout the social spectrum, largely among the working, rural, and middle classes. Evidence of this social shift among American soldiers can be found in the newspaper interviews of World-War-I marriage participants such as one in the *Saturday Evening Post*, in which one soldier Bernhard Ranger explained of the American husbands who remained in Paris after the war: "We come from every section of the United States, from every class and creed. Names range from Anderson to Zuckerman, from Galiaducei to Levy, from Bailey to Szlapka. Among us are Rotarians, Elks and Shriners, at least one Mormon, Mayflower descendants and sons of the steerage, A.B.'s, M.D.'s and D.S.C.'s, haves and have-nots, wets and drys—not many of the latter."[1] Even though an examination of American Navy World-War-I recruitment propaganda shows that many of members of the American Expeditionary Force (AEF) were drawn to enlist with the hope of an "opportunity to see the world,"[2] the majority of these participants differed greatly from their nineteenth-century counterparts who had been raised with private language tutors and in well-traveled families with far-reaching transnational social connections.

Shifting political and economic conditions at the turn of the twentieth century also meant a shift in broader cultural relationships between France and the United States. Therefore, for American soldiers, Europe took on a different meaning than it had in the nineteenth century when American elites went on grand tours in search of education, entertainment, and high cultural forms. Rather than the grandeur of art, architecture, and fancy dress that the elite class had coveted, American soldiers saw much of France as old and tired. Angela Petesch, a volunteer for the American Red Cross, for example, made the following observation after arriving in France with the Clubmobile Group H in August of 1944, ten weeks after D-Day: "They were way behind the times—women still washed clothes in the little streams and pound the garments with stones; the cows and pigs and chickens still live in the same building as the family. Quantities of the people still wear wooden shoes, and in general they have a very simple way of life."[3] As historian Mary Louis Roberts points out, such observations were often made in the war-torn countryside rather than of urban landscapes like Paris.[4] However, as Petesch explained, many of the same magniloquent sentiments were carried into urban spaces as well. During her time in Paris, she remarked: "There are no trains except the FE that the Army operates. Even right within the city of Paris there is no civilian postal service. Messages, if any, have to be delivered in person. And telephones in the country are non-existent."[5] In this manner, unlike their nineteenth-century counterparts, American soldiers cared little for the memory of aristocratic courts and were unimpressed with the crumbling chateaux.[6] After spending the night in one, Petesch complained: "The building itself is not so elegant as the word 'chateau' might imply. The floors and woodwork are terrible, and it is not [due to] the ravages of the war and enemy Germans."[7]

Additionally, even though working- or middle-class soldiers had not been members of an elite leisure class, those nineteenth-century cross-cultural interactions with American high society continued to resonate within the local French populations. The French therefore continued to apply national stereotypes of modernity, innovation, and especially wealth to the Americans that they encountered. Evidence of this continued ascription can be found in Eugène Brieux's 1920s play, *Les Américains chez nous*, in which notions of American energy, money, and industry are set against French tradition, memory, quality, and art.[8] Further, viewing American soldiers as wealthy like their nineteenth-century predecessors is not entirely amiss as historians Nancy Green and Mark Meigs have explained. According to them, even modest doughboys were far better off than the average French farmer.[9] In a letter to his parents during World War II, American soldier Alexander Hovsepian wrote: "Yesterday I bought our gang some cider [...] Even had a little chat with the girl (cute too). Paid 5 francs a canteen for it. A franc is 2c. When I figure I draw over 3,000 francs a month, it makes me feel like a millionaire."[10] Even American novelist Winston Churchill (not to be confused with the British statesman) called the American soldiers "millionaire privates who have aroused such burnings in the heart of the French *poilu*, with his five sous a day."[11] This monetary exaggeration of "millionaire" brings about an interesting interplay with socio-economics that should not be entirely discounted. While the majority of these men were certainly not "millionaires," they felt like it, and those they came into contact with perceived them as well- or even over-paid. Further, the American press frequently propagated this perception when attempting to explain to American audiences French women's attraction to American soldiers. One *New York Times* article speculated: "It is, of course, painful to suppose that any of the American soldier's charm depended upon the fatness of his purse, but it is also inevitable. In comparison with the 5 cents a day received by the poilu, or even the 35 cents a day of a Tommy, the American's minimum of $1 loomed pretty large. Nor did the latter make any bones about spending his wealth."[12]

This Franco-American marriage pattern was also largely characterized by growing global nationalism in the twentieth century. Even though many of the soldiers in the AEF during World War I had been first- or second-generation immigrants to the United States, in the context of the war, most increasingly saw their own identity through national lenses and, therefore, increasing self-identified as quintessentially *American*.[13] On this subject Ragner affirmed, "Quite naturally, we view the French side of problems with considerable leniency. Let no one infer, however, that our own citizenship and Americanism are thereby affected. We are incorrigibly American, to our wives among others. We are hypersensitive on that score."[14] He added, "Not a single member of the permanent AEF has forfeited his citizenship […] But though we stay on and die in France, we shall always be sojourners, guests. Our spiritual home is across the Atlantic."[15] The emotional elements of national self-description and attachment to the notion of "home" are interesting here. Similar sentiments can also be found in the Hovsepian's letters to his Russian immigrant parents during World War II. In one emotional letter to his father, he discussed the moment he sailed away to fight in France. He wrote:

> Why did we cry? I don't know about the other guys, but here I was alone, leaving my country, maybe for the last time. And then, I knew what my country meant to me. It was not a piece of geography any longer; it was very real in my heart. It was you and Mom, and our home, and our street, and the corner drug store, and the movie on Saturday night, and a ride to the beach with a girl on your arm. It was baseball, and radio, and your camera, and books, and a wonderful feeling when you wake up Sunday morning late knowing that you don't have to get up, and hear Mom cooking breakfast in the kitchen. Hell, it is everything a guy loves and lives for, and here I was, leaving it all […][16]

In his introspective description of what "his country" meant to him, each of these everyday elements and experiences become national symbols and rituals. Further, the attachment to the notion of "home" became increasingly nationalized in a way that differed greatly from those that crisscrossed the Atlantic during the previous century and was further intensified in the context of leaving for war.[17] In this way, an important tension between nineteenth-century cosmopolitanism and twentieth-century nationalism is brought forward in the broader temporal analysis of transnational-marriage patterns.[18]

Both the social shift in marriage participants to the middle, rural, and working classes and their increased tendency to self-describe through national frameworks provided the context for a heightened awareness of difference in cross-cultural wartime encounter. In this way, processes of subsequent self/other *distanciation* were even more profound than those in the nineteenth-century, elite transnational communities. Evidence of this heightened awareness and conception of difference in wartime encounters can be found in the accounts of soldiers in both wars. In a letter to his brothers, Hovsepian wrote of his arrival in France during World War II that from the moment the soldiers landed on the beaches it was obvious they were a different country and that for him, even air smelled different.[19] Likewise, when World-War-II soldier, Charles E. Frohman's company arrived, a group of them stopped to marvel at a French street sign. "It was the first distinctly French thing we had ever seen," he wrote. "It looked like something out of a fairytale book. It just didn't seem real."[20] Not only were notions of cultural difference heightened, but also that in coming to France they experienced something they might have only been imagined in "fairytale book" also demonstrates a considerable *distance* of difference.

This distance of national and cultural difference was even further reinforced during this period by the tightening of borders, anti-immigration movements, and the pseudoscientific classification of people into racialized categories, such as those found in the 1918 work of Madison Grant, *The Passing of the Great Race*. In his "hereditary history," Grant not only claimed that the people of Europe could be divided into distinctive biological categories, but also that through manipulation, and namely, conservation, superior moral, intellectual, and physical attributes of the "Nordic race" could and should be maintained—in the name of American nationalism.[21] While Grant's work remained rather marginal during World War I,[22] these notions of "innate differences" were, indeed, ascribed onto Franco-American marriage participants. In one *New York Times* article, for example, one contemporary commentator John R. Ellinston speculated that Franco-American wartime marriages would inevitably "fail" due to what he called "racial differences [that] promised incompatibility."²³ By juxtaposing what actually amounted to varied everyday cultural rituals and attitudes through the dichotomy of "Latin and Anglo-Saxon races," the author effectively insinuates that these differences were inherently embedded in the two societies. His claim calls into question the continued notion of a shared Atlantic culture that had developed in the previous centuries.²⁴

Yet, while national and cultural perceptions as well as changing global contexts at the onset of the twentieth century drastically changed the nature of cross-cultural encounter, and while Ellinston argued that participants were "too different" to expect a successful marriage with one another, American soldiers and French women still found themselves *longing for the "other"* through the wars. The following section examines this ongoing process.

War, Romance, and Sex: The Othering of French Women by American Soldiers

Conflicting Constructs of Wartime Engagement

During World War I, relationships between American soldiers and French women seem to have begun quickly after their initial encounters. Just months after the first American units began to land in France, the *Literary Digest* had already speculated that many marriages with local women would likely to occur. It declared, "Dispatches say [...] that when the war is over, France will have some sturdy Yankee citizens [...] that a good many of them will marry French wives can hardly be doubted."²⁵ As the war ended, another article in the *New York Times* went so far as to speculate that as many as 200,000 soldiers would stay in France "to marry French women" and because "they were charmed with French life."²⁶ While this number was, of course, a gross exaggeration, its supposition that many American soldiers were "charmed" by both French life and by French women suggests a broad fascination with not only the "other" but also the other's culture. Further evidence of widespread wartime relationships can be found in a 1919 edition of the American military newspaper *Stars and Stripes*, which printed an advertisement (Figure 3.1) for a translation guide that offered to help soldiers overcome language barriers during their time in France. However, rather than advertising more practical phrases such as those needed to accomplish everyday tasks, the guide, entitled "Compree? -Je t'aime" included "16 pages of snappy love stuff—in French and English" as well as various pick-up lines such as "Where are you going Bright Eyes?" and "When shall I see you again?"²⁷ While *Stars and Stripes* is often classified as a military newspaper, the extent to which it was state-sanctioned during the world wars is debated

Figure 3.1 Advertisement in *Stars and Stripes*, April 4, 1919.

among scholars familiar with the publication; therefore, one should question the extent to which its printing of an advertisement denotes promotion of its subject and should be cautious in concluding that the military attempted to perpetuate this fascination with local women. However, what is evident from the publication is that American soldiers in World War I seemed to have developed parallel and contradictory views of the war in which they were engaged—both as a destructive, devastating conflict and ironically, as an opportunity for *romantic* encounter. Viewing war as an opportunity for romance is perhaps unexpected given that war is most often associated with notions of violence, pillage, and even rape. However, that these conflicting views of engagement developed during World War I is less surprising when one considers the conditions in which transnational spaces of encounter were created. While small numbers of American soldiers, along with members of the Red Cross and Young Men's Christian Association (YMCA), began to arrive in France in the summer of 1917, the majority of the AEF did not arrive until the following year as the war was ending and remained there for an additional year until the summer of 1919.[28] Therefore, unlike during World War II, when encounter happened largely during active military engagement, during World War I, the greatest opportunity for encounter occurred outside the context of battle and in urban spaces that were well separated from the trenches. During his 1917 tour of World-War-I France, American novelist Winston Churchill for example, noted that Paris had been "saved from violation." "In spite of the soldiers thronging the sunlit streets," he explained, "Paris was seemingly the same Paris one had always known, gay—insouciance, pleasure bent. The luxury shops appeared to be thriving, the world-renowned restaurants to be doing business as usual; the expensive hotels were full."[29] The same type of spatial dichotomies cannot be found during the conflict in the 1940s, when cross-cultural encounter largely took place as military troops moved through villages and urban areas when pushing eastward through France to Germany.

Nonetheless, similar constructs of wartime participation as an opportunity for romantic encounter also continued into World War II as well, as later issues of *Stars and Stripes* demonstrate. One issue from September 9, 1944, for example, included an image (Figure 3.2) of several French women along with the caption: "Here's what we are fighting for."[30] That only women are depicted in the photo rather than children is telling—as is the fact that all of the women are smiling and reaching up at the camera rather than devastated by the effects of war. The corresponding article opens by boasting: "The French are nuts about the Yanks." It goes on to say that in winning the war, they won not only their gratitude but also their "love." By invoking images of opened-armed women and using emotion words like love, this publication suggests

Here's What We're Fighting For

THE French are nuts about the Yanks. This picture gives you the idea. Lots of GI's who never thought much about Freedom before are learning about it from the smiles and happy tears of folks who'd lost it for four black years.

 ※   ※   ※

Let's not kid ourselves. The honeymoon won't last forever. Some franc-happy go-getters will start gypping GI's and some dumb Joes are going to do things to disgrace our Army and get the French sore.

 ※   ※   ※

But most of us will stay on the ball. If we fight as hard to keep the goodwill of liberated peoples as we did to win it—there's hope for happier days.

 ※   ※   ※

War has a long list of entries on the debit side of the ledger—lives, money, misery. On the credit side there's this—the love and gratitude of one people toward another. It's the chance of a lifetime—and our kids' lifetime.

 ※   ※   ※

Let's not piddle it away.

Figure 3.2 "Here's What We're Fighting For," *Stars and Stripes*, September 9, 1944. Courtesy of Stars and Stripes, All Rights Reserved.

ways in which the notion of war as an opportunity for romance permeated both conflicts among American servicemen.

Popular World-War-I folk music, such as the song "Mademoiselle from Armentières," further demonstrates World-War-I soldiers' own perceptions of the construct of war as an opportunity for romantic encounters. Lyrics included lines like the following: "From gay Paree he heard guns roar, and all he learned was *je t'adore*"[31] and "You might forget the gas and shell but you will never forget the mademoiselle."[32] The song included over forty versus, and existed in many different versions. According to John Jacob Niles and Douglas Stuart Moore's 1929 collection of World-War-I songs, *The Songs My Mother Never Taught Me*, it had been adopted by the American troops from British soldiers who likely engaged in similar cross-cultural relationships with local women. Historian Mark Meigs argues that the song transcended both linguistic and cultural barriers because "hinky dinky," which was close to "hanky panky," was a term that most listeners understood as a description of a sexual act. Therefore, its use insinuated a proposition of sexual relations easily understood by both parties. What Meigs finds most notable about the song, however, is that similar to the dichotomy previously demonstrated by the *Stars and Stripes* images of war as both a conflict and an opportunity for romantic encounter, the song suggested that soldiers' experiences went beyond obligations of battle by placing personal and sentimental life in opposition to military duties.[33]

Sexualized and Romanticized Cultural Othering

But within this construct of war as an opportunity for romance, how were images of the othered French women and their perceived differences shaped by wartime encounter with American soldiers? Evidence of these processes is best noted in the ways in which participants described one another in varied forms of media and later personal accounts. Further, an examination of these discourses demonstrates not only how notions of difference were marked but also how these perceived differences provoked certain emotional responses. Here, as was the case in nineteenth-century elite transnational high society, these othering processes were accompanied by a preconditioned *cultural infatuation*—or affection for perceived culture itself. But during wartime, this infatuation manifested in very different forms. As the song suggests, rather than the elite high culture of art, architecture, and fancy dress of the nineteenth century, this *appreciation* for French culture during World War I became laced with notions of romance, sex, and pleasure—conceptions that were subsequently transcribed onto French women and their perceived difference. As a result, the attraction to French women was largely a romanticized and sexualized one. For example, the song lyrics of "Mademoiselle from Armentières," "If I get you chocolate, will you coucher or will you not," and "My Froggie girl was true to me. She was true to me, she was true to you, she was true to the whole damned army too, Hinky-dinky, Parlez-vous" suggest the creation of an image of the typical French woman as being both promiscuous and sometimes unfaithful.[34] However, in the process of othering French women, the distinctions between pleasure, sex, romance, longing, love, and even marriage often overlapped in contradictory ways.

In her work, *What Soldiers Do*, Mary Louise Roberts explores the sexual objectification of French women by American soldiers extensively. Roberts shows how soldiers exploited sexual fantasies based on preconceived notions of French women they already had. According to her, Americans viewed the Gallic race as "uncivilized, primitive and over-sexed" and therefore "made sex the defining element of French civilization."[35] However, the mere sexual objectification of French women by American soldiers is an incomplete explanation of marriage motivation, and it places female participants of these relationships in both passive and objectified roles. Therefore, deeper analysis into cultural and emotional constructs driving and shaping these relationships between French women and American soldiers is necessary. An examination of space is also important here. As historian of emotions Margrit Pernau shows in her work, "Space and Emotion: Building to Feel," different spaces often shape and are linked to certain emotions.[36] Therefore, it is important to examine how both spaces of war and the popular construct of places, such as Paris as a place of pleasure, effectively shaped the encounter between American soldiers and French women that led to marriage.

Origins of Sexualized Constructs

Such an inquiry first requires an examination into the roots of such constructs. Already during the nineteenth century, when Americans imagined the city of Paris as the seat of high culture, they also imagined it as a place of great temptation. One nineteenth-century guidebook, *Paris-Guide: par les principaux écrivains et artistes de la France 1867*, explained that this reputation was well-established around the world and that everyone knew of the famous Bal Mabille, an outdoor dancehall on the avenue Montaigne, which was, it explained, an "asile un peu bruyant de la jeunesse à son aurore, la curiosité des provinciaux, le rêve des couturières, la folie des étudiants, quelquefois aussi, mais en cachette, le caprice des femmes du monde" (asylum of noisy youth at dawn, the curiosity of the provincials, the dream of seamstresses, the madness of the students, sometimes also, but in secret, the impulse of the high society ladies of the world). According to the guidebook, this park, "a vu passer au clair du gaz tous les hommes les plus en renom des temps modernes; quelques-uns y ont dansé peut-être" (has seen all the most renowned men of modern times; some of them may have even danced there).[37] Likewise, *Paris at Night*, an English-language guidebook published in 1875, called Paris "the City of Pleasure" and pointed visitors to a range of brothels, dance halls, and gambling houses.[38] French historian Patrice Higonnet notes that by the 1890s, one could count roughly thirty burlesque shows in and around Paris. "Because of shows like this," he explains, "Paris became ever more closely associated with sexual transgression in the minds of Europe and of Protestant America."[39]

These constructs can be better positioned within the distanciation of the French "other" in relation to the American "self," and this nineteenth-century periodization of this process is important. Higonnet's literary examination of Paris in the American imagination traces the roots of these images even further into the past as he explains that this "sexualized American appreciation of the charms of Paris existed even before the Revolution of 1789. For John Adams, the immorality of the French aristocracy, both in Paris and in Versailles, was a matter of public knowledge,"[40] he also admits that during the eighteenth century, such images still remained peripheral and only spread more widely among the American imagination at the end of the nineteenth century. During the nineteenth century, American society underwent a series of social, religious, and moral reforms, in which puritan values became more deeply rooted. Set against these reforms, France's perceived sexual liberty became further marked in its cultural distinctions.

Hilary Kaiser likewise notes, that other ways in which the sexualized images of French women, in particular, became stereotyped in the American national imagination was through American's limited experiences with a handful of French women who, after the discovery of gold during the first half of the nineteenth century, worked as *les dames de comptoir* in the saloons and gambling houses in the American West.[41] French scholar Albert Benard de Russailh argues that through this very particular and limited kind of Franco-American encounter in the American West, "the French woman [became] [...] a new object of attention. Her way of walking, her lithe, graceful casualness and charming behavior that can only be found chez nous was an irresistible attraction. Men followed the French woman whenever she strolled down the street. For them, she was a rare curiosity, which they never tired of watching and admiring."[42] Even though most of the French women in the American West had worked as dancers or actresses, and only a few of them had been prostitutes, Annick Foucier explains: "There [was, nonetheless,] a very fine line between liberated woman, libertine, Courtesan, kept women, woman of easy virtue, and prostitute. And from one culture to the next, the distinctions get confused, depending on the woman's position in society, her possibilities for economic and emotional autonomy, the degree of social mobility in relation to marriage, and the relationship between money and sexuality."[43] When American men went to war in France, they took with them some of these preconceived and often misconstrued understandings with them, and subsequently the same forms of othering of the French woman in the American West had in many ways been transplanted across the Atlantic during the world wars.

As these sexualized images and representations of French women spread quickly throughout the AEF, they not only increased soldier curiosity of, or allure to, French women but they also shaped the cultural encounter that took place between the two groups. Just before arriving in France, Leslie Langville of the 42nd artillery division, for example, recalled: "According to the Lieutenant, we were in much danger of being raped the minute we put foot on French soil. Most of the fellows would have been willing victims of such treatment."[44] In this way, "wine, women, and song" became the unofficial anthem of the AEF stationed in France during and after World War I.[45] Further, sexualized images of Paris and French women coincided with romanticized images of the French in general. One American commentator noted in the American press: "The prime interest of the Anglo-Saxon in life is achievement, adventure, action. In French life, love is the supreme rite. All the Frenchman's education reading, observation train him to perfect himself in the art of making love."[46] This racialization of sexual mores shows how notions of difference became even further transcribed onto the "other" in cross-cultural encounter.

It should also be noted that while soldiers created and recreated cultural preconceptions (both romantic and sexualized) of French women through songs, comics, and photos in military publications such as *Stars and Stripes*, they also recreated and retold them through war stories between generations. In 1944, *Stars and Stripes* published the cartoon pictured in Figure 3.3. Here, as soldiers walk through a French town (denoted not only by the label on the top, but also by the wine on the table), their conversation is captured in the caption, "This is th' town my pappy told me about."[47]

Other examples of this generational transmission of cultural preconceptions can be found in one of Hovsepian's letters to his father. Here, he wrote of his mother's constant inquiries: "You shouldn't have told us all those stories about things you did in the first war. [Mom] still believes them."[48] The generational transfer of these sexualized preconceptions can also be found in the World-War-II accounts of Bernard Dargols. Dargols was a Parisian student who had been interning in New York when the conflict in France

Figure 3.3 "This is th' town my pappy told me about," *Stars and Stripes*, September 6, 1944. Copyright by Bill Mauldin (1944). Courtesy of Bill Mauldin Estate LLC.

began, and he decided to join the American Army. Because of his background, he was tasked with offering cultural lessons to other GIs before the D-Day landings in order to prepare them for what to expect in France. He recalled during a series of interviews that were later compiled and published by his granddaughter that during these lessons, his American comrades overwhelmed him with questions about French women and were eager to know if they were really as pretty as the men had heard.[49] Likewise, evidence of the generational transfer of these images can be noted in the discourses of the American population that remained in the United States during World War II. For example, in an interview with *Life Magazine* in 1944, an American woman named Nora Schuck expressed that she was worried about soldiers' indiscretions with local women when she said: "I didn't mind the fall of Paris so much as the capture of Armentières!" making a reference to the popular World-War-I song.[50]

Spatial and Emotional Analysis of Romanticized and Sexualized Othering

Soldiers in both wars played into these romanticized and sexualized constructs via their own performances during encounter. In a letter, World-War-I AEF member Otis Emmons Briggs explained: "The American soldier is having his hardest fight right now and thousands will not go home with their comrades. They will 'fall' wounded at the battle of Paris or Marseille or Bordeaux or any place where attractive women are. They 'fall' fighting alone, in a one-sided contest. And believe me, it is no easy fight with a real and constant temptation presenting herself in a most alluring form at almost every turn."[51] Likewise, the author of an article in the *Atlantic Constitution* declared: "I want to go on the record as saying both French and English girls went wild over our American men. Anyone who watched the developments over there will tell you the same thing. The Yank was a revelation. He was like a new toy. He was outspoken. He was full of fun. Laughing. Optimistic. He had supreme confidence in himself and sublime faith in everyone else."[52] In this way, soldiers propagated their own constructions of both women and war.

In further considering how, why and to what extent this kind of sexualized and romanticized othering took the form that it did, it is also important to consider the intersectionality of these cultural processes with gendered elements such as the hyper-masculinization of military service and with the emotional and rhetorical connections that are often made between war and sex (or between war and romance) specifically in military spaces and spaces of war. Here, as Frank Costigliola reminds us, men's quest for sexual adventure was a commonplace during wartime.[53] Likewise, military historian and World-War-II soldier Paul Fussell further examines the links between combat, emotion and sexual activity extensively in his 1975 work, *The Great War and Modern Memory*, in which he points to the writings of Marcel Proust who noticed that "war provokes an almost tropical flowering of sexual activity behind the lines which is the counterpart to the work of carnage which takes place at the front."[54] Further Wystan Hugh Auden's *The Age of Anxiety* (1947), explained: "In times of war even the crudest kind of positive affection between persons seems extraordinarily beautiful, a noble symbol of the peace and forgiveness of which the whole world stands so desperately in need"[55] Here, in the spaces of war, the lines between masculinity, sex, and emotion become difficult to distinguish.

Given this overlap, it is worth further questioning to what extent the sexualized othering of French women can be actually described as *positive othering* given that the enlaced and nuanced power dynamics make it harder to distinguish from other concepts like the "colonial gaze." This is even further complicated when we consider the most extreme extent to which the sexualization of French women was taken. For example, a 1945 article in *Life Magazine* warned: "In France, the hard feelings between the French people and the US soldiers were boiling over in riots and mutual recriminations. GIs in Le Harvre, angrily impatient to get home, rampaged through the town. The French were complaining that GIs acted more like conquerors than allies."[56] Instances of sexual violence in Europe were more extensively documented during World War II then they had been during World War I. One marriage participant, Pierrette S. recounted in a later interview that one of her classmates "was hitchhiking between Aix-en-Provence and Marseille [...] [and] was picked up by two black Americans, who raped and killed her." "It was horrible! [...] No, the Americans weren't all gentlemen!" she explained.[57] Sociologist and criminologist, J. Robert Lilly estimates that between 1942 and 1945, some 17,000 women and children in Britain, France, and Germany were victims of rape by American GIs.[58] And as Pierrette's account suggests, such instances were disproportionately attributed to racialized soldiers. In an attempt to challenge romanticized popular memory of the generous, protecting GI along with the grateful young French woman, both Judith Surkis and Mary Louise Roberts have produced extensive and riveting counter-narratives centered on wartime sexual violence.[59] Roberts argues that because soldiers often saw the Gallic race as "uncivilized" and "over-sexed," American soldiers exploited the myth of sexually available French women and committed theft, rape, and physical assault almost daily.[60] By intersecting gender and cultural analyses, both Roberts and Surkis similarly conclude that following the invasion of Normandy American men's sexual access to French women demonstrated the broader shifting power relations between the two societies—especially, insofar as soldiers understood their own role in the war's outcome. Sexual violence embedded within these kinds of gender and political power relations, therefore, resembles more closely the forms of othering studied by post-colonial and feminist scholars and provides an interesting contrast to the numerous romantic relationships that have been categorized as "handsome liberator/ grateful girl" narratives.

Nevertheless, while this extreme of sexual violence is important to consider in the examination of the sexualized forms othering of French women by American soldiers, for the purpose of this study, the analytical focus will rest on more consensual encounters and the ways in which they intersect with marriage motivation. More importantly, even though the great majority of the interactions between American soldiers and French women during both World War I and World War II could be best described as fleeting sexual encounters by their very nature, a closer analysis of soldiers' accounts demonstrates that many of them were far more embedded with emotions than one might initially expect.[61] The collected and published letters of World-War-II soldier Alexander Hovsepian, for example, provide notable insight into not only these emotions, but also their complexity within spaces of war. More importantly, his letters demonstrate that in the process of othering French women, the lines between sex, emotion, and even marriage overlapped in many contradictory ways.

Hovsepian, who joined the army after the attack on Pearl Harbor, was sent to Europe in 1944 as part of a combat intelligence unit. While the letters between him and his parents do not indicate his age, his mother described him as merely "a boy" who was both "young and underdeveloped."[62] During his time in France, he had numerous and varied sexual and emotional relationships with French women, each of which he detailed in letters to his father. These letters demonstrate many of the same themes already discussed, notably how hyper-masculinization of military service led to a quest for sexual activity—about which he wrote that "everybody [had been] talking about women all the time."[63] In another letter, he wrote that "French girls were easy to get," and in referencing one of the military's major concerns—the spread of sexually transmitted disease—he explained insouciantly: "I am not going to be so choosy from now on [...] I hear that Penicillin will cure G.C. 95% of the cases in one day."[64] However, a deeper analysis into his accounts reveals an interesting and perhaps unexpected emotional complexity to his proclivities and, undoubtedly, others like him.

The letter that describes his first sexual encounter with a French woman is the most telling. In it, he wrote:

> I had my first real experience with a woman last night [...] We went to a village, four of us, and were hell-bent on having a good time. The idea of having a good time here is pretty simple—you get drunk. You drink whether you like drinking or not, just for the hell of it [...] At first you feel like a great guy [...] but after a while you get awfully sad and mushy [...] So we went to a couple places and got pretty drunk, and

that left us awfully dissatisfied, and then a corporal we met at one place told us he knew where we could get a couple good girls, and not too expensive, so we thought it was a great idea.[65]

Here, the contradictory tension of "having a good time" and ultimate dissatisfaction demonstrates the ways in which soldiers used both drinking and women to create spatial dichotomies of their wartime experience. The "good time" of drinking and physical engagement with women provided a way to escape the spaces of active conflict. What is most notable in this passage, however, is that he thinks that he is going to engage in prostitution—an arrangement best characterized as a transaction or exchange in which emotions and sexual activity are typically viewed as mutually exclusive. During both World War I and World War II, American soldiers engaged so frequently in prostitution with French women that in each, French and American officials debated whether or not the American military should allow and oversee licensed brothels in locations near their camps as a way to combat venereal disease.[66] In this case, however, much to Hovsepian's surprise, he did not find himself in a brothel, but rather at farm house in the company of a family, their daughters, and a couple of their daughters' friends. He admits given his expectations, this made him feel both uneasy and ashamed; however, he was reluctant to leave because, according to him, he was the only one that could speak French, and the French family did not speak English. After a while however, his uneasy feelings wore out and he "fell in the groove", he explained. Then he continued:

> Before I knew it, one of the girls got on my lap and was kissing me and whispering all sorts of things to me, and I all of a sudden started to cry, tears rolling down my cheeks and she was trying to wipe them off, and it was so damned silly but I couldn't stop. I felt so sad and lonely. Then there was another girl trying to stop me from crying, and she was so sympathetic that she cried herself, and that made me feel even sadder. She gave me a glass of wine, and that was my end, because all of a sudden there was a blackout, and when I opened my eyes, everything was dark [...] then I felt somebody's arm on me, and I groped in the dark and I felt a girl lying next to me under the blanket. Well that was a new experience to me and I got terribly excited. She must have waken up because she pressed her body to mine, and it was so warm, and she kissed me, and before I knew it, it was all over.[67]

Unfortunately, the woman he was with remains as anonymous for the reader as she did for him, and her own expectations and experience likewise remain unknown. While the desperate conditions of war and lack of food in World-War-II France led many to participate in prostitution, it is impossible to know if this encounter was truly meant to be an economic exchange or if he wrongly assumed this. He later mentions that upon waking, he realized that she had not taken any of his money. Therefore, given the communication barrier, that he went there with incorrect assumptions is possible. Still, as the letter continued so too did his internal emotional struggle to come to terms with what just happened:

> [W]hen it was all over, I felt terribly ashamed and disgusted [...] it was so ugly and so different from how I imagined it would happen—that I was getting more and more disgusted and mad. I felt like somebody had robbed me. I was mad at the girl, and mad at myself for doing what I did—I knew that I would never be the same again. I was still pretty drunk and some of the silliest thoughts were going through my mind, like that I should go back and marry the girl and then I remembered that I didn't even know which of the four girls she was and even what her name was [...] and I was ashamed to ask the boys [...] I felt that they, too, were pretty depressed, even though we all talked big as if it was nothing, but a usual thing for us [...] I don't know if I would ever want to know another woman again, not the way I feel now.[68]

His invocation of marriage here is notable, and something that he does several times in his letters regarding various other relationships. It demonstrates the cultural constructs in which sex was linked to marital unions as well as the contrasting feelings of guilt and shame that were attributed to sexual engagements outside of those constructs. His internal emotional struggle is also perhaps indicative of the breakdown of traditional marriage and moral standards during wartime—standards that would only return in the 1950s as part of the "return to normalcy" social campaign.

Finally, in the closing of his letter, he not only linked sex with both notions of romance and as a rite of passage to masculinity, but he also showed how his emotional struggle was linked directly to the space of war:

> Well, anyway I am a man now, and damn it, I don't know whether to be proud or not. It wasn't very romantic—if anything it was silly. I am not ashamed—I had to go through it sooner or later, but why the hell couldn't it be nicer? But then, c'est la guerre, as we say here, and it seems that everything that is supposed to be fine and noble turns into dirt when it gets mixed with blood.[69]

That the lines between sex, emotion, and even marriage overlapped in opposing and contradictory ways is even more evident in the response letter from his father. It not only acknowledged the romantic expectations that his son had linked to sexual encounter, but it also indicates the shift in emotional standards surrounding the role of sex in courtship and love-based marriage as a proliferating practice:

> Love is the greatest creative force in the world—and love of a woman is the strongest and holiest of all forms of love—because woman is the holiest and most sacred of all God's creations [...]The poor girl who slept with you in a French barn wanted to make you happy, to make you forget the horrible things you have been through. She was more than a lover to you, she was sister and mother and wife, all rolled into one [...] It was a crude way of expressing her compassion to all you boys torn away from your homes and your loved ones [...] Years will pass. You will fall in love and marry—and then you will know the overwhelming power of pure love, the greatest of all human emotions [...] But never forget that poor French girl, think of her with respect and reverence—because she was a woman in the purest and most sacred sense of the word, giving away all she had in an awkward and crude attempt to alleviate the pain of loneliness when you needed this most. After every war they build monuments to unknown soldiers. Let there be a monument in your heart to an unknown woman—and keep this monument beautiful and clean at all times.[70]

Here, the emotional nuance expressed by the American servicemen like Hovseptian who documented their experiences complicates our understanding of the nature of wartime sexual and romantic relationships and establishes something of a middle ground between the valorization of the American soldier in Europe on the one hand and the critique of the sexual rapacity associated with war established by Roberts on the other.

Shortly after this first encounter, Hovsepian's other letters to his father regarding relationships with other women demonstrate more closely sentiments of longing based on positive othering processes, and it seems that he quickly heeded his father's advice. He also warns his father, not to "worry about [his] love affairs." He wrote: "I *am* careful. I am not an innocent boy anymore, it's true, but I'm not a promiscuous bastard either."

In the same letter, he describes his last relationship with another French woman named Julianne. Here, he wrote:

> Each time she passed me, I slowly turned my head and watched her figure glide through the room [...] She had a gorgeous figure. The kind you see in Greek statues. She had the face of a Greek goddess. But her eyes were like smoldering embers. She had the eye of a tiger. They made me shudder to look at them. They didn't belong on that face [...] She was the type of woman that personifies the word "woman" [...] I was fascinated. If I had to marry her to get her, I would have done it at the drop of a hat [...] Well, Pop, you can guess the rest. But what you'd never guess was that I really fell in love with her—like you read in the books and in the movies.[71]

In characterizing Julianne as "a Greek goddess" he noted what he perceives as foreign and almost exotic qualities that make her attractive to him. Here, his notions of romantic love in this context were very idealized and storybook-like, and again, he invoked marriage, though he would not marry her or any French woman. While Hovsepian writes of several relationships which other French women, it should be noted that he rarely described them as French, simply as women—some of them by name, others not. What is even more interesting, however, is once he arrived in Luxembourg and Germany, he never mentioned further relationships with women in those places. By contrast, he actually continued to discuss the French women he left behind.

It should be further reiterated here that soldiers' performance (and subsequent propagations) of the sexualized and romanticized constructs of not only women but their own roles in encounter were linked directly to spatial dichotomies of war. Here, Paul Fussell explains: "The reason why theater and modern war seem so compatible is that modern wars are fought by conscripted armies, whose members know they are only temporarily playing their ill-learned parts [...] in an attempt to distance themselves from the annihilations occurring around them." According to Fussell war was much like theater in that the life of the soldier was not real life; "You were never you. The 'I' part of you was somewhere else," he explains. Moreover, this sense of theater also offered a means of interpretation and familiarity in a search for meaning and structure.[72] Therefore, if we further examine the emotional dimensions we can observe the ways in which soldiers attempted to reconcile these kinds of very contrasted emotions on this "theatrical stage"—on one hand, the excitement of liberation and grateful women waiting for them contrasted with fear as the war was not entirely over, on the other. For example, Hovsepian attempted to explain this emotional reconciliation in one of his many letters to his father. He wrote:

> The strain of war sure does something to you. They say you get used to it, but I guess it's all a lot of baloney because you can't get used to a thing which isn't normal [...] When you start each day without knowing whether you go to bed the same night, or whether other boys in your section will be alive or dead [...] believe me, you're better off without thinking too much about it [...] It's only when you're pulled back from the front and out of danger that all those thoughts and feelings which were kept back hit you like a ton of bricks. You feel like laughing, shouting, rolling on the ground, kissing every girl you meet, getting drunk and telling everyone that you're alive and to hell with everything else.[73]

By juxtaposing these two spaces—one of war and one of women—soldiers were able to use the latter as a way to escape the realities and emotions of the former. In another letter, Hovsepian similarly recounted:

> Pat and I had a pass to a swell big city [...] We had a huge dinner, drank champagne, flirted with some beautiful French girls. They came over to our able. Pat and I can speak French very well now. Never have any trouble anywhere. The girls offered to show us the famous spots in the city [...] We gave them each a big chocolate bar [...] They saw us to the trucks when it was time to go. Just as we were going they threw their arms around us and kissed us right in front of about four truck loads of soldiers. Did they whistle and did we blush! But it was fun to feel a girl's arm around your neck.[74]

Of one girl in particular he revealed that only after two days with her, she made him forget the war entirely.[75] Likewise, after being wounded in the east of France, World-War-II soldier Joe Sacco explained of a visit from a girl that he had met in a nearby village:

> The flowers were nice but it was seeing Monique that cheered me up. We'd known each other only a few weeks, but I'd changed a great deal in that time. The days had gone by quickly, yet the transformation within had been profound. Since landing at Normandy, I'd seen horrors on a magnitude I could have never imagined and had been changed by the sadness, the anger, and the fear that surrounds me. Doubt and uncertainty had become my constant companions. Sorrow and death had haunted me without reprieve. But now I felt different

in a way I didn't know it was possible to ever feel. With a word, with a gesture, with a smile and a kiss, Monique had touched my heart and reconstructed my soul.[76]

Emotions of War and the Othering of American Soldiers

War as opportunity for both romantic encounter and marriage between American soldiers and French women was a bilateral construct; however, the process through which French women othered American soldiers differed significantly from the ways they had been othered by their partners. For example, during World War I, Denyse Dorville of Paris, who would meet and marry AEF service member Henry Marston of Overbrook in April 1918, explained to a reporter for *Literary Digest*: "I met my husband quite by chance; it was a real romance! [...] He was using his leave to study singing [...] in Paris [...] we met through the window, just like that! We used to hear him practice and one day my brother [...] called to him across the window [...] and spoke to him. We knew he was American. It was the fashion to be hospitable to American officers and men. In fact, we adored them!"[77] Likewise, World-War-II bride Denise J. Rossow explained in an article that she wrote for the *Chicago Tribune*: "In September 1944 Ray asked if I would marry him. I replied, 'Why not?' Since 1942 I admit I was really taken by the Americans. They seemed so different. For the most part they were young, full of life."[78] In both accounts, notions of difference remain central to both cross-cultural attraction and marriage motivations. But how were the differences of American soldiers marked by French women, and in what ways did these differences provoke emotional responses that would lead to marriage?

In the case of French women, this emotional process of othering was deeply embedded within the spaces of war and the emotions that the war had prompted. Among the local French population, emotions like fear, uncertainty, and the longing for stability under German invasion and occupation during World War II were soon contrasted against the overwhelming excitement and exhilaration of liberation. This emotional shift provided an important context in which Franco-American encounter and marriages would manifest. In her self-published memoir, transnational-marriage participant Liz Lawson provides a glimpse into the emotional turbulence of this shift. When the German army invaded Paris, her family like many others fled to the countryside. When they were finally able to return to their home in the occupied territory, she explained that "there was a certain sadness and melancholia hanging in the air" and every day sounds were muffled "as if people wanted to hide their feelings from the occupier."[79] For another marriage participant Jeannine Ricou-Allunis, occupation, defeat and restrictions on foodstuffs somehow had taken away France's *Frenchness*. She explained in her memoir: "The worst was that they deprived us of food. You don't do that to French people."[80] On the same subject Lawson wrote: "Can one imagine France without its wonderfully light, crisp baguettes of bread early in the morning when the aroma of their baking would lilt the spirit of the most morose minds? During the war years French bread was transformed into a dark heavy mass of dough and when cut, the loaf would expose very unorthodox contents, small strings, particles of stone, a dead fly, a piece of rubber band!"[81] Further, as many of her neighbors joined the civilian occupation force (or the collaboration), most people were overcome by feelings of distrust and suspicion. According to Lawson, those whose favorite pastime had been to debate politics were soon "shuttered" as such exchanges became dangerous. To this she said: "Silence was advisable and it proved a great hardship for the French people who always enjoyed a debate on political issues."[82]

These negative emotions of occupation further intensified the subsequent euphoria and excitement that was then created by the arrival of the American soldiers. This emotional contrast is described in Lawson's memoir. She wrote:

> The days that followed the D-Day landings were shrouded in our memories with the emotions that one feels when hope is so near yet so uncertain and when the courage of many men sets the path to final victory [...] We wanted to believe that the Allies were fighting for democracy and freedom and we were filled with gratitude. From D Day on, the American soldier and everyone who was involved in the final battles became our hero, and we were ready to give him everything we had and celebrate his arrival with the joy and enthusiasm we felt they deserved.[83]

However, the emotional processes driving the othering of and fascination with American soldiers went far beyond mere gratitude for their role in the liberation of French cities from German occupation. As Charles Lemeland of Glatigny, who was twelve years old at the time of the D-Day landings, recounted in a later interview, anticipation of the Americans arrival quickly evolved into fascination and enchantment, even for him as a young boy. He recounted:

> On April 29th a gray, cool and tense Tuesday, we heard about the Allied landings. It was not a surprise. The Americans had landed, we were told, but that raised a number of questions. When would they arrive in Glatigny, where we were staying? How did American soldiers really look? What kind of uniform did they wear? What guns and equipment would they have? What would their faces be like? What was their style as soldiers? We had to wait exactly one month for the answers.

When he did finally observe some of the soldiers in the town of Barneville, Lemeland described them as "friendly, good-humored, and good-looking." He continued:

> [T]hey were quite popular, especially with women. Best of all, they did not look or act like fanatical, professional soldiers. As if they did not take the war quite seriously or, at least, not all the time. They had a great talent for enjoying themselves whenever they could. We were fascinated by their demeanor, their gestures. In a word, they were "cool." The way they got into their cars and drove was classy, with a touch of wildness [...] They were definitely a different breed of cats. With the American soldiers it was the wonderful world of laughter, play, and permissiveness: candy galore, the thrill of getting inside tanks and other fascinating machinery and touching all those levers and pedals, posing for pictures, looking at pictures of relatives, of girlfriends usually in bathing suits and appearing to us like movie stars! [...] The Eldorado had come to us. The Americans were nothing but demi-gods haloed with a kind of supernatural prestige.[84]

For Lemeland, the American soldiers exhibited an awe-invoking quality. Here, their perceived difference was marked by their lighthearted demeanor, as well as what he interpreted as elegance and class. That he described them as similar to "movie stars" and "demi-gods" depicts the ways in which othering of American soldiers took the form of not only fascination and enchantment but also idolization in many respects. Such conceptions were also likely shaped by the cultural representations of actual movie stars. As Darglos noted, before going to New York for his prewar internship, the only prior interaction that most French people had had with Americans had been through the prism of American popular cultural forms such as literature, music, and film. According to him, before World War II, his entire American "universe" had been comprised of Benny Goodman, Frank Sinatra, Ella Fitzgerald, Fred Astaire, Duke Ellington, Glenn Miller, and Louis Armstrong.[85]

Further, the striking and curious difference of the American soldier was distinctly marked by his military uniform, which provided a clear materialization of distinction. In a later interview, one World-War-II-marriage participant, Marcelle S., who was born in Oran, Algeria, explained of her American husband in his uniform, "Moray was the most gorgeous officer! I took one look at him and said, 'I don't believe this!' It was one of those things. I fell head over heels."[86] Likewise, Jeannine Ricou-Allunis recounted the first time she saw her husband remarking specifically that "he was good looking, and he wore a beautiful uniform." She continued in her memoir to explain:

"Our eyes were like that - we never saw such good-looking men in our life."[87] For some women, especially those who had engaged in relatively short courting periods, the military uniform became a perpetual display of their American partners' physical appearance and identity. Jennette Davis of Granville, for example, was only fifteen years old when she met her husband. After a short courtship, they continued their relationship through written correspondence until they met again in Paris five years later. When she saw him, she recounted that she did not recognize him at first because he was not wearing his uniform.[88] Though the military uniform provided a clear materialization of difference and distinction, it also simultaneously served as a clear sign of the nation-state, and attraction to it meant that in a rather paradoxical way, nationalism led to transnationalism through these wartime coupling processes.

As Lemeland remarked, young French women were especially taken by the awe-invoking enchantment of the American soldiers. For them, the excitement of liberation paired with an apparent celebrity-like magnetism—marked by the uniform—created an environment that both fostered and facilitated transnational relationships. As Lawson continued in her memoir, she provided a further glimpse into the depth of the emotional experiences young women like her felt when they first encountered American soldiers. One day, she had been riding her bike to the next village to get some bread for dinner, and she ran into an American convoy for the first time. She wrote:

> I felt faint with excitement. I could have jumped and embraced them hugging their oil-smeared faces and telling them how happy and free I now felt. I wanted to cry, shedding tears I had kept under control for too long. I wanted to scream at the top of my lungs *Vive les Américains!* But I did nothing but stare speechless and dumbfounded. I was totally overcome by my emotions.[89]

While Lawson was left quietly confounded in her first encounter, other young women actively sought out American soldiers for the purpose of engaging them in their courting customs. For example, during his later interview, Lemeland recounted some of his observations regarding the enthusiasm of the young women that he knew. He said: "The Americans were unbelievably successful among French girls. There's no other way to say this. My sister, who was only fifteen, didn't stop talking about them with her friends from school. My brother and I would see them endlessly plotting how to get close to the young liberators."[90]

A brief comparison of the liberation celebrations during both World War I and World War II demonstrates generational shifts in cultural attitudes regarding the ways in which men and women interacted publicly during such post-conflict merriments. Even though one World-War-I soldier's journal entry from November 14,1918 explained that "there was a big celebration with lots of pretty women everywhere," a later interview with that soldier's Franco-American daughter, Liliane, suggests that it was not the same kind of "kissing celebration" that would take place in World War II. She claimed: "At that time, an 18-year old girl didn't jump into the arms of people, didn't fling their arms round people's necks; she didn't have boyfriends left and right."[91] According to historian, Mary Louise Roberts, it was not until the mid-twentieth century, that "the Victorian restrictions of sexual continence and self-control had largely disappeared from white middle class American society, particularly among the younger generation." By that time, "heterosexual pleasure and sexual satisfaction were defined as important for personal happiness as well as a successful marriage."[92] Likewise, in their work *Intimate Matters: A History of Sexuality in America*, John D'Emilio and Estelle Freedman characterize the period beginning in 1920s to mid-century as one of sexual liberalism in the public sphere.[93] Therefore, the ways in which courtship behaviors and sexuality were publicly displayed by transnational couples likely differed greatly between the two conflicts.

The broader cultural fascination that fostered processes of positive othering and longing for the other in cross-cultural encounter was further complicated by the rise of anti-Americanism in France during both the interwar years and the allied bombing campaigns of World War II, which targeted and subsequently destroyed local infrastructure such as bridges, roads, and railways.[94] This led to contradictory emotions of resentment, fear, anger, loss, distrust, and suspicion of the American soldiers. Jacques Petit, who was an adolescent at the time of the American invasion, explained in his journal how the "romantic enthusiasm" of the Americans arrival quickly evolved into an uncontrollable fear as his town was destroyed by the bombardment.[95] According to Roberts, in 1944, 35,317 civilians were killed by the allied campaign and thousands of homes and farms were destroyed.[96] As Hovsepian made his way through the Norman peninsula he noted this destruction in a letter to his parents that even though he applicated the beauty of the countryside, he noted that in some places everything had been destroyed. Of allied culpability, he states: "Boy, I didn't think we could do so much damage."[97]

In a full examination of the process of positive othering, one should consider to what extent these sentiments of fear, anger, and distrust were indicative of the emotions felt by the French women who went on to marry American soldiers. Marriage participant Jeannine Ricou-Allunis discussed extensively the bombardment in her memoir; however, she never mentions feelings of resentment for the American soldiers responsible. She wrote:

> Orleans was bad, very bad. On some streets there was nothing left, such as the Les Aubrais, near the station. The bombings killed many people. Some of my friends were killed. Sometimes when the bombs were not exploded, they just laid there on the street. But you know, we just walked over them. We were not worried about it. I cannot explain the feeling; I think we were not feeling anymore when there was so much going on. You lose the fear. It becomes everyday life.[98]

Likewise, Liz Lawson explained in her memoir that even though fear had overtaken their lives as bombing and air raids frequently sent them to the metro tunnels for shelter in the night, they still rooted for the Allied forces and believed the sacrifice of so many sleepless nights would be worth the freedom that would follow their victory.[99] Even Andrée McLatcher of Caen, another transnational-marriage participant whose childhood home had been demolished in the allied bombing explained in a later interview:

> We loved our house, but it was completely destroyed when the Allies bombed Le Havre in September 1944 [...] I know they wanted to get rid of the Germans, but most of them had already left. Thousands of civilians were killed, and all sorts of buildings, including schools, hospitals and churches were destroyed. There were fires and rubble everywhere. It was awful. Luckily none of my family members were killed. A lot of people from Normandy are still angry about the bombing of Le Havre. [But] my family accepted what happened because my father told us it wasn't the Allies' fault.[100]

While contrasting feelings of fear and resentment among the French population during the bombing campaign are visible, as these passages suggest, for those women that entered into marriages with American soldiers, such resentment remained peripheral within a broader spectrum of emotions invoked by war and liberation.

As they made their way from places such as Normandy or Marseille to the interior, American soldiers in World-War-II France also got caught up in this excitement that followed their arrival and played well into the role that had been imagined for them (and by them). For example,

George Hook of Middleton, Ohio, who later married a French woman, explained in an interview:

> I must say it was an emotional thrill to liberate a French town. After the fighting was over and all the Germans had been killed or captured, or had fled, the streets were suddenly filled with joyous crowds of people who appeared from nowhere [...] In one town a pretty young girl climbed up on my tank and presented me with a small French flag she had made and kept for the day of liberation. It is still one of my most treasured possessions.[101]

Likewise, World-War-II soldier and member of the 92nd Battalion, Joe Sacco explained:

> Of special importance in the war being waged [...] was getting to the next town before the infantry so that we could be the first to find and grateful-to-be-liberated girls. Sometimes we would let the infantrymen fight up to the edge of a town, and then we'd go in ahead to start setting phone lines. It wasn't the safest way to operate, but the prospect of discovering pretty girls made us more willing to take the risks [...] Each town was fanaticized to be a dream town [...] the town in which lived nothing but beautiful French women, all anxiously waiting for the day they would meet a handsome young American soldier and be swept off of their feet.[102]

Of course, the city that held the most promise for them was Paris. As one American private explained, it was the liberation of the city of Paris that saw "the greatest night the world has ever known." Invoking the World-War-I idiom, he called it "a glorious night of wine, women, and song."[103] Even though the French Forces of the Interior marched down the Champs d'Elysees first, it was still the American soldiers that found themselves at the center of so much attention. One Parisian woman Raymonde Liska, who also went on to marry an American soldier, recounted further details as she remembered them in a later interview:

> On our way home, when we reached the Caulaincourt Bridge near the Montmartre Cemetery, we saw two American soldiers in a sidecar. They were lost and had stopped on the bridge to ask some passers-by how to get to the Place de la Concorde. First one woman stepped up to talk to them, then three, then six, then 15, 20 - you can imagine the scene. All the women wanted to kiss the soldiers, who were soon covered

in lipstick! [...] Those women were so happy to see the Americans, so very happy [...] And a lot of the women were very pretty [...] they were also still very coquette; they tried to dress nicely and they wore make-up. Those American boys didn't know what hit them. They had lipstick on their foreheads, on their cheeks. Everybody wanted to touch and kiss them because they came from another world.[104]

The last line of this passage again suggests the importance of perceived difference in mutual attraction on both sides. However, the role of kissing here was one of cultural negotiation and, as Roberts notes, sometimes misunderstanding. Here, she argues that as the French frequently used the *bisou* as simple greeting, many of the soldiers may have misinterpreted this gesture in their own othering process of French women. However, Liska's remark that these particular women were *"coquette"* and dressed nicely and wearing make-up seems also indicative that they were engaging in coupling practices. Therefore, perhaps a better interpretation can be found in the statement of another young French women who explained, "We were all young, in love, and full of hope."[105]

Franco-American encounter and processes of transnational coupling remained a profoundly emotional experience, much as it had in those of the nineteenth century. While Westerners in the nineteenth century had already come to view emotional- or love-based courtship and marriage as ideal, by the mid-twentieth century, such notions became customary across social spectrums. However, even though economic arrangements may not have been the primary motivating factor for marriage participation, many female participants nonetheless remained aware of their social and economic situations as a result of the wars. Yet, this economic interpretation, while valid, still fails to explain the emotional or cultural motivations of both parties engaged in cross-cultural courtship during wartime. As I have shown in this chapter, the cultural and emotion-latent constructs that largely drove Franco-American infatuated encounter to marriage during the world wars included processes of positive othering by both sides. Despite increasingly seeing their own identities through national lenses, notions of perceived difference remained the driving forces of transnational coupling during the world wars, much like they had in the nineteenth century. But here, the romanticized sexualization of French women, along with the idolization of American soldiers created for both sides a conception of the conflicts that surrounded them as both destructive and, at the same time, momentary blissful. The ways in which the subsequent courtships proceeded and transcended national boundaries after these initial infatuated encounters is the focus of the next chapter.

Notes

1. Bernhard Ragner, "The Permanent AEF," *Saturday Evening Post*, November 11, 1939.
2. Joplin-Pugh Advertising Agency, *Here Is Opportunity See the World, Serve Your Country, Save Your Money: United States Navy World War One Propaganda*, 1918 1914, Prints and Photographs Division, Library of Congress Washington, D.C. 20540 USA; Charles E. Ruttan, *A Wonderful Opportunity for You: United States Navy World War One Propaganda*, 1917, George F. Tyler Poster Collection, Temple University Libraries, Special Collections Research Center.
3. Angela Petesch, *War through the Hole of a Donut* (Madison, WI: Hunter Halverson Press, 2006), 145.
4. Roberts, *What Soldiers Do*, 50.
5. Petesch, *War through the Hole of a Donut*, 149–50.
6. Ernie Pyle, "Brave Men," *Stars and Stripes*, September 2, 1944.
7. Petesch, *War through the Hole of a Donut*, 151.
8. Eugène Brieux, *Les Américains chez nous: comédie en trois actes* (La Petite Illustration Théatrale, 1920).
9. Green, *The Other Americans in Paris*, 230; Meigs, *Optimism at Armageddon*, 114–15.
10. Aramais Akob Hovsepian, *Your Son and Mine*. (New York: Duell, Sloan, and Pearce, 1950), 79 Excerpt(s) from YOUR SON AND MINE by Aramais Hovesepian, copyright © 1950, copyright © renewed 1977 by Aramais Akob Hovsepian. Used by permission of Dutton, an imprint of Penguin Publishing Group, a division of Penguin Random House LLC. All rights reserved.
11. Winston Churchill, *A Traveller in War-Time: With an Essay on the American Contribution and the Democratic Idea* (New York: The Macmillan Company, 1918), 13.
12. Ellinston, "Paths of a French War Bride Are Rocky."
13. Harriet H. Macdonald, "At the War Brides' Home," *Independent 99*, September 6, 1919, 329.
14. Ragner, "The Permanent AEF," 38.
15. Ragner, "The Permanent AEF," 40.
16. Hovsepian, *Your Son and Mine*, 71.
17. More on nationalism as a collective emotion can be found in Barbara H. Rosenwein's work on "emotional communities." Barbara H. Rosenwein, Maureen C Miller, and Edward Wheatley, *Emotions, Communities, and Difference in Medieval Europe: Essays in Honor of Barbara H. Rosenwein* (London: Routledge, 2017).
18. This tension is also at the heart of Rodgers, *Atlantic Crossings*, which shows that American cosmopolitanism came to a close following WWII.
19. Hovsepian, *Your Son and Mine*, 79.
20. Howard H. Peckham and Shirley A. Snyder, *Letters from Fighting Hoosiers*, (Bloomington: Indiana War History Commission, 1948), 119.
21. Madison Grant and Henry Fairfield Osborn, *The Passing of the Great Race: Or, the Basis of European History* (New York: Charles Scribner's Sons, 1916), viii–ix.
22. Jonathan Peter Spiro, *Defending the Master Race: Conservation, Eugenics, and the Legacy of Madison Grant* (Burlington, VT; Hanover, NH: University of Vermont Press ; Published by University Press of New England, 2009), 167.
23. Ellinston, "Paths of a French War Bride Are Rocky."
24. R. R. Palmer and American Council of Learned Societies, *The Age of the Democratic Revolution a Political History of Europe and America, 1760–1800* (Princeton, NJ: Princeton University Press, 1959).

25 "Franco-Yanko Romance," *Literary Digest*, November 10, 1917.
26 "Cupid's Success in AEF: Expected 200,000 Soldiers Will Stay in France, Most Marrying French Girls," *New York Times*, January 30, 1919.
27 *Stars and Stripes*, April 4, 1919, 6; cited in Zeiger, *Entangling Alliances*, 19.
28 Churchill, *A Traveller in War-Time*, 3.
29 Churchill, *A Traveller in War-Time*, 14.
30 *Stars and Stripes*, September 9, 1944. Cited in Roberts, *What Soldiers Do*, 64.
31 John Jacob Niles and Douglas Stuart Moore, *The Songs My Mother Never Taught Me* (New York: Macaulay, 1929), 18.
32 Billy Murray and Ed Smalle, *What Has Become of Hinky Dinky Parlay Voo* (audio recording), 1924.
33 Meigs, *Optimism at Armageddon*, 106.
34 Niles and Moore, *The Songs My Mother Never Taught Me*, 21.
35 Roberts, *What Soldiers Do*, 20.
36 Pernau, "Space and Emotion: Building to Feel."
37 *Paris-Guide. 2 / par les principaux écrivains et artistes de la France*, vol. 2 (Paris: Librairie Internationale, 1867), 1249, http://gallica.bnf.fr/ark:/12148/bpt6k200160r. For image see: Provost. Lithographe, "Le Bal Mabille [Estampe]," (Paris, Ledot Jeune), département Estampes et photographie, Bibliothèque François Mitterrand. http://gallica.bnf.fr/ark:/12148/btv1b53026346c/f1.item.
38 *Paris at Night: Sketches and Mysteries of Paris High Life and Demi-Monde. Nocturnal Amusements: How to Know Them! How to Enjoy Them!! How to Appreciate Them!!!.* (Boston: Boston and Paris Publ. Co., 1875), http://hdl.handle.net/2027/ucw.ark:/13960/t2j687m1v.
39 Patrice L. R. Higonnet, *Paris: Capital of the World* (Cambridge MA: Harvard University Press, 2002), 301–2.
40 Patrice L. R. Higonnet, *Paris: Capital of the World*, 321.
41 Kaiser, *French War Brides in America*, 155.
42 Albert Benard de Russailh and Sylvie Bostsarron Chevalley, *Journal de voyage en Californie à l'époque de la ruée vers l'or: 1850–1852* (Paris: A. Montaigne, 1980), 205.
43 Annick Foucrier, *Le rêve californien: migrants français sur la côte Pacifique, XVIIIe-XXe siècles* (Paris: Belin, 1999), 164.
44 Leslie Langille, *Men of the Rainbow*, (Chicago, IL: The O'Sullivan Publishing House, 1933); cited in George Browne, *An American Soldier in World War I*, ed. David L. Snead (Lincoln, NE: University of Nebraska Press, 2006), 43; James H Hallas, *Doughboy War: The American Expeditionary Force in World War I* (Boulder, CO: Lynne Rienner Publishers, 2000).
45 Martin Marix Evans, *American Voices of World War I: Primary Source Documents, 1917–1920* (London: Fitzroy Dearborn Publishers, 2001); Don V. Paradis, *The World War I Memoirs of Don V. Paradis, Gunnery Sergeant, USMC*, edited by Peter F. Owen (self-published: Lt Col Peter F. Owen, 2010), 29.
46 Ellinston, "Paths of a French War Bride Are Rocky."
47 "This is th' town my pappy told me about," *Stars and Stripes*, Stars and Stripes, September 6, 1944. Cited in Roberts, *What Soldiers Do*, 3.
48 Hovsepian, *Your Son and Mine*, 86.
49 Bernard Darglos, *Bernard Dargols, un GI français à Omaha Beach*, ed. Caroline Jolivet (Rennes: OUEST FRANCE, 2012), 68–70.
50 "Some Iowa Girls Didn't Like That Kissing in Paris," *Life*, September 25, 1944. Cited in Roberts, *What Soldiers Do*, 70–71.

51 Quoted in Meigs, *Optimism at Armageddon*, 112.
52 Jane Dixon, "It's Love's Blue Monday for the Doughboy Now Who Took Himself a War Bride," *The Atlanta Constitution*, September 14, 1919.
53 Frank Costigliola, "'Mixed Up' and 'Contact': Culture and Emotion among the Allies in the Second World War," *The International History Review* 20, no. 4 (December 1998): 799.
54 Fussell, *The Great War and Modern Memory*, 271.
55 W. H. Auden, *The Age of Anxiety: A Baroque Eclogue* (Princeton University Press, 2011), 88.
56 "GIs In Paris Flock to Pig Alley," *Life Magazine*, November 26, 1945, 29.
57 Interview with Pierrette S. in Kaiser, *French War Brides in America*, 140.
58 J. Robert Lilly, *La face cachée des GIs: les viols commis par des soldats américains en France, en Angleterre et en Allemagne pendant la Seconde Guerre mondiale, 1942–1945* (Paris: Payot, 2003), 43; Anonymous, *A Woman in Berlin.* (London: Virago, 2011); and Gabriele Köpp, *Warum war ich bloß ein Mädchen? das Trauma einer Flucht 1945* (München: Knaur-Taschenbuch-Verl., 2012) both provide first-hand accounts of the rape of German woman during Russian occupation of Germany.
59 Roberts, *What Soldiers Do*, 110; Judith Surkis, "Sex, Sovereignty, and Transnational Intimacies," *The American Historical Review* 115, no. 4 (October 2010): 1089–96.
60 Roberts, *What Soldiers Do*, 20, 109.
61 United State Army report in Walker, *Venereal Disease in the American Expeditionary Forces*, 101 showed that seventy-one percent of American soldiers claimed to have had sexual relationships with French women while serving in the American Expeditionary Forces during World War I. Similar data is unavailable for World War II.
62 Hovsepian, *Your Son and Mine*, xi.
63 Hovsepian, *Your Son and Mine*, 100.
64 Hovsepian, *Your Son and Mine*, 114.
65 Hovsepian, *Your Son and Mine*, 100–101.
66 Edward M Coffman, *The War to End All Wars: The American Military Experience in World War I.* (Lexington: The University Press of Kentucky, 2014), 133 cites February 1918 letter from Premier Clemenceau to GHQ, in which such arrangements are suggested. When the letter was transmitted to Secretary Baker, he responded famously by saying, "For God's sake, Raymond, don't show this to the President or he'll stop the war." Roberts, *What Soldiers Do*, 1–2 cites WWII exchange between Le Havre mayor, Pierre Voisin, and American general commander Colonel Weed. The request was denied for fear that news of military-sanctioned promiscuity would spread back in the United States.
67 Hovsepian, *Your Son and Mine*, 102.
68 Hovsepian, *Your Son and Mine*, 103.
69 Hovsepian, *Your Son and Mine*, 104.
70 Hovsepian, *Your Son and Mine*, 105–6.
71 Hovsepian, *Your Son and Mine*, 179.
72 Fussell, *The Great War and Modern Memory*, 191, 193, 199.
73 Hovsepian, *Your Son and Mine*, 99.
74 Hovsepian, *Your Son and Mine*, 109.
75 Hovsepian, *Your Son and Mine*, 120.
76 Jack Sacco, *Where the Birds Never Sing: The True Story of the 92nd Signal Battalion and the Liberation of Dachau* (New York: Regan Books, 2003), 241.

77 "French Envoys of Cupid in America," *Literary Digest*, February 14, 1920, 60.
78 Denise J. Rossow, "French War Bride," *Chicago Tribune*, December 16, 1999, sec. Voice of the People (Letter).
79 Liz Lawson, *Memoirs of a French War Bride, 1940–1950* (Santa Cruz, CA: n.p., 1998), 17, 19.
80 Jeannine Ricou-Allunis, *Memoir of a French War Bride* (Bloomington, IN: Author House, 2004), 17.
81 Lawson, *Memoirs of a French War Bride, 1940–1950*, 30.
82 Lawson, *Memoirs of a French War Bride*, 19.
83 Lawson, *Memoirs of a French War Bride*, 69.
84 Interview with Charles Lemeland in Hilary Kaiser, *WWII Voices: American GIs and the French Women Who Married Them* (Scottsdale: Summertime Publications Inc., 2011), 57–59.
85 Darglos, *Bernard Dargols, un GI français à Omaha Beach*, 25.
86 Interview with Marcelle S. in Kaiser, *French War Brides in America*, 67.
87 Ricou-Allunis, *Memoir of a French War Bride*, 99.
88 Interview with Jennette Davis in Kaiser, *WWII Voices*, 127.
89 Lawson, *Memoirs of a French War Bride, 1940–1950*, 73.
90 Interview with Aubert Lemeland in Kaiser, *WWII Voices*, 61.
91 Interview with Liliane Schroeder in Kaiser, *French War Brides in America*, 19.
92 Roberts, *What Soldiers Do*, 53–54.
93 John D'Emilio and Estelle Freedman, *Intimate Matters: A History of Sexuality in America*, 1st ed. (New York: Harper & Row, 1988), Part IV.
94 For more on anti-American sentiment in France between the world wars see Green, *The Other Americans in Paris*.
95 Petit, *Au coeur de la bataille de Normandie*, 9.
96 Roberts, *What Soldiers Do*, 21.
97 Hovsepian, *Your Son and Mine*, 80.
98 Ricou-Allunis, *Memoir of a French War Bride*, 26–27.
99 Lawson, *Memoirs of a French War Bride, 1940–1950*, 26.
100 Interview with Andrée McLatcher in Kaiser, *WWII Voices*, 129.
101 Interview with George Hook in Kaiser, *WWII Voices*, 66–67.
102 Sacco, *Where the Birds Never Sing*, 199.
103 Quoted in Levenstein, *We'll Always Have Paris American Tourists in France Since 1930*, 75.
104 Interview with Raymonde Liska in Kaiser, *WWII Voices*, 141–42.
105 Interview with Pierrette S. in *French War Brides in America*, 142.

Chapter 4

TRANSNATIONAL COURTSHIP IN SPACES OF WAR

Throughout, this study has built upon Wen-Shan Yang and Melody Chia-Wen Lu's concept of *transnational marriage*, which successfully situates the concept of *cross-border marriage* within a context of wider transnational processes by placing the analytical focus on the transnational networks and spaces from which marriages emerged.[1] Based on that working definition, in the case of wartime marriages during the twentieth century, the relative absence of a transnational community or social network among marriage participants, such as that which produced elite marriages in the nineteenth century, creates a methodological imperative to locate and define new transnational spaces that were created during the world wars. Therefore, in what follows, the focus shifts from wartime othering as an emotional process to a spatial analysis of transnational courtship and marriage.

This chapter is divided into four parts. In the first part, I attempt to locate and trace transnational cultural formation across and within multiple sites of wartime encounter by examining where and how soldiers and local women met and courted one another. Here, I argue that because most couples did not share a common language, other forms of mediated cultural cues, such as dancing, provided the translinguistic means of communication that became important cultural devices in courting rituals and transnational coupling. In this fashion, public dances, like those organized by the American Red Cross, came to serve as one of the most important examples of wartime transnational spaces that produced Franco-American marriages. In the second part of this chapter, I further explore subsequent courtship rituals among participants as well as the important role of their families in the cultural negotiation of these spaces. Finally, the third and fourth parts of this chapter examine how those transnational spaces of courtship and marriage existed in opposition to national spaces. Through an analysis of the conditions and frameworks that transnational couples had to navigate in order to form recognized matrimonial unions, I argue that state and military regulations, as well as the national criticisms of wartime Franco-American marriages further solidified participants' conceptions of the national borders that they attempted to cross. Here, not only did state and legal structures indirectly force couples to choose to enter into marriage after shortened periods of courtship in ways national couples were not, but also national apparatuses used notions of an *ideal* marriage as being a *national* one in their criticisms as a way to reconstruct and redefine the nation and national belonging in the twentieth century.

Locating Transnational Spaces of War

Examining where and how soldiers and local women met and courted one another allows us to both locate and map transnational cultural formation across and within multiple sites of wartime encounter. By identifying these spatial typologies and determining which of those spaces can be classified as transnational spaces, we are not only able to move beyond national frameworks of history, but also, and more specifically, can examine the cultural dimensions of transnational marriage motivation during this period. Because of the vastly different spatial contexts of World War I and II, as well as the availability of sources on which this analysis is based, the sites of encounter during each war will be dealt with separately in this section.

Transnational Spaces of Courtship during World War I

During the World War I, where and how soldiers and local women met and courted one another varied greatly, and as Susan Zeiger shows in her work *Entangling Alliances: Foreign War Brides and American Soldiers in the Twentieth Century*, these settings were often linked to both the social circumstance and military rank of the American soldier.[2] For middle- and working-class soldiers in the AEF, casual transnational encounters with French women largely occurred in urban public spaces such as streets, parks, and cafés. World-War-I soldier Robert Scudder, for example, met a girl in a park as she was walking with her friends. They arranged a date to the movies one week later, and soon after he met her parents. Within a couple of months, he asked her to marry him.[3] In 1917, another American soldier explained in an interview with a reporter from the *Literary Digest* that he had been frequenting a small café in Paris for days just because there was a girl there that had sparked his interest. During the interview he revealed enthusiastically: "Why she wouldn't let me walk home with her last night but said maybe she would tonight!"[4] Likewise, during a later interview with the *Sunday Evening Post* in 1939, AEF service-member and transnational-marriage participant himself, Bernhard Ranger depicted a similar story of a fellow American soldier, Sergeant Major Elhert Lee Dodds:

> [H]e knew not a single word of French and, alone in Paris, scuttled to the first haven he encountered, the Pension Simonet, which advertised English spoken. He was in such trepidation that he did not even notice the comely cashier, Yvonne Simonet, daughter of the proprietor. She, however, noticed him and caused her mother to gasp, an hour later, by announcing that she felt sure 'the American in No. 37' would take her away.[5]

Officers, by contrast, often met women at formal events and through established social networks. One French woman, Marie-Jeanne, met her husband at a reception held for American soldiers in Nice that was hosted by Colonel Webb C. Hayes, son of the former American president. His wife, Mrs. Hayes had been specifically looking for young French women to entertain their AEF guests and invited Marie-Jeanne on the recommendation of a mutual acquaintance. In a later interview with Hilary Kaiser, her daughter Myriam, explained: "Maman was very vivacious and lively [and] my father fell in love with her immediately. So the next day he arrived at my grandparents' home with an armful of roses. My grandmother opened the door, and there was a young man with a huge bunch of flowers. This sort of thing wasn't done at the time! But he was allowed to come in."[6]

In his *Sunday Evening Post* interview, Bernhard C also depicted another story of a couple who had not even met in person before commencing a courtship. According to him, a First Division soldier had submitted a poem to the *New York Herald, Paris edition* in 1917, and when a young lady from Agen read the "eleven graceful lines," she "wrote her appreciation to the warrior-poet." After a year of correspondence between Paris and the trenches, they finally met, and as Ragner described, "a whirl-wind courtship ensued" and they were married shortly after Armistice.[7] In this case, the site of the cross-cultural space of encounter was not in a physical location such as a café, but rather within what one might describe as a literary space. Nonetheless, the process of its construction occurred in the same fashion as the other transnational spaces of courtship, only outside of physical proximity.

Like the others, this story of a "whirl-wind" romance is depicted here not only as a chance encounter but also one that sparked a rather immediate and forceful emotional reaction. Ragner attempted to explain this by arguing that it was "destiny" that had played the most obvious role in how and where American soldiers met French women. Nonetheless, that transnational-marriage participants often depicted their own stories as chance encounters suggests that they were perhaps unaware of the cultural spaces that they themselves were creating.

Unfortunately, because these limited descriptions of encounters during World War I are so brief, a full analysis of the cultural characteristics of these transnational spaces that the actors created becomes difficult for the historian. However, Ranger's references to the linguistic boundaries of these encounters provides both a suitable and thought-provoking entry point for the further untangling of some of their more nuanced cultural dynamics. Such linguistic references are numerous in both World War I and World War II accounts. In the same *Sunday Evening Post* interview, another World-War-I, transnational-marriage participant F. B. Huger recounted this story of encounter: "I met my wife on the beach at Cannes. I spoke no French, she no English, and I really can't understand how it all happened, but here we are."[8] Likewise, during World War II, a soldier of the 92nd Signal Battalion, Joe Sacco, in later interviews collected and published by his son, reported that one of his comrades had begun a relationship with the daughter of a local mayor. "She didn't speak English, and he only knew what French he'd studied in high school, so they weren't able to have much in the way of meaningful conversations. Still, they liked each other's company enough to go for afternoon walks."[9] While many of these casual encounters were likely awkward at first, one writer for the *Literary Digest* in 1917 claimed that linguistic barriers actually facilitated cross-cultural romances more than it hindered them. The author explains: "The difference in language seems to form no bar; in fact, the kindly efforts of each to learn the language of the other acts as an aid."[10] Likewise, World-War-I, transnational-marriage participants Margurite Ferrard and William Wiles explained during an interview in their new home in Philadelphia after the war that even after their marriage he still did not speak French, nor she English, but "no words are needed in [their] radiant little Franco-American household."[11]

This absence of common language is important for two reasons. First, it demonstrates the emotional and cultural expectations of contemporaries who engaged in transnational courtships. When cultural encounter that produces marriage goes beyond language, perceived notions of difference are even further highlighted. Therefore, one can again conclude that processes of positive othering and the emotion of longing for association with the other continued to remain central in the processes of transnational coupling in this wartime context. Second, it raises interesting methodological questions about the theory of emotions history, the ways in which emotions history is intertwined with cultural history, and the role of language in emotional constructions. Notable emotions historians Susan Matt and Peter Stearns argue that emotions cannot exist independently from language as individuals define emotions in the process of expressing them.[12] These assertions are largely based on the constructionist theory of emotions—which, according to the Max Plank Institute for Human Development, maintains that, "feelings and their expressions are shaped by culture and learned or acquired in various social contexts. What somebody can and may feel (and show) in a given situation, towards certain people or things, depends on social norms and rules. It is thus historically variable and open to change."[13] While the research that is presented here, unfortunately, does not go far enough to successfully contribute to the debate of whether emotions are universal and innate or culturally constructed and variable, it does demonstrate some of the analytical limitations of attempting to understand the ways in which those historical actors understood the mediated feelings of others in the past. In the case of Franco-American marriages during wartime, when education background, social circumstance and national self-identification created a context in which cross-border-marriage participants did not share a common language (unlike their well-traveled, well-educated, nineteenth-century, elite counterparts), the historian must be cautious of reducing language to its oral components. Therefore, in examining the cultural and emotional dimensions of these transnational spaces, one must seek out and examine other forms of nonverbal language and mediated cultural cues that provided the translinguistic means communication in courting practices.

Transnational Spaces of World War II

During World War II, one of the most notable of these nonverbal constructs was dancing. In 1944, *Stars and Stripes* printed an image of an American soldier dancing with a local young French woman and titled the image "Savee [sic] Jitterbug Mademoiselle?" The image included the following caption: "You may not speak French, and they don't savee English, but Cpl. Rossario Tallient of Brooklyn demonstrates there is a universal language as he teaches the French cutie to jitterbug in the streets of liberated city."[14] This caption demonstrates how what was considered "the universal language" of dancing became central in transnational coupling and courting rituals. In this fashion, public dances, like those organized by the American Red Cross, came to serve as one of the most notable examples of the wartime transnational spaces that produced Franco-American marriages. For both American men and French women, dances provided an opportunity for not only entertainment but also for coupling with the "other." In an interview with Harvey and Mona Levenstein, one World-War-II American soldier Ernie Ricci [pseud.] confirmed that the "dance halls were packed with carousing GIs."[15] Likewise World-War-II, transnational-marriage participant, Jennette Davis, explained in a later interview of the other girls in her town: "I think quite a few girls from Granville married GIs [...] the Granville casino had a lot of dances and shows on Sundays, and that's where most of the girls and the GIs would meet."[16] While transnational cultural formation occurred across and within multiple sites of encounter during World War II, such as on top of a liberating tank, in the street or metro, in their homes over a meal, at film showings, or at an army base where they worked, examining Red Cross dances as a space of transnationality provides one of the most ideal opportunities for uncovering mediated cultural cues that provided a translinguistic means of communication in courting practices.

In organizing dances, the American Red Cross played a significant—though perhaps unintended—role in transnational coupling processes and the creation of transnational space. During World War II, the American Red Cross mobilized and joined troops in Europe in an effort to provide both relief aid and "compassionate support" to servicemen. Angela Petesch, a Red Cross volunteer who arrived in World-War-II France with the Clubmobile Group H in August of 1944 explained: "One of our organizations greatest accomplishments was bringing the Red Cross to the men in isolated areas rather than waiting until the men got to the Red Cross."[17] Scattered around France, these volunteer groups provided mobile recreational clubs, entertainment and "simple pleasures of home"—such as the donuts that Petesch served—to soldiers who were unable to make it to leave areas. While President Eisenhower called these efforts the "friendly hand of this nation reaching across the sea to sustain its fighting men,"[18] what was meant to serve as a national agency, came instead to serve as a facilitator of one of the most important transnational spaces for wartime marriage participants. In a later interview, one of these participants, Jacqueline B.-P., explained how she had met her American husband at such an event: "At that time, after the war, we'd go [to] American Red Cross dances [...] I was young and innocent at the time. I thought he was sexy and had a lot of charm. And it's true that he really was charming, [...] I thought I loved him!"[19] Like the spaces created during World War I, encounter with the "other" at dances is depicted here as producing a rather immediate and forceful emotional reaction; however, in this case, unlike the former, it is not often depicted as a chance encounter but often an intentional one.

Local dances and gatherings had been banned in French towns under German occupation. While many young French people still managed to hold some small and informal gatherings during that time, liberation brought with it a sense of freedom from oppression. In this way, liberation by the allied forces contributed to both the popularity of the Red Cross dances and the emotional experiences of French girls who attended them. One young woman from Marseille who married an American soldier explained in a later interview: "When the Americans came, the first thing they did was to hold dances and to invite the local girls from Marseille. It was all chaperoned and very respectable. The American Red Cross organized everything."[20] Another French woman who wrote extensively about her relationship and marriage in a self-published memoir, Liz Lawson, also met her American GI husband, Warren, at a Red Cross dance. She explained:

> A ripple effect of the newly gained freedom was to launch young people on a search for social pleasures that had been illegal during the occupation. Dancing in public places was one of them [...] Now public dancing was authorized, and the well-attended parties were under the sponsorship of the American Red Cross, which requisitioned dance halls in big hotels and hired well-known bands to play for the GIs.[21]

The dances hosted by the American Red Cross often took place during the evening or on weekend afternoons. Because the American forces usually prohibited fraternization with female American volunteers like those serving as nurses or in the Clubmobile groups,[22] the Red Cross actively sought local French women to attend these events. These local women, however, did not need much convincing. Jeannine Ricou-Allunis, who also wrote extensively about her marriage in her memoir, recounted in it the evening she met her husband at a Red Cross dance. "After five years, on May 8, 1945, the war was over. I wasn't feeling very good. I was sick, but I told my dad and my grandmother, 'No matter what, I'm going to dance with everybody.'"[23] Some like, Jacqueline C. S. of Châteaubriant, had parallel motives for attending. She explained: "We went to the dances to meet Americans, but also because of the refreshments and food."[24] Others, like Lawson, viewed the dances as an opportunity for far more. In her memoir she wrote:

> My friend Christiane and I attended the parties with great expectation. We went to as many as possible so long as it did not interfere with our studies [...] I still remember clearly the Sunday afternoon when I entered the big dance hall at the Crillon near the Champs-Elysees [...] The girls were near the front door, a bit shy to enter such an imposing place, hesitant to start a new acquaintance that seemed often to be a gamble. It was like throwing the dice and watching the winning number come up. If only the right partner would step forward and ask each one of us to dance! We had already created the imaginary person. In our minds, he would be tall, good looking, friendly and polite—the perfect gentleman. Of course, we didn't have to dance more than one dance with the same person if we didn't care for our partner. We didn't even

have to complete a succession of dances, usually four or five, before we would excuse ourselves with a legitimate reason for not wanting to pursue the acquaintance.[25]

Here, her emotional expectations demonstrate how the Red Cross dances acted as a quasi-transnational-marriage market, much like the balls and dinners of the nineteenth century had for elite transnational high society. For many, like for Lawson, attending such an event was about much more than dancing and entertainment linked to the excitement of liberation, it was about looking for a potential marriage partner in the othered American soldier. Her use of the word "gamble" connotes both the hurried nature in which such encounters took place and the impersonal aspects of the nonhuman affection of cultural infatuation and positive othering. Finally, this account demonstrates how women like her exercised a tremendous amount of personal choice in their coupling processes.

Moreover, like the elite transnational balls and dinners of the nineteenth century, the Red Cross dances during World War II came to be characterized by important cultural forms that regulated both social interaction and pleasure through mediated cultural codes. Understanding the cultural rituals that developed here are essential for further uncovering how marriages and courtships emerged from spaces of transnationality. Here, Lawson's memoir provides an important glimpse into some of these cultural codes, as she understood them. She wrote:

> So many subtle things were involved in dancing with a stranger! The way he came to you, his smile, the tone of his voice as he introduced himself, his one hand on your back, the other hand being held at the proper level, the way he would draw his partner to him and hold tight, but not too tight, the expertise of his steps [...] The informality of the dances eliminated more complex introductions. One simply moved forward, smiled and let oneself be drawn into the rhythm of the dance [...][26]

With regards to the dance that she shared with her would-be husband she says that they immediately felt comfortable together and that "a tacit harmony seemed to exist between [their] steps." As Lawson's depiction suggests, the cultural facets of the act of dancing produced a profoundly emotional experience for many of the transnational couples. Further, the ways in which Lawson attributes meaning to the personal proximity and the physical contact tells us much about how actors came to understand the mediated emotions of others in ways that transcended linguistic boundaries. Here, the unspoken "harmony" of her and her would-be-husband's steps, as well as what she describes as the instant emotional sensation of comfort and ease suggests that marriage participants developed intuitive skills that they used to evaluate potential emotional connections with their partners. Further, that "the informality of the dances eliminated more complex introductions" connotes how existing cultural understandings from more local contexts created the dimensions in which the emotions and actions of others were understood. In the same fashion, it also demonstrates some of the changes these codes underwent as they were renegotiated and applied to transnational (or transcultural) spaces. That, as she notes, such negotiations worked for some of her dancing partners and not others, suggests the varying degrees in which this process occurred as well as the varying degrees in which others were able to apply meaning to such cultural signals.

Courting Practices in Transnational Spaces and the Role of the Family

But how did relationships progress from an emotionally charged construct such as dancing to the act of marriage? The following sections examine not only the subsequent courtship rituals in these culturally negotiated spaces but also the role of the participants' families within them as well. After Ricou-Allunis met her husband, Albert, at a dance, he offered to walk her home. Of the progression of the relationship, she recounted:

> We walked home and he had a little dictionary [...] We sat in front of the house and he showed [it to] me and told me the names of things. And guess what, he told me he's going to marry me. I thought, my God, that guy must be crazy. I had just met him a few hours ago. When I went in, my grandmother asked me, 'Who were you talking to in the front?' I said, 'Well, an American soldier. He tells me he's going to marry me. He's crazy.' My grandmother started laughing and said, 'Be careful, Jeannine. Lots of times we marry those crazy guys.'[27]

When Albert returned to her home the next day, her father was less than pleased. The role of the family in courting practices is important here. While relationships formed between marriage participants, the families still sometimes played an important role.

It is important to note that many of the young French women that participated in these marriages were adolescents when the war began. According to the directress of one of the hostess houses in New York that helped relocate the new brides to be with their husbands in the United States, the average age of French brides during World War I was between seventeen and twenty.[28]

A similar average age range also characterized those during World War II,[29] and one marriage participant Jeanette Davis was only fifteen when she met her husband, John.[30] Another World-War-II marriage participant, Nicole explained that the American soldiers were the first men she ever went out with.[31] Further, World-War-II marriage participant Jacqueline C. S. explained in an interview that they were obliged to go out with the Americans in groups in order to secure the authorization of their families.[32]

The dominant would-be role of the French family in these transnational relationships was not unknown to the soldier participants. In June of 1944, *Stars and Stripes* published an article, entitled "So you're going to France," which declared the following: "It's not true that all French women are easy. Any guy who has the idea that the way to make friends and influence Frenchmen is to slip up alongside of the first good-looking gal he sees and slip her a quick pat on the fanny is going to be in for trouble." A cartoon on the same page shows a GI with a French girl. In the image the couple is being followed by a large group of her French relatives. The caption reads, "French cuties are well chaperoned."[33] After meeting a girl in Alsace, Sacco explained that a number of men in his unit had courted girls there. With regards to one of them he recounted: "Hodges had struck up a romance with the daughter of the mayor" and when they went on afternoon walks, they "were chaperoned by the girl's mother, little sister and aunt who followed several steps behind the love birds, watching their every move. Within days the escort grew to include an uncle, a couple of cousins and the mayor himself. Eventually other members of the 92nd joined the parade while Hodges and his mademoiselle happily walked along smiling but hardly saying a word."[34] However, he recounts the story like an oddity, implying that many of the American were unaccustomed to this social convention.

During World War I, the role of the family extended to the United States when some French families requested letters of reference from the soldiers' familial and social networks. During World War I, one member of the AEF from Philadelphia had been courting a young woman named Madeleine. Their daughter explained in a later interview that despite having been "in good favor with the whole family" they requested that he send them references from his church back home.[35] Likewise, the daughter of another World-War-I couple similarly explained that in order to convince her grandfather, her father was also required to get letters of reference from both his family and his church.[36] Therefore, while transnational marriage participants in both world wars exercised a tremendous amount of personal choice in both their partner selection and their courting practices, the role of their larger families remained significant in the processes of cultural negotiations within spaces of encounter and courtship.

Transnational Courtship to Transnational Marriage (and Might-Have-Been Marriages)

Amorous encounter that had been intensified by the contrasting emotions of war and liberation, hypermasculinity of military service, mutual curiosity, fascination, positive othering, and cultural infatuation led to countless romantic and sexual encounters between American soldiers and local French women during both World War I and World War II. However, only some of these transnational relationships produced marriages. As the lyrics of the popular World-War-I song suggest, "Quand la guerre est fini[e], les américains parti[s], mademoiselle seule au lit, bouncing the new baby,"[37] the reality for many French women in both wars was that they would be left behind as soldiers' regiments continued on or soldiers were demobilized and returned to the United States. Sacco explained what it was like to leave the girl, Monique, with whom he had developed an emotional relationship, when the 92nd Battalion left Alsace-Lorraine. He recounted: "We spent the last minutes talking about how we would see each other again, and about how I would come back for her after the war and how she would come to Alabama with me. She made me promise a hundred times that I wouldn't get hurt. I hugged her and tried to reassure her, but I didn't know what would happen to me as the war progressed from here." He nonetheless promised he would return for her. They embraced one final time, and his unit departed. He continued: "I can never forget her face, her smile, her tears as we pulled away—she standing beside the road, waving hugging her mother's arm, looking directly into my eyes even as the distance between us increased, wiping a stream of tears from her beautiful face and then [...] hidden behind dust and trucks and men of war."[38] Likewise, in the letters to his father, Hovsepian recounted a similar experience. He wrote:

> There is a difference between going out with girls, necking and having fun, and the way I felt toward Jeannie. It was not kid stuff anymore; it was man-and-woman stuff, and I suddenly felt like a man feels towards his wife, I guess [...] Well then we got the orders to pull out of these parts. We knew it was our last night and we were sad [...] I promised her to write to her often, and then come back to see her when the war was over, and I meant it too. The next A.M. when we were loading on the trucks she stood there crying, watching us [...] the truck started and she wouldn't let go. She kept hanging on [...] we pulled out and there she stood in the middle of the road waving at me with great big tears rolling down her face [...]. It was so sad leaving her there crying.[39]

While Hovsepian invoked marriage and marriage-like terms numerous times in his letters about various sexual and emotional relationships with French women, neither he nor Sacco entered into matrimonial contracts with any of their French partners. Nonetheless, these passages are suggestive of a profoundly emotional courtship experience that should not be discounted simply because an act of marriage did not occur. Further, in examining transnational marriages, these passages create an inquisitional imperative for the further examination of the ways in which transnational spaces of courtship existed in opposition to the national spaces that participants occupied. By examining the external structures and frameworks that transnational couples had to navigate in order to form recognized matrimonial unions, I argue that state and military regulations, as well as the conditions of war not only played a role in whether or not a marriage would take place but also further solidified participants' conceptions of the national borders that they attempted to cross.

While neither Sacco nor Hovsepian ever went back to marry the girls they left behind, those who did either did so with a sense of urgency and or did so by continuing the courtship through correspondence. World-War-II marriage participant Jennette Davis, for example, corresponded with her American GI, John, for five years before they met again when he returned to Paris.[40] Likewise, Andrée McLatcher only spent three consecutive Saturdays with her would-be GI husband before he was sent elsewhere. They corresponded for approximately one year before deciding to marry.[41] By contrast, those who married quickly soon found their marriages at the center of critiques by national onlookers who propagated notions that wartime unions had been hurriedly undertaken without full regard for the inevitable "consequences." In the August 2, 1925 issue of the *New York Times*, John Ellingston called the Franco-American marriages of World War I "marriages of haste, under impulse of abnormal excitement and of ignorance."[42] Similarly, the *Literary Digest* claimed that French mothers had been "flooding the mails with letters of inquiry as to the status of their daughters who have been so rash as to enter into matrimonial alliances with that khaki-clad youths [...] from the other side of the ocean."[43] And in 1919, one American woman who had been serving in World-War-I France attempted to explain the transnational courtship-to-marriage process to the *Atlanta Constitution*. She said: "I have known cases wherein a doughboy strolled down a boulevard in Paris, was picked up by a French girl [...] had a few glasses of wine, and broke out with 'wouldn't you like to take a little trip to America dearie—' 'Oui—I go—très bien' gushed the girl [...] Off they went to the nearest civil authority [...] and were married."[44] Even Hilary Kaiser drew similar conclusions when she noted that one of the major themes that she found among the marriage participants she interviewed was "a certain amount of naïveté and unconsciousness on the part of the young war brides." She explains: "They made the hasty decision to marry a man they hardly knew, to leave their native land and to immigrate to America, often without considering the consequences should it not work out [...] [they] had romantic notions that everything would be fine once they were together, that love would 'conquer all'."[45]

This perception of the process demonstrated by both Kaiser and the *Atlanta Constitution* was relatively overly simplified, and while it may have been indicative of contemporary national views of the wartime unions, and perhaps indicative of what were relatively short courting periods among couples, this notion of "hasty, naïve" marriages fails to account for the complicated administrative and emotional processes that many couples went through in order to form marital unions during wartime. For example, one of Kaiser's interviewees, Jeanne-Marie L. C. explained in detail her decision to enter into a marital union so quickly:

> I was very surprised my parents didn't object to our marrying. But they told me there was one condition: I had to wait until the end of the war. So, we got officially engaged and were going to wait. But shortly after our engagement, someone told Tom that during the post-war period [...] it would be just as impossible for him to come back [...] to get me as it would be for me to go to the United States. So my parents agreed to our marrying rather quickly [...] We started the paperwork in January 1944. However, that was when the American army began realizing that a lot of GIs had married undesirable women—sick ones and others—and that they were all going to be coming to the United States. So the army [...] decided to make it much more difficult to obtain authorizations to marry. We had to start the paperwork all over again [...] I also had to be interviewed by all of my fiancé's superior officers. We wanted to get married in July and hoped the papers would arrive in time. But by the time the papers finally arrived, the landing in France had started, and Tom was put on a two-hour alert, so we had to keep waiting. Then one day Tom arrived at my house and announced: 'Guess what? We have permission! We're getting married on the 11th.' It was September 5 or 6, so we had to work fast.[46]

American-Red-Cross volunteer Angela Petesch also explained some of the more practical considerations as to why such "hasty" undertakings were sometimes necessary. She wrote: "Planning a marriage under conditions [of wartime] presents many problems. In the first place, nobody knows where the bride and groom might be at any future date or where the ceremony will be performed. The poor boy can get only a 48-hour pass at most. Then there is the transportation problem [...]"⁴⁷ Here, one might also consider a shift away from an interpretation of naivety on the part of marriage participants and, as Jeanne-Marie L. C.'s account suggests, consider the ways in which state and legal structures indirectly forced couples to choose to enter into marriage after shortened periods of courtship in ways national couples were not. Moreover, transnational couples during the world wars were bound by not only military regulation but also by stricter immigration laws that their elite counterparts had been in the nineteenth century. Therefore, for those twentieth-century couples that wished to continue courtships in close physical proximity, an act of marriage transcended national borders in ways that courtship did not.

It should also be noted that not all marriages occurred in the haste of wartime. Elenor Kiler, who oversaw the work of the Young Women's Christian Association (YWCA) to help French women join their husbands in the United States after World War I revealed to a *New York Times* reporter in 1921 that "romances that started during the war [were] still resulting in marriages." "Only last week," she explained, "a young woman came through here to join her fiancé in California. They had met and became engaged during the war, while he was still overseas. A highly accomplished girl, she had a splendidly paid position with a famous French house in Paris and was reluctant to leave. Finally, her fiancé wrote us to meet her, and she went on to begin life in California."⁴⁸ Of course, the notion of what was or was not an appropriate pre-marriage courtship period is also culturally, socially, and even individually variant. For example, one 1920 article in the *Literary Digest* claimed: "Under French laws there cannot be any marrying in haste [...] French laws are strict. No elopements are possible, what with the parties obliged to have lived in the same household at least four weeks, the posting of marriage bans at least sixteen days before at the mairie (town hall), and the production of birth certificates to prove that you were born!"⁴⁹ Petesch also claimed that the Army required a sixty-day waiting period before wedding could take place.⁵⁰ Likewise, in a later interview, World-War-II marriage participant Marcelle S. recalled that she and her husband Morry (who had been stationed in Algeria) had to wait a "ninety-day 'cooling-off' period" before she could get any of the needed papers. After such time, she was also interviewed before they were allowed to proceed. However, she admits that her husband's captain had been supportive of their relationship.⁵¹

The likelihood that a marriage would occur was dependent on several structural factors that participants had to navigate—one of them, as stated in the previous passage, was the support of commanding officers. During both World War I and World War II, marriages between American soldiers and local women posed a problem for the American military. As Mark Meigs explains during World War I, this was not only because the military believed that these women would become dependent on the army and would require transport to the United States after the war, but also because marriage fostered a loyalty that was self-serving rather than for the organizational military collective.[52] This opposition to marriage is demonstrated in military correspondence. For example, one cavalry colonel reported on March 19, 1918:

> When Private W. asked permission to marry I refused, as I did in other cases, on the ground that this was no time to be undertaking new responsibilities and obligations; that we were over here to fight when the time came; and to spend the rest of the time getting ready for it and not to marry and raise families. If Private W. is allowed to marry this girl it will lead to a number of other cases just exactly like this. I have been through the whole thing twice before in Cuba and the Philippines.[53]

Similarly, in a wartime memo from Judge Advocate General to the AEF, W. A. Bethel stated that "under present conditions marriage of American soldiers to French girls, is prejudicial to military interests." However, he continued:

> The matter of prohibiting marriage is a very delicate one, since it is the policy of our country to encourage matrimony, and the view has always been taken, heretofore, that marriage is a personal privilege with which the Government, in general, has no right to interfere. A military order forbidding matrimony would, in time of peace, in my opinion, be illegal, and such, I think is the view that has always been taken. As a temporary measure, in time of war, when personal rights must give way to the needs of the State, I believe such an order is legal and appropriate, although some, of course may take the contrary view.[54]

No such order was issued, however, and conflicting views of marriage as an individual freedom and as a threat to a successful military campaign led to confusion regarding how to deal with the AEF's "marriage problem" in World-War-I France. In that confusion, some couples managed to marry successfully on their own. Others requested officers' permission, while others fell into the administrative maze of misinformation and redirection. In a letter to General Pershing, Sargent Orley Hill wrote: "I have permission to ask the General for permission to marry. Officers of my regiment cannot give me the permission and I am asking you this great favor Sir.

The French authorities say I must have permission from you. Sir hoping to get the permission by mail [...] I hope this is not asking too much of you Sir."[55] While some commanding officers refused permission to marry, others simply refused permission for leave during which time a marriage was meant to take place. By contrast, it is also important to note that some officers were supportive of the matrimonial endeavors of their soldiers. *Time Magazine*, for example featured a World-War-II rest area in the Riviera and explained that the "GIs 'heaven' was staffed with officers ready to do anything to make the soldier happy: they have even arranged weddings."[56]

Unfamiliarity with French marriage laws also created an obstacle for couples wishing to marry. In 1919, the *Literary Digest* published an article, entitled "Cupid Has Had to Print a Set of Rules for the Doughboys in France" that explained for American readers the complicated processes through which soldiers and their brides would have to endure before a wedding could take place. It explained that French law, which defined marriage as a civil contract, required civil registration documents that proved identity including birth certificates, which many soldiers were unable to produce in time, as marriages procedures in the United States rarely included such requirement. French law also required the publication of bans or intent for a certain period of time before a marital contract could be enacted, typically ten to sixteen days. One of the parties was required to reside in the town where the marriages would take place for a minimum period of one month and was required to prove residency by a certificate of domicile. An affidavit from the American consul was also required, which was to be written in French and legalized by the French Ministry of Foreign Affairs. This document certified the birth of the American, whether or not he had ever been previously married, if divorced those details as well, that he is of marrying age in the state from which he comes, that he does not require the consent of his parents, and that the publishing of bans in the United States is not required.[57] Some French municipalities agreed to accept sworn affidavit from American officers in place of some of the requirements listed earlier—a measure that kept American officers involved even in French administrative marriage procedures.[58]

Yet, while some structures hindered the practice of marriage in wartime, others helped to facilitate it. Groups such as the YWCA and the Red Cross were notable in these efforts, both directly and indirectly. The Red Cross had not only organized the dances where many couples met and began courtships, it also assisted soldiers in obtaining the letters of reference for French families who might have been suspicious of the men courting their daughters.[59] Further, Public Law 271 also known as the War Brides Act allowed for new wives to benefit from transportation provided by the U.S.

Army and enter the United States as nonquota immigrants after World War II. The American Red Cross not only assisted with paperwork for entry into the United States but also gave the brides cultural training to prepare them for their lives there.[60] The YWCA arranged for the new brides to be housed in Hostess Houses, which had originally been established for American women, but were converted to temporary shelters for the French brides of American servicemen as they awaited transport to the United States. The YWCA was also charged by the army with transporting new brides (and often children) to the United States and looking after them at ports of departure in France.[61] Lastly, they provided other kinds of assistance, even financial assistance in the form of loans, until soldier husbands were discharged from the army.[62] World-War-II marriage participant Jeanne Marie L. C. explained in a later interview that when she arrived in New York the Red Cross not only greeted them, housed them in what she considered to be a luxurious hotel, but also took them on several visits and excursions.[63] Finally, the YWCA also helped to establish social clubs in the United States for recently arrived brides, such as the *Union des femmes de France* in Boston, which offered not only a social network but also English and child-care classes.[64]

Reinforcing National Borders and Defining Marriage through Public Opinion and National Critiques

The legal and military restrictions faced by wartime marriage participants were not the only force that further solidified their conceptions of the national borders that they attempted to cross. As many participants soon discovered after their marriages took place, so too would external public opinions of their unions reinforce these barriers. The sexualized reputation and gendered national stereotypes of French women exacerbated national criticisms in the United States and affected the post-marriage migration processes of marriage participants. As Zeiger shows in her examination of World-War-I marriage and immigration regulation, France's risqué reputation was often set against a period of progressive moral reform in America, and with an army that was supposed to be "pure and clear through and through."[65] Interviews with World-War-II participants demonstrate that these views persisted well into the middle of the century. Jacqueline B.-P., for example, explained in a later interview that Americans often perceived French women like her as "ooh la la girls."[66] Likewise, another World-War-II marriage participant, Jeanne-Marie L. C. said of her personal experiences after moving to the United States that most of the women there ignored them, and the men ogled them.[67] Newspaper headlines such as "Yank Must Prove

French Wife Has Good Character" and "New Order Refuses To Take Girls To The U.S. Unless They Are Ladies" confirm how these views influenced the immigration structures that couples had to navigate. Immigration officials in New York, for example, requested that the husband's commanding officer send a statement that the wife was of "reputable character."[68] Such sentiments also infiltrated the agencies meant to assist in the wartime marriage and post-marriage migration processes. For example, in a memo to Emmet White of the American Red Cross's Department of Civil Relief, Elizabeth Hutchin complained that the French brides were "far from a desirable class of citizens" argued the army should "cease to furnish transportation" for them as soon as possible.[69] Zeiger concludes that such criticism and suspicion of World-War-I marriages were not only representative of but also linked to early-twentieth-century nativism and anti-immigration movements in the United States.

However, a broader temporal and geographical analysis of national critiques of transnational marriages shows that these criticisms are neither surprising nor a development particular to the early- and mid-twentieth century and its anti-immigration climate. As the first part of this work has shown, the view that the women of wartime transnational marriages were "foreign war brides" who may or may not have been "desirable," fails to fully consider that other transnational marriage participants of various backgrounds and social statuses faced similar national criticism at different moments in the past. Therefore, I contend that the perceived role of the practice of marriage in the making of national culture as well as its relationship to the state need to be more systematically considered. As Nancy F. Cott has shown, the practice of marriage is an essential aspect in the making of the nation-state, as it underlines national belonging, establishes cohesion, and sets national moral standards.[70] However, when families construct themselves beyond national borders, they fail to fit into national narratives of identity. Therefore, an attempt is made by both the state and national apparatuses to shape relationships according to national agendas and criteria by defining what are or are not acceptable family formation practices.[71] Such sentiments are then permeated through public discourse as part of the imagining of the national community.[72]

As with the elite Franco-American marriages in the nineteenth century, the American press, which sensationalized story of the "war bride", was largely responsible for perpetuating national criticisms, which further solidified participants' conceptions of the borders that they crossed. The 1919 *New York Times* article that had grossly exaggerated that as many as 200,000 World-War-I soldiers would stay in France "to marry French women," for example, had caused such an outrage among the American public that the publication was compelled to correct it only a few months later in another article, entitled "Doughboys and French Girls: Not Many of Them are Marrying, and Soldiers Long for Their Homes."[73] What is most interesting, however, is the justification used for the national resentment. In the latter article, the author explained that "American mothers, wives, and sweethearts" were "suffering" at the thought that they will be abandoned for "French girls." This is curious when set against the nineteenth-century titled marriages, which were viewed as "problematic" because of the ideological juxtaposition of American republicanism and European aristocracy and because, according to onlookers like Gustavus Myers, American heiresses were taking money out of the United States and pouring it into Europe.[74] By contrast, in the case of the twentieth-century wartime marriages, the national reaction is far more personal and far more emotional as such unions were perceived as leaving "poor American girls left crying and alone." The same image of "the girl back home" was also used during World War II. For example, in 1944, in response to iconic images of soldiers kissing French women during liberation celebrations, *Life* claimed, "Some Iowa Girls Didn't Like That Kissing in Paris" and quoted one Mrs. Hubert Hanson, who complained: "I want him to save his kisses for me."[75]

Other forms of critiques tell us much about the cultural attitudes surrounding the practice of marriage. In 1919, the *Atlanta Constitution*, published an article entitled, "It's Love's Blue Monday for the Doughboy Now Who Took Himself a War Bride", which was based on an interview with an American woman, Byrd McFall, who had been aiding French women with their transfers to the United States after World War I. Here, she and Jane Dixon, the article's author, depicted the image of a "good wholesome American boy" who had fallen victim to the "dangerous, money-seeking French woman"—both of whom were "foolish and irresponsible."[76] By othering French women as loose gold-diggers, they attempted to illegitimatize wartime marriages between French women and American soldiers as merely based on economic considerations. Like in the case of elite transnational marriages of the nineteenth century, when a marriage was criticized as being solely motivated by financial arrangements, it was, for the most part, an attempt to render the union as illegitimate or at least, less legitimate than the emotional-based alternative. That means that if economic-based marriages were viewed as illegitimate, love-based marriages were perceived as the normative cultural ideal. Further, even though McFall admitted that there may have been some "beautiful unions between American fighters and the women of our allies," she claimed that "there were more sordid, ugly matings" suggesting that lustful or sexually based marriages were also viewed as less legitimate.

Finally, these national discussions and critiques of wartime transnational marriages largely focused on what was perceived to be inevitable disappointment and rejection. Shortly after World War I, an incident in St. Maries, Idaho where "three French war brides tearfully begged to go back to France" provided a baseline for rumors and news reports that most of the brides, after having settled in the U.S., were unhappy and homesick.[77] The *Literary Digest* asserted in an article entitled, "French Envoys of Cupid in America" that plenty of French women were returning to France "disillusioned" after divorce or abandonment.[78] Already on September 2, 1919, the *New York Times* claimed that at least sixty-two French brides had returned to their old homes after obtaining divorces from their husbands because they could not adapt to the American way of life and speculated that the number was probably greater. Similarly in a 1947 letter to the Minister of Foreign Affairs, the French Ambassador Henri Bonnet claimed that various French consulates had received about 50 requests for repatriation from "disillusioned" French brides and estimated that 100 more requests were expected by the end of the year.[79] While the exact number of divorces over the course of both periods are hard to ascertain, Kaiser also notes that about half of her World-War-II interviewees had later divorced. However, by the time that she conducted most of her interviews in the 1990s, the American divorce rate had already risen to about one in two marriages, leaving her rate of divorce among French war brides about the same as the American national average.[80] Further, as sociologist Thomas Monahan shows, most marriages contracted during and after periods of war—when more traditional structures are in disarray and what were perceived has moral standards had temporarily broken down—often show greater susceptibility to divorce.[81]

What is most interesting, however, is the ways in which the notion of undoubtedly foreseeable divorce and disappointment were used to further national criticisms of wartime transnational marriages. For example, in response to the increasing number of Franco-American marriages during World War I, Dixon claimed confidently in the *Atlanta Constitution* that "mixed marriages, unions between girls of other nationalities and American boys, do not, as a rule, bring happiness. The countries are too widely separated in customs, in tradition."[82] This critique creates an interesting paradox as the same notions of *difference* that had attracted many participants to the "other" in the first place were being used by national audiences to condemn their relationships to "inevitable failure." This notion that national differences in customs could not bring happiness in transnational marriages, as well as the continued use of the image of "the girl back home" demonstrates that national critiques stemmed less from the views of French women as over-sexed, undesirable immigrants, and more from prevailing notions that *ideal* marriages were culturally homogenous, *national* marriages. In the broader temporal comparison of this work, this represents an interesting shift. While elite transnational marriage participants faced criticism from American audiences because their marriages into European aristocracy were viewed as contrary to the national prerogative of American republicanism, they were never critiqued for being too culturally different to "succeed." By contrast, in the case of twentieth-century wartime marriages, notions of culture were even further linked with national identity and nationalism.

Notes

1. Yang and Lu, *Asian Cross-Border Marriage Migration*.
2. Zeiger, *Entangling Alliances*, 17.
3. Zeiger, *Entangling Alliances*, 17.
4. "Franco-Yanko Romance," 46.
5. Ragner, "The Permanent AEF."
6. Interview with Myriam H. in Kaiser, *French War Brides in America*, 11.
7. Ragner, "The Permanent AEF," depicting the story of Mademoiselle Hélène Siegel, who would later become Mrs. Myer.
8. Ragner, "The Permanent AEF."
9. Sacco, *Where the Birds Never Sing*, 244.
10. "Franco-Yanko Romance," 46–47.
11. "French Envoys of Cupid in America."
12. Matt and Stearns, *Doing Emotions History*, 43.
13. "History of Emotions | Max Planck Institute for Human Development," accessed November 30, 2016, https://www.mpib-berlin.mpg.de/en/research/history-of-emotions.
14. "Savee Jitterbug Mademoiselle?," *Stars and Stripes*, August 24, 1944.
15. Interview with Ernie Ricci [pseud.] in Levenstein, *We'll Always Have Paris*, 78.
16. Interview with Jennette Davis in Kaiser, *WWII Voices*, 127.
17. Petesch, *War Through the Hole of a Donut*, vii–viii.
18. Petesch, *War Through the Hole of a Donut*, 135.
19. Interview with Jacqueline B-P. in Kaiser, *French War Brides in America*, 114.
20. Interview with Pierrette S. in Kaiser, *French War Brides in America*, 140.
21. Lawson, *Memoirs of a French War Bride, 1940–1950*, 82.
22. Petesch, *War Through the Hole of a Donut*, 168.
23. Ricou-Allunis, *Memoir of a French War Bride*, 34.
24. Interview with Jacqueline C. S. in Kaiser, *French War Brides in America*, 41.
25. Lawson, *Memoirs of a French War Bride, 1940–1950*, 83.
26. Lawson, *Memoirs of a French War Bride*, 83–84.
27. Ricou-Allunis, *Memoir of a French War Bride*, 36.
28. Macdonald, "At the War Brides' Home."
29. Virden, *Good-Bye, Piccadilly*, 1.
30. Interview with Jeanette Davis in Kaiser, *French War Brides in America*, 125.
31. Interview with Nicole in Kaiser, *French War Brides in America*, 48.
32. Interview with Jacqueline C. S. in Kaiser, *French War Brides in America*, 41.

33 "So You're Going to France," *Stars and Stripes*, June 15, 1944.
34 Sacco, *Where the Birds Never Sing*, 244.
35 Interview with Therese H. in Kaiser, *French War Brides in America*, 5.
36 Interview with Myriam H. in Kaiser, *French War Brides in America*, 11.
37 Niles and Moore, *The Songs My Mother Never Taught Me*, 56–57.
38 Sacco, *Where the Birds Never Sing*, 250–51.
39 Hovsepian, *Your Son and Mine*, 120.
40 Interview with Jeanette Davis in Kaiser, *French War Brides in America*, 126.
41 Interview with Andrée McLatcher in Kaiser, *WWII Voices*, 131.
42 Ellinston, "Paths of a French War Bride Are Rocky."
43 "Cupid Has Had to Print a Set of Rules for the Doughboys in France," 78.
44 Dixon, "It's Love's Blue Monday for the Doughboy Now Who Took Himself a War Bride."
45 Kaiser, *French War Brides in America*, 150.
46 Interview with Jeanne-Marie L. C. in Kaiser, *French War Brides in America*, 58–59.
47 Petesch, *War Through the Hole of a Donut*, 171.
48 "French War Brides Happy in America," *New York Times*, December 4, 1921.
49 "French Envoys of Cupid in America," 57.
50 Petesch, *War Through the Hole of a Donut*, 185.
51 Interview with Marcelle S. in Kaiser, *French War Brides in America*, 68–68.
52 Meigs, *Optimism at Armageddon*, 125.
53 Kellogg, *Marriage of Soldiers*, 4–5. Also cited in Meigs, *Optimism at Armageddon*, 127.
54 Quoted in Zeiger, *Entangling Alliances*, 29.
55 Quoted in Zeiger, *Entangling Alliances*, 28.
56 "U.S. At War: G.I. Heaven," *Time Magazine*, June 18, 1945.
57 "Cupid Has Had to Print a Set of Rules for the Doughboys in France."
58 Zeiger, *Entangling Alliances*, 36.
59 Zeiger, *Entangling Alliances*, 34.
60 Kaiser, *French War Brides in America*, xxxvii–xxxviii.
61 "French Envoys of Cupid in America," 57.
62 Nina Mjagkij, "YMCA," in *The United States in the First World War: An Encyclopedia*, ed. Paul L. Miles and Anne Cipriano Venzon (Taylor & Francis, 1999), 811.
63 Interview with Jeanne Marie L. C. in Kaiser, *French War Brides in America*, 59.
64 "French War Brides Happy in America."
65 Zeiger, *Entangling Alliances*, 13.
66 Interview with Jacqueline B-P. in Kaiser, *French War Brides in America*, 118.
67 Interview with Jeanne-Marie L. C. in Kaiser, *French War Brides in America*, 61–62.
68 Zeiger, *Entangling Alliances*, 43.
69 Quoted in Zeiger, *Entangling Alliances*, 39; Original citation: Elizabeth Hutchin, "Memo to Emmet W. White, Department of Civil Relief, American Red Cross" October 31, 1919, RG 200, American Red Cross Papers, National Archives and Records Administration.
70 Cott, *Public Vows*, 5.
71 Williams, *Global Marriage*.
72 Benedict Anderson, *Imagined Communities: Reflections on the Origin and Spread of Nationalism* (London; New York: Verso, 2006).
73 "Cupid's Success in AEF"; "Doughboys and French Girls: Not Many of Them Are Marrying, and the Soldiers Long for Their Homes," *New York Times*, May 11, 1919.

74 Myers, *History of the Great American Fortunes*, 1936, 92.
75 "Some Iowa Girls Didn't Like That Kissing in Paris," *Life Magazine*, September 25, 1944.
76 Dixon, "It's Love's Blue Monday for the Doughboy Now Who Took Himself a War Bride."
77 "French War Brides Happy in America."
78 "French Envoys of Cupid in America."
79 Letter from Henri Bonnet to Leon Blum, January 8, 1947, 3. Quoted in Kaiser, *French War Brides in America*, xxxi.
80 U.S. Bureau of the Census, Current Population Reports, "Marriage, Divorce, and Remarriage in the 1990's" (U.S. Government Printing Office, Washington, DC, 1992), 1. According to Jean-Paul Sardon, "L'évolution Du Divorce En France," *Population* 51, no. 3 (1996): 726, the rate of divorce in France around the same time that Kaiser conducted her interviews was 1 in every 2.8 marriages. In 1946, the divorce rate in France had been 1 in every 4.5 marriages.
81 Thomas P. Monahan, "The Changing Probability of Divorce," *American Sociology Review* 5, no. 4 (August 1940): 545.
82 Dixon, "It's Love's Blue Monday for the Doughboy Now Who Took Himself a War Bride."

CONCLUSION

History written within the framework of the nation is as distorted as it is incomplete. From these caged perspectives, instances of transnational coupling and marriage were too often treated as curious anomalies that violated norms and could only be explained by the economic motives of the participants. The marriages examined here however were deeply embedded in a profound cultural relationship between these two societies. Of course, these subjects were only a small subset of a larger population that occupied the Atlantic space, but by carving out these small moments in the past, and examining them through cultural and emotional lens, a more fruitful historical perspective of recent discussions about the nature of transnational cultures and the definitions of marriage and family formation emerges.

This book has provided an examination of two different patterns of Franco-American marriage that occurred in two very different historical contexts. In the nineteenth century, transnational marriages between France and the United States largely occurred between wealthy, elite Americans and those that they perceived to be their socio-economic equivalent—European aristocrats. Linked within same social networks, these elite transnational-marriage participants often spoke the same languages, shared common values, read similar literature, and performed similar cultural rituals. This paired with their unrestricted movement between different urban centers such as New York, London, and Paris meant that their marital unions often emerged out of spaces that were not entirely defined by national boundaries. The coming of World War I then effectively ended elite domination of the transnational space that existed between France and the United States and allowed for a geographic mobility of the working, rural, and middle classes who engaged in the conflict. By bringing an entire new group of people into the sphere of transnationality, World War I and its consequences changed not only the power relations between France and the United States but also the dimensions of broader cultural encounters and social spaces that existed between the two. In this context, wartime-marriage participants were not members of a socially homogenized, transnational social network that effortlessly carved out an existence and moved freely beyond national boundaries as their nineteenth-century counterparts had but were instead American soldiers and local French women who were largely restricted by both the conflict around them and the national boundaries that were tangibly manifested in their everyday lives. However, even though marriage participants perceived national borders differently in each context, the human tendency to connect and couple in both cases, nonetheless largely superseded the borders that had been constructed between them. And despite the very different settings, the similarities that emerge in the stories of these two patterns are striking.

Most notably, both patterns were the result of emotionally charged cultural encounters that occurred in identifiable and mappable transnational spaces. With regards to titled marriages, rather than the result of mere strategic socioeconomic calculations on the part of American women and their families in an attempt to gain social honor and prestige in places such as fashionable New York, these marriages were instead the result of social interaction within elite transnational social networks and spaces that existed between the United States and Europe, among those who chiefly identified with others of similar economic and social status rather than national origin. Here, the extravagant social events of transnational high society, such as the costume balls and dinners came to serve as not only a stage for Franco-American cross-cultural encounters but also a cultural mechanism for elite coupling. Likewise, in the second part, rather than simply a solution to the devastating demographic dilemma faced by French women following the military deaths of French men, Franco-American marriages in the context of war were also largely driven by important cultural and emotional elements within wartime cross-cultural encounter. Just like in nineteenth-century ballrooms, the construct of dancing became an important cultural device in courtship interaction, and Red Cross dances came to serve as a quasi-transnational-marriage market much like the extravagant high society dinners and balls at the Tuileries and the American legation had. Through a careful analysis of first-hand descriptions, it is clear that even though many wartime courtships and marriages were viewed as undertaken in haste, they were not undertaken without ritual.

Even more, in both nineteenth- and twentieth-century contexts, emotions mattered. At the intersection of cross-cultural encounter and transnational coupling in both contexts stood a profoundly emotional experience. Within all these social spaces, emotional processes of cultural othering isolated positive characteristics and produced emotions of mutual fascination and longing for association with the perceived "other." In this way, attraction to notions of difference created strong emotional responses and largely remained the driving force of marriage and coupling processes in both contexts.

By participating in a transnational marriage, participants bound themselves not only to their spouse but also to the culture of that spouse. Motivations for transnational marriage were, therefore, still strategic but were largely based on preconceived notions of what participants believed the other culture to be. Because the emotional experience was so intertwined with cross-cultural interaction, the marriages that emerged from these spaces can be, in many respects, characterized as even more (rather than less) emotional than their national counterparts. This is notable because even during two different phases of the culmination of the national project, transnational-marriage participants, driven by this attraction to difference as well as cultural infatuation, preferred to marry across national lines rather than within them. This provokes important questions regarding Benedict Anderson's concept of the nation as an imagined community. Embedded within this notion of an imagined community conceived as a "deep, horizontal comradeship," Anderson presents the idea of a strong emotional bond.[1] However, in these two patterns of transnational marriage—one of them rooted in the context of hyper-nationalism—the strong emotional bond stretches well outside of that national polity.

How transnational spaces of encounter and courtship existed alongside or in opposition to national spaces also requires further consideration. In both cases, couples and their marriages attracted significant criticism from national communities, often for being financially motivated. In the first case, American heiresses were criticized as being "title hunters," and in the second, French women were viewed as "dangerous and money-seeking." Despite these labels however, couples in each of these patterns rarely crossed class lines. Instead in each case, this critique was largely an attempt to render the union as illegitimate or at least, less legitimate than the alternative, and it created an important dichotomy when describing marriage as a practice—either one married for love or one married for money and status. This reveals important elements of contemporary emotional standards in both the nineteenth and twentieth centuries because the underlying assumption of such critiques rested on the notion that normative cultural ideal was therefore an emotional union, rather than an economic one.

National critiques also worked to further solidify conceptions of borders and highlight an important development with regards to the role of marriage and the making of national cohesion and belonging. In the first part national critiques largely stemmed from American, rather than French, public discourse, and primarily rested on the juxtaposition of American republican ideals with European monarchy and aristocracy. For those criticizing the marriages, the problem was not so much that American women married French men, but simply that these French men were members of a titled nobility. Such unions were, therefore, contradictory to the American national project distinguished by its "classless society." In the context of the twentieth-century wartime marriages, public reaction was even far more rooted in national identity and nationalism, as critics largely drew on images of "the girl back home" abandoned by the American soldier who took a French wife and on the notions that national differences in cultures and customs meant that most transnational, wartime unions were destined to fail. Here, unlike in the first part, *ideal* marriages were, therefore, perceived of as culturally homogenous, *national* marriages, and national apparatuses used this notion of an ideal marriage as a way to reconstruct and redefine the nation and national belonging in the twentieth century.

It is without a doubt that there are numerous historical and methodological questions that this book has left unanswered. Spaces of transnational marriage for example provide an especially important avenue for future research. In an effort to expand the definition of marriage to include preceding courtship and coupling practices, this work has largely focused on the spaces leading up to marriage as well as questions of marriage motivation; however, the resulting transnational spaces and communities that were produced *by* these marriages also provokes interesting methodological questions. While the topic of transnational families as a subject of inquiry in both transnational and migration studies has continued to progress over the last decades, the concept is often been characterized by couples and families *separated* by national borders and stretched across long distances by migration processes.[2] Yet, when marriages, such as those examined here, transcend national boundaries, each resulted in the creation of its own third, transnational space within the intimate space of the family or familial household. While this intimate familial space can be characterized as a negotiated space, it is not necessarily one that can be reduced to its component parts. Therefore, further spatial analysis into the post-marriage households of transnational-marriage participants' families provide great analytical value for further research. Potential questions in a historical analysis might include the following: What are the cultural and emotional dimensions of these post-marriage, transnational-familial spaces? How did practices of childrearing differ in these spaces compared to national ones?[3] How did childrearing practices take place in consideration of the variable dimensions of language, education, social practices, symbols, and rituals? Could Barbara H. Rosenwein's concept of "emotional communities" be further applied and broadened to include transnational families and the transcultural dimensions within them? Finally, the resulting post-marriage social networks are also intriguing, and the extent to which marriages produce new transnational communities rather than just emerge from them could also be potentially fruitful.

The question of language within transnational coupling processes and spaces of transnationality also provokes interesting questions about emotions history. While titled marriage participants were raised with private language tutors and in well-traveled families, wartime-marriage participants by contrast often struggled to communicate with those with whom they coupled. For the historian, these language barriers highlight important emotional and cultural elements of transnational spaces in the twentieth century. Here, when cultural encounter that produced marriage went beyond a shared language, it came to serve as clear marker of difference. In this way, language (and language difference) became an important element in cultural othering. While in other national/migration histories, linguistic variations clearly marked "the outsider," in this case, they were perceived in positive ways that even facilitated cross-cultural coupling. Further, the assumption of historians of emotions is that culture and language create the dimensions in which emotions are understood. However, in the forming of translinguistic intimate relationships, emotions superseded language. This raises important methodological questions about the theory of emotions history, the ways in which emotions history is intertwined with cultural history and the role of language in emotional constructions. The emotional processes linked to language and sound (or representations of language and sound), therefore, present a potentially fruitful avenue for future research as well. This work has also only begun to explore some of these larger methodological questions regarding the theories of emotions and their applicability and usefulness to transnational perspectives of history writing, and the relationship between culture and emotions in transnational spaces requires further exploration.

Finally, while this work has already placed transnational-marriage patterns within the broader global shift from nineteenth-century nation-making to twentieth-century hyper-nationalism, the following question also seems pertinent: How would the role of coupling and marriage in and out of the framework of the national project change if applied to broader shifts of transnational interconnectedness as global currents continued to evolve into the twenty-first century? What other transnational-marriage patterns could provide a window into that analysis? In what ways did conceptions of the borders shift in the context of not only political, economic, and diplomatic integration, but also in the context of information and communication advancements?

Another notable marriage pattern that provides an interesting opening for continued research during this later period is that of university students on international exchange programs between France and the United States. Here, students created their own transnational social networks in university spaces, and complex extensions of those networks likely also provided the stage for transnational marriages. In this way, international education came to serve as another form of global class formation and created a different kind of elite class in various ways. Yet, at the same time, even though these later twentieth-century university social spaces took on a very different form then they had during the period of wartime hyper-nationalism, they continued to exist in opposition to national spaces as students still faced similar national immigration and administrative hurdles in contracting marriages comparable to those during wartime.

Finally, cultural othering as an emotional process and shifting cultural relations between France and the United States during the second half of the twentieth century also provoke interesting questions regarding the temporality of cultural infatuation and the ways in which cultural imagery continued to create emotional responses. Throughout both the nineteenth and twentieth century, there were many sites in which this infatuation was manifested. In the nineteenth century, it was in society papers, travel literature, elite costume balls, and social events. During the twentieth century, these sites that perpetuated cultural stereotypes shifted to music, film, and advertisements. Yet, what is interesting is that the processes of sexual and romanticized othering shifted from French women and was transcribed onto French men, as notions of the "French lover" permeated the American imagination. One 1961 newspaper article in the *Chicago Tribune*, for example, explained that the "Paris of song and story" had intrigued "American women in search of romance" for years and asks if "French Men [were really] THAT Perfect."[4] In what ways is this fluidity of gendered national stereotypes best contextualized within the broader setting of changing emotional standards as they relate to marriage and courtship practices and rituals into the second half of the twentieth century? I hypothesize that the overarching argument would likely remain that same: That the story of these marriages, which transcend national, cultural, and linguistic boundaries, is most certainly a *love story*; however, it is not only a love story limited to the connections between individuals, but also one characterized by a cultural love affair between French and American societies.

Notes

1 Anderson, *Imagined Communities*, 7.
2 Christiane Harzig, Dirk Hoerder, and Donna R. Gabaccia, *What Is Migration History?* (Cambridge, UK; Malden, MA: Polity, 2009), 124–26; I Levin, "Living Apart Together: A New Family Form," *Current Sociology* 52 (2004): 223–40.
3 Gabrielle Varro, *La femme transplantée: une étude du mariage franco-américain en France et le bilinguisme des enfants* (Presses Univ. Septentrion, 1984) addresses this question in a sociological examination of Franco-American families during the 1980s.
4 "Are French Men THAT Perfect?," *Chicago Tribune*, January 15, 1961.

BIBLIOGRAPHY

Archival Sources

New York Public Library, New York, United States
Annie J. Bradley Diary
Laura J. Libbey Diary
    Vol 3 Visit to Europe.
Levi P Morton Papers Series
    Series VII, Scrapbook Vol 4A, 4B, 5, and 6
    Box 1, Folder "Correspondence 1881 July"
    Box 1, Folder "Correspondence 1882 January"
    Box 2, Folder "Correspondence 1883 January–1888 December"
    Box 2, Folder "Correspondence 1884 May"
    Box 7 Social Correspondence, Folder "Accepts and Regrets, Ball 1884 April 24"
    Box 8, Folder Political Papers, Minister to France, Speeches of Previous Ministers
    Box 8, Letterbook Vol. 2, March 11, 1884–April 25, 1885

New York Genealogical and Biographical Society Collection

Massachusetts Historical Society, Boston, Massachusetts, United States
Annie Fields Papers

Library of Congress, Washington, DC, United States
Prints and Photographs Division

Temple University Library, Special Collections Research Center, Philadelphia, Pennsylvania, United States
George F. Tyler Poster Collection

Bibliothèque nationale de France, Paris, France
Département Estampes et Photographie
    RESERVE FT 4-QB-370

Paris Musées / Musée Carnavalet – Histoire de Paris
Département Estampes et Photographie
    K4520

Bibliothèque de l'Institut National d'Histoire de l'Art
Département Estampes et Photographie
    NUM OC 52

Government Documents

Hill, Joseph A. *Marriage and Divorce: 1887–1906*. Edited by The United States Department of Commerce and Labor Bureau of the Census. Washington: Government Printing Office, 1908.
Kellogg, Albert B. *Marriage of Soldiers*. Washington, DC: Historical Section, Army War College, 1942.
S. N. D. North, Director. *Special Reports: Marriage and Divorce, 1867–1906, Part One: Summary, Laws, Foreign Statistics*. Washington: U.S. Government Printing Office, 1909.
U.S. Bureau of the Census, Current Population Reports. "Marriage, Divorce, and Remarriage in the 1990's." U.S. Government Printing Office, Washington DC, 1992.
Walker, George. *Venereal Disease in the American Expeditionary Forces*. Baltimore: Medical Standard Book Co., 1922.

Newspapers/Magazines

American Sociology Review, 1940
Appleton's Journal: A Magazine of General Literature, 1875
Boston Post, 1884
Chicago Tribune, 1882, 1961, 1999
Figaro, 1881
Gaulois, 1883, 1895
Independent, 99, 1919
La Patrie, 1882
Life Magazine, 1945
Literary Digest, 1917, 1919, 1920
Milwaukee Journal Sentinel, 1929
Morning News, 1884
The New York Times, 1895, 1899, 1903, 1907, 1908, 1913, 1919, 1921, 1925
New-York Tribune, 1882
New York Daily Tribune: War Ships Sunk in Samoa, Library of Tribune Extras, 1889
Omaha World Herald, 1909
Paris Comet: Anglo-American Fortnightly Magazine, 1927
Paris Harold, 1939
Revue de Paris, 1935
San Francisco Call, 1905
The Saturday Evening Post, 1939
Stars and Stripes, 1919, 1944
The American Journal of International Law, 1907
The Atlanta Journal-Constitution, 1919
The North American Review, 1890
The Pittsburgh Press, 1900, 1901, 1915
Town Topics, Journal of Society, 1887, 1889, 1891, 1916, 1919
Truth, 1884

Published Primary Sources

Anonymous. *A Woman in Berlin*. London: Virago, 2011.
Brieux, Eugène. *Les Américains chez nous: comédie en trois actes*. La Petite Illustration Théâtrale, 1920.

Browne, George. *An American Soldier in World War I*. Edited by David L. Snead. Lincoln, NE: University of Nebraska Press, 2006.

Canudo, Ricciotto. *Mon âme pourpre roman de la forêt et du fleuve*. Paris: la Renaissance du livre, 1918.

Castellane, Boni. *Comment j'ai découvert l'Amérique; mémoires*. Paris: G. Crès et cie, 1924.

———. *How I Discovered America*. New York: Alfred A. Knopf, 1924.

Cauwes, Albert. *Des rapports du mariage avec la nationalité*. Paris: L. Larose & Farcel, 1901.

Chambliss, William H, and Foster, Laura E. *Chambliss Diary, Or, Society as It Really Is*. New York: Chambliss & Co., 1895.

Churchill, Winston. A Traveller in War-Time: With an Essay on the American Contribution and the Democratic Idea. New York: The Macmillan Company, 1918.

Claretie, Jules. *L'Américaine*. Chicago: W. B. Conkey, 1893.

Conway, John Joseph. *Footprints of Famous Americans in Paris*. London; New York: John Lane; John Lane Co., 1912.

Croffut, W. A. *The Vanderbilts and the Story of Their Fortune*. London: Belford, Clarke, 1886.

Darglos, Bernard. *Bernard Dargols, un GI français à Omaha Beach*, edited by Caroline Jolivet. Rennes: OUEST FRANCE, 2012.

Davis, Richard Harding. *About Paris*. New York: Harper & Brothers, 1895. http://hdl.handle.net/2027/uc2.ark:/13960/t49p36786.

Du Saussay, Victorien. *La traite des blancs: mariages franco-américains: roman de passion*. Paris: Librairie des publications modernes, 1900.

Fitzgerald, F. Scott. "Babylon Revisited." *Best Short Stories of ... and the* Yearbook of the American Short Story. Boston: Houghton Mifflin Co., 1931, 122–42.

Grant, Madison, and Henry Fairfield Osborn. *The Passing of the Great Race: Or, the Basis of European History*. New York: Charles Scribner's Sons, 1916.

Hegermann-Lindencrone, L. de. *In the Courts of Memory, 1858–1875: From* Contemporary Letters. New York: Harper & Bros., 1912.

Hermant, Abel. *Les transatlantiques*. Paris: Michel, 1927.

Houghton, Walter Raleigh. *American Etiquette and Rules of Politeness*. Chicago: Rand, McNally, 1882.

Hovsepian, Aramais Akob. *Your Son and Mine*. New York: Duell, Sloan, and Pearce, 1950.

Huber, Michel. *La population de la France pendant la guerre, avec un appendice sur Les revenus avant et après la guerre*. Paris; New Haven: Les Presses universitaires de France; Yale University Press, 1931.

Irving, Washington, William P. Trent, George S. Hellman, and Mass. Bibliophile Society. *The Journals of Washington Irving*. Vol 3. Boston: Bibliophile Society, 1919.

James, Henry. *The American*. London: Macmillan and Co., 1878.

Jeune, Susan Mary Elizabeth Stewart-Mackenzie. *Memories of Fifty Years*. London: E. Arnold, 1909.

Josephy, Helen, and Mary Margaret McBride. *Paris Is a Woman's Town*. New York: Coward-McCann Inc., 1929.

Köpp, Gabriele. *Warum war ich bloß ein Mädchen? das Trauma einer Flucht 1945*. München: Knaur-Taschenbuch-Verl., 2012.

Langille, Leslie. *Men of the Rainbow*. Chicago: The O'Sullivan Publishing House, 1933.

Lawson, Liz. *Memoirs of a French War Bride, 1940–1950*. Santa Cruz, CA: [self-published], 1998.

McAllister, Ward, *Society as I Have Found It*. New York: Cassell Pub. Co., 1890.

Murray, Billy, and Ed Smalle. *What Has Become of Hinky Dinky Parlay Voo* (audio recording), 1924.

Myers, Gustavus. *History of the Great American Fortunes*. Vol. 3. New York: The Modern Library, 1909.

Niles, John Jacob, and Douglas Stuart Moore. *The Songs My Mother Never Taught Me.* New York: Macaulay, 1929.
Oral history interviews collected, edited, and published in Kaiser, Hilary. *French War Brides in America: An Oral History.* Westport, CT: Praeger Publishers, 2008 and *WWII Voices: American GIs and the French Women Who Married Them.* Scottsdale, AZ: Summertime Publications Inc., 2011.
Paradis, Don V. *The World War I Memoirs of Don V. Paradis, Gunnery Sergeant, USMC,* edited by Peter F. Owen (self-published: Lt. Col. Peter F. Owen), 2010.
Paris at Night: Sketches and Mysteries of Paris High Life and Demi-Monde. Nocturnal Amusements: How to Know Them! How to Enjoy Them!! How to Appreciate Them!!!. Boston: Boston and Paris Publ. Co., 1875. http://hdl.handle.net/2027/ucw.ark:/13960/t2j687m1v.
Paris-Guide. 2 / par les principaux écrivains et artistes de la France. Vol. 2. Paris: Librairie Internationale, 1867. http://gallica.bnf.fr/ark:/12148/bpt6k200160r.
Peckham, Howard H., and Shirley A. Snyder. *Letters from Fighting Hoosiers.* Bloomington: Indiana War History Commission, 1948.
Petesch, Angela. *War through the Hole of a Donut.* Madison, WI: Hunter Halverson Press, 2006.
Petit, Jacques. *Au coeur de la bataille de Normandie: souvenirs d'un adolescent de Saint-Lô à Avranches: été 1944.* Louviers: Ed. Ysec, 2004.
Pulitzer, Ralph. *New York Society on Parade.* New York; London: Harper & Bros., 1910.
Ricou-Allunis, Jeannine. *Memoir of a French War Bride.* Bloomington, IN: Author House, 2004.
Sacco, Jack, and Mazal Holocaust Collection. *Where the Birds Never Sing: The True Story of the 92nd Signal Battalion and the Liberation of Dachau.* New York: Regan Books, 2003.
Saffell, William Thomas Roberts. *The Bonaparte-Patterson Marriage in 1803, and the Secret Correspondence on the Subject Never Before Made Public.* Philadelphia: The Proprietor, 1873.
Seeger, Alan. *Letters and Diary of Alan Seeger.* New York: Charles Scribner, 1917.
Social Register Association (U.S.). *Social Register, New York,* 1892.
Tilly, Comte Alexandre de. *Mémoires du comte Alexandre de Tilly, pour servir à l'histoire des moeurs de la fin du 18me siècle.* Paris: Chez les Marchands de Nouveautés, 1828.
Titled Americans. a List of American Ladies Who Have Married Foreigners of Rank. New York: Street & Smith, 1890.
Van Dyke, Henry. "America for Me." In *Poems of Henry Van Dyke.* New York, Charles Scribner's Sons, 1911. http://www.potw.org/archive/potw308.html.
Wharton, Edith. *A Backward Glance.* New York; London: D. Appleton-Century Co., 1934.
———. *French Ways and Their Meaning.* New York; London: D. Appleton and Company, 1919.
———. *The Custom of the Country,* New York: Charles Scribner's Sons, 1913.

Secondary Sources

Adam, Thomas. *Buying Respectability: Philanthropy and Urban Society in Transnational Perspective, 1840s to 1930s.* Bloomington: Indiana University Press, 2009.
Almond, Gabriel A. *Plutocracy and Politics in New York City.* Boulder, CO: Westview Press, 1998.
Anderson, Benedict. *Imagined Communities: Reflections on the Origin and Spread of Nationalism.* London; New York: Verso, 2006.
Auden, W. H. *The Age of Anxiety: A Baroque Eclogue.* Princeton University Press, 2011.
Bailey, William G. *Americans in Paris, 1900–1930: A Selected, Annotated Bibliography.* New York: Greenwood Press, 1989.

Beauvoir, Simone de, and H. M. Parshley. *The Second Sex*. New York: Alfred A. Knopf, 1993.
Beckert, Sven. "Die Kultur Des Kapitals: Bürgerliche Kultur in New York Und Hamburg Im 19. Jahrhundert." In *Vorträge Aus Dem Warburg-Haus*, edited by Warburg-Haus, 4: 143–75. Berlin: Akademie, 2000.
Beckert, Sven, and Julia B Rosenbaum. *The American Bourgeoisie: Distinction and Identity in the Nineteenth Century*. New York: Palgrave Macmillan, 2010.
Beevor, Antony, and Artemis Cooper. *Paris after the Liberation, 1944–1949*. New York: Doubleday, 1994.
Bell, Millicent. "Edith Wharton in France." In *Wretched Exotic: Essays on Edith Wharton in Europe*, edited by Katherine Joslin and Alan Price. New York: P. Lang, 1993.
Bhabha, Homi K. *The Location of Culture*. London; New York: Routledge, 1994.
Blower, Brooke Lindy. *Becoming Americans in Paris Transatlantic Politics and Culture between the World Wars*. Oxford and New York: Oxford University Press, 2011.
Bologne, Jean Claude. *Histoire du couple*. Paris: Perrin, 2016.
Bourdieu, Pierre. *Distinction: A Social Critique of the Judgment of Taste*. London: Routledge & Kegan Paul, 1986.
———. *The Field of Cultural Production*. Edited by Randal Johnson. 1st edition. New York: Columbia University Press, 1993.
Brandon, Ruth. *The Dollar Princesses*. London: Weidenfeld and Nicolson, 1980.
Bredbenner, Candice Lewis. *A Nationality of Her Own Women, Marriage, and the Law of Citizenship*. Berkeley: University of California Press, 1998.
Brons, Lajos L. "Othering, an Analysis." *Transscience* 6, no. 1 (2015): 69–90.
Camiscioli, Elisa. *Reproducing the French Race: Immigration, Intimacy, and Embodiment in the Early Twentieth Century*. Durham: Duke University Press, 2009.
Canaday, Margot. *The Straight State: Sexuality and Citizenship in Twentieth-Century America*. Princeton, NJ: Princeton University Press, 2009.
Charsley, Katharine. *Transnational Marriage: New Perspectives from Europe and Beyond*. New York: Routledge, 2012.
Coffman, Edward M. *The War to End All Wars: The American Military Experience in World War I*. Lexington: The University Press of Kentucky, 2014.
"Concluding Roundtable." *International Conference on Intermarriage and Mixedness: New Research Challenges on Intermarriage and Mixedness in Europe and Beyond*. Sorbonne, Maison de la Recherche, Paris, November, 2015.
Coontz, Stephanie. *Marriage, a History: From Obedience to Intimacy or How Love Conquered Marriage*. New York: Viking, 2005.
Cooper, Dana. *Informal Ambassadors: American Women, Transatlantic Marriages, and Anglo-American Relations, 1865–1945*. Kent State University Press, 2014.
Corbin, Alain, and Pascal Ory. *Une histoire des sens*. Paris: Robert Laffont, 2016.
Costigliola, Frank. "'Mixed Up' and 'Contact': Culture and Emotion among the Allies in the Second World War." *The International History Review* 20, no. 4 (December 1998): 791–805.
Cott, Nancy F. *Public Vows: A History of Marriage and the Nation*. Cambridge, MA: Harvard University Press, 2000.
Delbaere-Garant, Jeanne. "Paris." In *Henry James: The Vision of France*. Liège: Presses universitaires de Liège, 1970. http://books.openedition.org/pulg/906
Demartini, Anne-Emmanuelle, Anne-Claude Ambroise-Rendu, Hélène Eck, and Nicole Edelman. *Émotions contemporaines: XIXe–XXIe siècles*. Paris: A. Colin, 2014.

D'Emilio, John, and Estelle Freedman. *Intimate Matters: A History of Sexuality in America*. 1st ed. New York: Harper & Row, 1988.

Eliot, Elizabeth. *Heiresses and Coronets*. New York: McDowell, 1959.

Evans, Martin Marix. *American Voices of World War I: Primary Source Documents, 1917–1920*. London and New York: Routledge, 2014.

Forsdick, Charles. "Travelling Concepts: Postcolonial Approaches to Exoticism and Diversity." In *Travel in Twentieth-Century French and Francophone Cultures: "The Persistence of Diversity."* Oxford: Oxford University Press, 2010.

Foucrier, Annick. *Le rêve californien: migrants français sur la côte Pacifique, XVIIIe–XXe siècles*. Paris: Belin, 1999.

Fox, Stephen Russell. *The Ocean Railway: Isambard Kingdom Brunel, Samuel Cunard, and the Revolutionary World of the Great Atlantic Steamships*. London: Harper Perennial, 2004.

Fussell, Paul. *The Great War and Modern Memory*. New York: Oxford University Press, 1975.

Gayatri Chakravorty Spivak. "Can the Subaltern Speak?" In *Marxism and the Interpretation of Culture*, edited by Cary Nelson and Lawrence Grossberg, 271–313. Urbana: University of Illinois Press, 1988.

Gillis, John R. *For Better, for Worse: British Marriages, 1600 to the Present*. New York: Oxford University Press, 1985.

Grayzel, Susan R. *Women's Identities at War: Gender, Motherhood, and Politics in Britain and France during the First World War*. Chapel Hill, NC: University of North Carolina Press, 1999.

Green, Nancy L. *The Other Americans in Paris: Businessmen, Countesses, Wayward Youth, 1880–1941*. Chicago: The University of Chicago Press, 2014.

Hallas, James H. *Doughboy War: The American Expeditionary Force in World War I*. Boulder, CO: Lynne Rienner Publishers, 2000.

Harzig, Christiane, Dirk Hoerder, and Donna R Gabaccia. *What Is Migration History?* Cambridge, UK and Malden, MA: Polity, 2009.

Hegel, Georg Wilhelm Friedrich, Hans-Friedrich Wessels, and Heinrich Clairmont. *Phänomenologie des Geistes*. Hamburg: F. Meiner Verlag, 1988.

Higonnet, Patrice L. R. *Paris: Capital of the World*. Cambridge, MA: Harvard University Press, 2002.

Hillerin, Laure. *Pour le plaisir & pour le pire: la vie tumultueuse d'Anna Gould et Boni de Castellane*. Paris: Flammarion, 2019.

"History of Emotions | Max Planck Institute for Human Development." Accessed November 30, 2016. https://www.mpib-berlin.mpg.de/en/research/history-of-emotions

Homberger, Eric. *Mrs. Astor's New York: Money and Social Power in a Gilded Age*. New Haven: Yale University Press, 2002.

I-Mien, Tsiang. "The Question of Expatriation in America Prior to 1907." In *The Johns Hopkins Univerity Studies in Historical and Political Science*. LX 3. Baltimore: The Johns Hopkins Press, 1942.

Jackson, Peter, Phil Crang, and Claire Dwyer. *Transnational Spaces*. London and New York: Routledge, 2004.

Jaher, Frederic Cople. "Style and Status: High Society in Late-Nineteenth-Century New York." In *The Rich, the Wellborn, and the Powerful: Elites and Upper Classes in History*, edited by Frederic Cople Jaher, 258–84. Secaucus, NJ: Citadel Press, 1975.

Judith Surkis. "Sex, Sovereignty, and Transnational Intimacies." *The American Historical Review* 115, no. 4 (October 2010): 1089–96.

Kaiser, Hilary. *French War Brides in America: An Oral History*. Westport, CT: Praeger Publishers, 2008.

———. *WWII Voices: American GIs and the French Women Who Married Them.* Scottsdale: Summertime Publications Inc, 2011.
Kehoe, Elisabeth. *The Titled Americans: Three American Sisters and the British Aristocratic World into Which They Married.* New York: Atlantic Monthly Press, 2004.
Kershaw, Ian. *To Hell and Back: Europe, 1914–1949.* London: Penguin Books, 2016.
Kim, Bok-Lim C. "Asian Wives of U.S. Servicemen: Women in Shadows." *Amerasia Journal* 4, no. 1 (1977): 91–115.
Leach, Edmund. "The Social Anthropology of Marriage and Mating." In *Mating and Marriage*, edited by Vernon Reynolds and John Kellett. Oxford and New York: Oxford University Press, 1991.
Lee, Hermione. *Edith Wharton.* New York: Alfred A. Knopf, 2007.
Levenstein, Harvey A. *Seductive Journey: American Tourists in France from Jefferson to the Jazz Age.* Chicago: University of Chicago Press, 1998.
———. *We'll Always Have Paris American Tourists in France Since 1930.* Chicago: University of Chicago Press, 2004.
Levin, I. "Living Apart Together: A New Family Form." *Current Sociology* 52 (2004): 223–40.
Lilly, J. Robert. *La face cachée des GIs: les viols commis par des soldats américains en France, en Angleterre et en Allemagne pendant la Seconde Guerre mondiale, 1942–1945.* Paris: Payot, 2003.
Mac Coll, Gail, and Carol Wallace. *To Marry an English Lord.* New York: Workman Pub., 1989.
Matt, Susan J, and Peter N Stearns. *Doing Emotions History.* Urbana: University of Illinois Press, 2014.
Mayer, Arno. *La persistance de l'ancien régime: L'Europe de 1848 a la grande guerre.* Paris: Flammarion, 1983.
McNeil, Frances. *Sisters of Fortune.* Sutton: Severn House, 2007.
Meigs, Mark. *Optimism at Armageddon: Voices of American Participants in the First World War.* Washington Square, NY: New York University Press, 1997.
Mjagkij, Nina. "YMCA." In *The United States in the First World War: An Encyclopedia*, edited by Paul L. Miles and Anne Cipriano Venzon, 811. Taylor & Francis, 1999.
Montgomery, Maureen E. *"Gilded Prostitution": Status, Money, and Transatlantic Marriages, 1870–1914.* London; New York: Routledge, 1989.
———. "'Natural Distinction': The American Bourgeois Search for Distinctive Signs in Europe." In *The American Bourgeoisie: Distinction and Identity in the Nineteenth Century*, edited by Sven Beckert and Julia B. Rosenbaum, 27–44. New York: Palgrave Macmillan, 2010.
Morris, Lloyd R. *Incredible New York; High Life and Low Life of the Last Hundred Years.* New York: Random House, 1951.
Moya, Jose. "The Historical Emergence and Massification of International Families in Europe and Its Diaspora." In *Transregional and Transnational Families in Europe and Beyond: Experiences Since the Middle Ages*, edited by Christopher H. Johnson, David Warren Sabean, Simon Teuscher, and Francesca Trivellato. New York: Berghahn Books, 2011.
Muñoz-Perez, Francisco. "Mariages d'étrangers et mariages mixtes en France: Évolution depuis la Première Guerre." *Population* (French Edition) 39, no. 3 (1984): 427–62.
Neyrand, Gérard, Marine M'Sili, France, and Direction de la population et des migrations. *Mariages mixtes et nationalité française: les Français par mariage et leurs conjoints.* Paris: Ed. l'Harmattan, 1995.
Nicholson, Virginia. *Singled Out: How Two Million Women Survived without Men after the First World War.* London: Viking, 2007.

Nicolosi, Ann Marie. "'We Do Not Want Our Girls to Marry Foreigners': Gender, Race, and American Citizenship." *NWSA Journal* 13, no. 3 Gender and Social Policy: Local to Global (2001): 1–21.

Nussbaum, Martha Craven. *Upheavals of Thought: The Intelligence of Emotions.* Cambridge and New York: Cambridge University Press, 2001.

Palmer, R. R., and American Council of Learned Societies. *The Age of the Democratic Revolution a Political History of Europe and America, 1760–1800.* Princeton, NJ: Princeton University Press, 1959.

Pernau, Margrit. "Space and Emotion: Building to Feel." *History Compass* 12, no. 7 (2014): 541–49.

Phillips, Roderick. *Untying the Knot: A Short History of Divorce.* Cambridge: Cambridge University Press, 1991.

Puy de Clinchamps, Philippe du, and Patrice du Puy de Clinchamps. *La noblesse.* Paris: L'Intermédiaire des chercheurs et curieux, 1996.

Reddy, William M. *The Making of Romantic Love: Longing and Sexuality in Europe, South Asia, and Japan, 900–1200 CE.* Chicago: University of Chicago Press, 2012.

———. *The Navigation of Feeling a Framework for the History of Emotions.* Cambridge, UK and New York: Cambridge University Press, 2001.

Rennella, Mark. *The Boston Cosmopolitans: International Travel and American Arts and Letters.* 1st ed. New York: Palgrave Macmillan, 2008.

Rieker, Yvonne. "Love Crossing Borders: Changing Patterns of Courtship and Gender Relations among Italian Migrants in Germany." In *Intimacy and Italian Migration: Gender and Domestic Lives in a Mobile World*, 113–23. New York: Fordham University Press, 2011.

Roberts, Mary Louise. *What Soldiers Do: Sex and the American GI in World War II France.* Chicago: University of Chicago Press, 2013.

Rodgers, Daniel. *Atlantic Crossings: Social Politics in a Progressive Age.* Cambridge, MA: Belknap Press of Harvard University Press, 1998.

Rosenwein, Barbara H, Maureen C Miller, and Edward Wheatley. *Emotions, Communities, and Difference in Medieval Europe: Essays in Honor of Barbara H. Rosenwein.* London: Routledge, 2017.

Russailh, Albert Benard de, and Sylvie Bostsarron Chevalley. *Journal de voyage en Californie à l'époque de la ruée vers l'or: 1850–1852.* Paris: A. Montaigne, 1980.

Said, Edward W. *Orientalism.* New York: Vintage Books, 1979.

Saint-Simon, F. de, E. de Seréville, and E. de Seréville. *Dictionnaire de La Noblesse Française: Supplément.* Paris: Éditions Contrepoint, 1977.

Sardon, Jean-Paul. "L'évolution Du Divorce En France." *Population* 51, no. 3 (1996): 717–49.

Schutte, Kimberly. *Women, Rank, and Marriage in the British Aristocracy, 1485–2000: An Open Elite?* Basingstoke: Palgrave Macmillan, 2014.

Seidel Menchi, Silvana, Emlyn Eisenach, and Charles Donahue. *Marriage in Europe, 1400–1800.* Toronto: University of Toronto Press, 2016.

Seigel, Micol. "Beyond Compare: Comparative Method after the Transnational Turn." *Radical History Review* 2005, no. 91 (December 21, 2005): 62–90.

Shaw, Alison, and Katharine Charsely. "Rishtas: Adding Emotion to Strategy in Understanding British Pakistani Transnational Marriages." *Global Networks* 6, no. 4 (2006): 405–21.

Sheehan, James J. "Reviewed Work: The Persistence of the Old Régime. Europe to the Great War by Arno J. Mayer." *Social History* 8, no. 1 (January 1983): 111–12.

Shukert, Elfrieda Berthiaume, and Barbara Smith Scibetta. *War Brides of World War II*. Novato, CA: Presidio Press, 1988.
Sims, Jessica Mai, and Runnymede Trust. *Mixed Heritage: Identity, Policy and Practice*. London: Runnymede Trust, 2007.
Spicer, Paul. *The Temptress: The Scandalous Life of Alice De Janze and the Mysterious Death of Lord Erroll*. New York: St. Martin's Griffin, 2011.
Spiro, Jonathan Peter. *Defending the Master Race: Conservation, Eugenics, and the Legacy of Madison Grant*. Burlington, VT; Hanover, NH: University of Vermont Press; Published by University Press of New England, 2009.
Spivak, Gayatri Chakravorty. "The Rani of Sirmur: An Essay in Reading the Archives." *History and Theory* 24, no. 3 (1985): 247–72.
Strääf, Maria. "In between Cultures: Franco-American Encounters in the Work of Edith Wharton." Linköping University, Department of Culture and Communication, 2008.
Tannenbaum, Edward R. "Reviewed Work: The Persistence of the Old Régime. Europe to the Great War by Arno J. Mayer." *The American Historical Review* 87, no. 2 (April 1982): 439–40.
Texier, Alain. *Qu'est-ce que la noblesse?* Paris: Le Grand livre du mois, 2000.
Thompson, E. P. *La Formation de la classe ouvrière anglaise*. Paris: Gallimard: Le Seuil, 1988.
Torpey, John. *The Invention of the Passport: Surveillance, Citizenship, and the State*. Cambridge, UK and New York: Cambridge University Press, 2000.
Toyota, Mika. "Editorial Introduction: International Marriage, Rights and the State in East and Southeast Asia." *Citizenship Studies* 12, no. 1 (2008): 1–7.
Tulard, Jean. *Napoléon et la noblesse d'Empire: avec la liste des membres de la noblesse impériale, 1808–1815*. Paris: Tallandier, 2003.
Tyrrell, Ian. *Transnational Nation: United States History in Global Perspective since 1789*. Basingstoke: Palgrave Macmillan, 2007.
Valette, Régis. *Catalogue de la noblesse française contemporaine*. Paris: R. Laffont, 1977.
Varro, Gabrielle. *La femme transplantée: une étude du mariage franco-américain en France et le bilinguisme des enfants*. Presses Univ. Septentrion, 1984.
Veblen, Thorstein. *The Theory of the Leisure Class. 1899*. Repr. ed., New York: A. M. Kelley, Bookseller, 1965.
Virden, Jenel. *Good-Bye, Piccadilly: British War Brides in America*. Urbana: University of Illinois Press, 1996.
Werner, Anja. *The Transatlantic World of Higher Education: Americans at German Universities, 1776–1914*. European Studies in American History, Vol. 4. New York: Berghahn Books, 2013.
Williams, Lucy. *Global Marriage: Cross-Border Marriage Migration in Global Context*. Basingstoke; New York: Palgrave Macmillan, 2010.
Williams, Teresa K. "Marriage between Japanese Women and US. Servicemen since World War II." *Amerasia Journal* 17, no. 1 (1991): 135–54.
Wray, Helena. *Regulating Marriage Migration into the UK: A Stranger in the Home*. Farnham, Surrey, England; Burlington, VT: Ashgate, 2011.
Yang, Wen-Shan, and Melody Chia-Wen Lu. *Asian Cross-Border Marriage Migration: Demographic Patterns and Social Issues*. Amsterdam: Amsterdam University Press, 2010.
Zeiger, Susan. *Entangling Alliances: Foreign War Brides and American Soldiers in the Twentieth Century*. New York: New York University Press, 2010.

INDEX

Adam, Juliette 58
Adam, Thomas 19, 26n10
Adams, John 93
Age of Revolutions 7
Alabama 127
American Congress 41
American Expatriation Act 40
American Expeditionary Forces (AEF) 13, 84, 86, 89, 94, 96, 104, 118, 119, 126, 131
American Red Cross 85, 89, 117, 121–23, 133, 134
ancien régime 30, 69
Anderson, Benedict 138n72, 143, 146n1
Anthropologist 1
Aristocracy 12, 20, 21, 43, 44, 58, 60, 72, 93, 135, 137, 143
Armstrong, Louis 106
Asian Cross-Border Marriage Migration: Demographic Patterns and Social Issues 4
Atlanta Constitution 128, 129, 135, 136
Atlantic 2, 12, 28, 29, 31, 36, 43, 55, 56, 58, 86–88, 94, 141
Auden, Wystan Hugh 96, 114n5
  The Age of Anxiety 96

Baily, William G. 71
Beckert, Sven 29, 47n11, 47n12
Bell, Millicent 55
Bethel, W.A. 131
Bhabha, Homi K. 15n15
Bologne, Jean Claude
  Histoire du couple 14n1
Bonaparte, Jérôme 17
Bonnet, Henri 78, 136

Bradley, Annie 30
Brandon, Ruth 25n8

Cameron, Catherine 68
Castellane, Boni de 21, 23, 26n17, 37, 39– 41, 43, 58, 61, 64, 65, 67–69
Catholic Church 8, 70
Catholicism 69
Cauwes, Albert 41, 49n66, 49n67, 50n68
Central Music Hall 28
Chambliss, William H. 18, 20, 25n5, 44
Charsley, Katharine 4, 15n13, 15n32, 26n31
  British sociologist 4
  Transnational Marriage: New Perspectives from Europe and Beyond 4
Chateau de Petit Val 29
Churchill, Winston 85, 89, 112n11, 113n28
Claretie, Jules 69, 75n66
Clinton, Cornelia 17
Clinton, George 17
Coffman, Edward M. 114n66
Contractualization 3, 4
Coontz, Stephanie 1, 6–9, 14n2, 14n4, 15n16, 15n19, 15n22, 15n26, 15n30, 68, 69, 75n62, 75n68
  Marriage, a History: From Obedience to Intimacy or How Love Conquered Marriage 1
Corrigan, Archbishop Michael 41
Costigliola, Frank 96, 114n53

Cott, Nancy 3, 14n9, 134, 138n70
  Public Vows: A History of Marriage and the Nation 3
Courtship rituals 1, 7, 117, 125
Cross-border marriage 3, 4, 24, 40, 56, 121
Cultural history 4, 24, 120, 145
Cultural infatuation 24, 53, 56, 59, 61, 91, 124, 127, 143, 146

Darglos, Bernard 106, 113n49, 115n85
Darrow, Margaret 8
Davis, Jennette 107, 115n88, 121, 126, 128
Davis, Richard Harding 23, 26n25, 44, 46
Department of Civil Relief 134
Division of labor 6
Dixon, Jane 114n52, 135, 136, 138n44, 139n76, 139n82
Duke of Marlborough 22
Du Saussay, Victorien
  La traite des blancs: mariages franco-américains\roman de passion 25n6

Economic liberalism 31
Egalitarian 7
Eliot, Elizabeth 25n2, 47n25, 32, 67, 74n42, 74n58
Ellinston, John R. 80n5, 87, 88, 112n12, 112n23, 113n46
European nobility 39

Fields, Annie 30, 47n17, 47n18
Fitzgerald, Ella 106
Foster, Laura E. 25n5
France
  "certain political men" of 58
  abolition of monarchy 22
  American visitors and residents 21
  and French culture 59
  and Great Britain 71
  and the United States 2, 11, 12, 17, 54, 69, 72, 83, 84, 141, 145, 146
  anti-Americanism 108
  Clubmobile Group H 122
  Pittsburg Press 43
  political position of nobility 21
Franco-Prussian War 31, 33

Freedman, Estelle 108, 115n93
French Ministry of Foreign Affairs 132
French nobility 4, 11, 22, 38
French Revolution 17, 72
Frohman, Charles E. 87
Fussell, Paul 79, 81n15, 96, 102, 114n54, 114n72
  The Great War and Modern Memory 96

Genêt, Edmond-Charles 17
German invasion 12, 84, 104
Global nationalism 86
Goodman, Benny 106
Gould, Anna 23, 37, 38, 40, 42–44, 64, 67, 68
Gould, Frank J. 37, 44
Grand Tours 30, 38, 84
Grant, Madison 87
  "Nordic race" 87
  The Passing of the Great Race 87
Great War 70
Green, Nancy 21, 26n13, 26n18, 44, 47n22, 49n50, 50n85, 59, 71, 73n20, 75n82, 85, 112n9
  The Other Americans in Paris 21

Harbor, Pearl 98
Hegel, Georg Wilhelm Friedrich 54, 72n3
Heterosexual couples 10
Higonnet, Patrice 93
Homberger, Eric 36, 39, 48n41, 49n59
Hovsepian, Alexander 85–87, 94, 98, 99, 101–103, 108, 112n16, 113n48, 114n63, 114n65, 114n68, 114n71, 114n75, 115n97, 127, 128, 138n39
Huger, F. B. 120
Hutchin, Elizabeth 134
Hyper-nationalism 2, 11, 77, 143, 145, 146

Immigration 31, 78, 133, 134, 146
  anti-immigration 87, 134
  laws 130
Individualism 7
Industrial Revolution 27
International marriage 3, 4, 43

INDEX

Jacqueline, C. S. 126
Jaher, Frederic Cople 19
  The Rich, the Wellborn, and the Powerful: Elites and Upper Classes in History 19, 26n9
James, Henry 44
Jaray, Gabriel-Louis 71
Jerome, Clara 32
Jerome, Jennie 32
Jewish and Greco-Roman law 6

Kaiser, Hilary 80n6, 81n14, 93, 113n41, 119, 128, 129, 136

Langille, Leslie 113n44
Lawson, Liz 104, 105, 107, 109, 115n79, 115n80, 118n81, 115n89, 115n99, 123, 124, 137n21, 137n25
Leach, Edmund 1, 14n3
Lee, Hermonie 55, 73n8
Lewis, Sinclair 45
  Dodsworth 45
Libbey, Laura J. 30, 47n19
Life Magazine 96, 97
Lilly, J. Robert 114n58
  Sociologist and criminologist 97
Literary Digest 77, 88, 104, 118, 120, 128, 130, 132, 136
Livingston, Elizabeth 17
Lu, Melody Chia-Wen 4, 14n12, 117

Marquis of Anglesey 38
Marriage
  "a set of legal rules" 1
  "private agreement" 7
  based on notions 7
  commitment 1
  connectedness of individuals 1
  cross-cultural interaction 12
  economic and political institution 6
  emotional evolution of 6, 13
  Franco-American 2, 12, 13, 18, 23, 24, 27, 34, 40, 53, 54, 70–72, 75n75, 77, 80, 83, 84, 86, 87, 104, 117, 118, 121, 128, 134, 136, 141, 142
  longue durée 9
  microcosm 2
  modern 3
  monogamous and indissoluble 6
Married Women's Independent Citizenship Act 42
Max Plank Institute for Human Development 121
Mayer, Arno J. 21
  The Persistence of the Old Regime 21
Meigs, Mark 85, 91, 113n33, 114n51, 131
Metropolitan Opera House 36
Meyers, Gustavus 17, 20, 24
Migration
  history 145
  "push-pull" explanations 5
  studies 144
Minister of Foreign Affairs 136
Monahan, Thomas P. 136, 139n81
Montgomery, Maureen 28, 47n4, 55
Morton, Helen 38, 42, 43
Moulton, Lillie 29–33
Mutual curiosity 127
Myers, Gustavus 25n3, 26n33, 74n46, 135, 139n74

National Assembly 20
National borders 2, 3, 11, 31, 38–46, 70, 77, 128, 130, 133–37, 142, 144
National frameworks 3, 4, 12, 64, 83, 87, 118
National spaces 13, 24, 34, 36, 117, 120, 128, 143, 146
New York Herald 71, 119
New York Times 42, 43, 63, 86–88, 128, 130, 134, 136
New York Tribune 33

Othering 9, 54

Paris Comet 28
Paris society 22, 43
Pernau, Margrit 92
  "Space and Emotion: Building to Feel" 15n14, 92, 113n36
Petesch, Angela 85, 112n3, 112n5, 112n7, 122, 129, 130, 137n17, 137n18, 138n47, 138n50
Petit, Jacques 108, 115n95

Philips, Roderick 7, 8, 15n29, 26n27
  Untying the Knot: A Short History Of Divorce 8
Positive othering 12, 56, 58, 59, 62, 97, 101, 108, 111, 120, 124, 127

Red Cross dances 13, 122–24, 142
Reddy, William 6, 7, 9, 15n21, 15n27, 15n35, 15n36
  longing for association 9
  The Making of Romantic Love: Longing and Sexuality in Europe, South Asia, and Japan 6
Resistance 78
Ricou-Allunis, Jeannine 104, 106, 108, 115n80, 15n87, 15n98, 123, 125, 137n23, 137n27
Rieker, Yvonne 7, 8, 15n28
Rodgers, Daniel 14n6, 26n30
Rosenwein, Barbara H. 112n17, 144
Rossow, Denise J. 104
  Chicago Tribune 104, 146

Schutte, Kimberly 8, 15n20, 36, 62, 64
  "overtly arranged marriages" 36
  Women, Rank, and Marriage in the British Aristocracy, 1485–2000: An Open Elite? 8
Scudder, Robert 118
Second Empire 18, 20, 32
Sexual liberalism 108
Sexual violence 97, 98
Sheehan, James J. 21, 26n16
Social characterizations 1
Social interaction 11, 36, 53, 64, 124, 142
Social invention 1
Social networks 1, 5, 11–13, 27, 29, 33, 68, 77, 79, 84, 117, 119, 126, 133, 141, 142, 144, 145
Social practice 1, 2, 13, 144
Social values 2
Spatial analysis 9, 13, 117, 144
Stars and Stripes 77, 88–91, 94, 121, 126
Storrs, Emery A. 28

Stowe, Harriett Beecher 22
Surkis, Judith 97

Third Republic 20, 69
Thompson, E.P. 24, 26n29
Torpey, John 31, 47n21, 47n23
  The Invention of the Passport: Surveillance, Citizenship, and the State 31
Town Topics 20, 43, 67, 70
Transatlantic circulation and mobility 2
Transatlantic mobility 11, 12, 27
Transatlantic system 2
Transcultural dimensions 144
Transnational community 9, 11, 13, 24, 27, 29–31, 33, 38, 39, 56, 61–64, 71, 77, 87, 117, 144
Transnational marriage 2–6, 8, 10, 13, 14n12, 17, 21, 24, 31, 36, 39, 46, 54, 56, 62, 68, 78, 79, 84, 117, 118, 126, 128, 134–37, 141, 143–45
Transnational spaces
  and communities 11, 144
  and social networks 5
  as elite social events 33
  courting practices 125
  cultural and emotional dimensions 6, 11, 12, 53, 121
  cultural elements of 145
  cultural othering 56, 57, 59
  domination 72
  emotional dimensions of elite 53
  encounter and courtship 11, 143
  marriage and courtship 4, 5, 13
  of courtship 118, 119, 128
  wartime 117, 121, 122

U.S. Army 132–33

Wharton, Edith 22, 26n21, 43, 45, 47n7, 50n76, 54, 55, 59, 72n1
Williams, Lucy 14n8, 14n10
World War I 21, 54, 71, 72, 78, 80, 83, 84, 86–89, 91, 94, 96–99, 104, 107, 108, 110, 118, 120, 122, 125–28, 130, 131, 133–36, 141

World War II 12, 71, 78, 80, 84–87, 89, 90, 94, 96–100, 103, 104, 106–10, 120–22, 124, 126–28, 130–33, 135, 136

World wars 2, 10, 12, 13, 77, 83, 88, 94, 111, 117, 126, 130

Yang, Wen-Shan 4, 14n12, 117, 137n1

Young Men's Christian Association (YMCA) 89

Young Women's Christian Association (YWCA) 130, 132, 133

Zeiger, Susan 118
  Entangling Alliances: Foreign War Brides and American Soldiers in the Twentieth Century 118

www.ingramcontent.com/pod-product-compliance
Lightning Source LLC
Chambersburg PA
CBHW021144230426
43667CB00005B/246